PopLit, PopCult
and *The X-Files*

PopLit, PopCult
and *The X-Files*

A Critical Exploration

by Jan Delasara

McFarland & Company, Inc., Publishers

Jefferson, North Carolina, and London

Library of Congress Cataloguing-in-Publication Data

Delasara, Jan, 1943–
    PopLit, PopCult and The X-Files : a critical exploration
/ by Jan Delasara.
        p.   cm.
    Includes bibliographical references and index.
    ISBN 0-7864-0789-1 (soft cover : 50# alkaline paper) ∞
    1. X-files (Television program).   2. Popular culture —
United States.   I. Title.
PN1992.77.X22 D45 2000
791.45'72 — dc21   00-24225

British Library cataloguing data are available

Cover background art © 2000 Lauri Lynnxe Murphy

Manufactured in the United States of America

McFarland & Company, Inc., Publishers
  Box 611, Jefferson, North Carolina 28640
    www.mcfarlandpub.com

Contents

Preface

Frye and Baker's *Harper's Handbook to Literature* defines *popular culture* as material culture or artistic works with a general appeal, works not defined as high culture. The first example the authors offer is "a television series." The *Handbook* further defines *popular literature* as that which transmutes mythic archetypes into "the literary coin of a particular time and place." Such popular works can, the authors point out, be simple or quite complex. Genre fictions in particular (such as science fiction or mystery) are "often unsophisticated in the way they handle materials, *although they need not be* [emphasis added]. When [these works] are well-written and challenge the conventions of the genre, they sometimes rise to a more general and longer-lasting popularity." Academic aficionados of popular literature are fond of reminding their skeptical colleagues that the Greek tragedies were a popular form, that Shakespeare himself was a writer of "popular literature," and that Charles Dickens' novels appeared in newspapers in serial form for popular audiences.

Although we can't know how *The X-Files* television series will be judged in the future, any critical study undertaken now will show future audiences and researchers how this popular literary work was received and understood in its own day. Many who pursue research in the area of popular literature realize that there is a wide gap between popular writing about the popular arts and the academic analysis and criticism of these forms. "Fan"-oriented writing, at its worst, is unfocused, superficial, anecdotal, personality-driven, and not text-centered. It is largely unconcerned about appreciation or aesthetic qualities. And the widely read reviews and entertainment pieces about popular television and motion pictures are brief, spontaneous and ephemeral — even though sometimes quite perceptive. On the other hand, academic writing about TV shows and movies can be quite specialized and dense — and

1

therefore it tends to play to small houses, buried in academic journals or shared with a few people in presentations at arcane professional conferences. This situation creates a space, even a need, for serious book-length examinations of popular dramatic texts and forms, analytical explorations that can be understood and even enjoyed by a non-specialized but literate and interested readership.

The television series *The X-Files* is a prime candidate for such an analysis. According to audience surveys, many of its viewers are college educated, but not necessarily by way of English programs. One aim of the study is to give such viewers a reference that covers from five to seven years of the series and presents it as a comprehensible whole. Another aim is to analyze and interpret the series as text, assessing its aesthetic qualities and its socio-political position, while at the same time considering the relationship of its form and content to an expanded network of influences which coexist and interpenetrate with it during the decade of the 1990s. I set out to write a wide-based but focused, informative and understandable study of a popular television series, using the terminology of literary analysis sparingly, employing a modicum of close reading when required, and applying some selected, relevant theoretical constructs. When necessary I define constructs and literary terms; in other instances I assume that the context is clear enough to give the approximate meaning. Generally, I try to use a common-language vocabulary in readable sentences not overburdened with academic jargon.

The value of the finished study depends to a large extent on the relevant literary, social and theoretical connections it reveals. Making these connections, I believe, is important cultural work, because it promotes a dialogue and fosters ties between the academic world and the community of educated readers at large.

Further, I strongly believe in the value of taking a close look at popular forms of drama that have the impact of myth, which *The X-Files* does. When we examine these stories in their socio-historical context; when we display their parts, how these parts work together, and to what effect; when we make explicit their implied premises and principles, then we can enrich viewers' understanding and appreciation, and perhaps stimulate them to serious thought about the values these myths communicate and the lessons about life they teach. And, yes, I feel that *The X-Files* is worthy of such study. The series is a unique cultural product which offers both escape and engagement, but it is not *only* popular. It is also complex, powerful and artistically conceived. My close examination has caused me to enjoy it more, and this enjoyment is crucial. The analysis which goes along with any kind of critical writing should have an emotional component. It ought to be a pleasurable activity in itself or be directed toward an appealing goal. So I have worked for a balance between the extremes of dispassionate objectivity and emotional subjectivity. While something is undoubtedly lost in the compromises needed to conjoin these two approaches to critical inquiry, much more, I think, is gained by their directed and dynamic interplay. That interplay is what I hope I have achieved.

I should probably explain a few choices made in writing this book and putting the parts together. First, I made an arbitrary decision to refer to C. G. B. Spender as "The Smoking Man" in most cases, sometimes varying that name with "CSM," and on rare occasions using his entire formal designation of "the Cigarette Smoking Man." I have also taken the liberty of calling "X" (the character) "Mr. X" when I thought that the X alone might be confusing. To orient readers and provide references that can be consulted as necessary, Chapter One begins with an overview of the ongoing plot of the family/conspiracy mythos. Then, in the appendices, I have included two lists of episode titles. The first lists episodes in the order originally shown, along with notes on some of the issues and motifs featured in each one. The second listing is of titles in alphabetical order, cross-referenced with their season number and order of appearance.

In addition to sources duly credited in my bibliography, I would like to further acknowledge the contributions of several people whose materials have found their way into this study: Roxanne Carol for her overview of alien races; BRANTON for his DULCE BOOK, published on the Internet by EagleNet; Timothy Masterson for his expertise and insights regarding numerological principles; and Stephen Mehler and Theresa Crater, both of whom have provided valuable information and ideas along the way. Further, my colleague Riki Matthews gave me invaluable assistance in manuscript editing and indexing. I must also express my gratitude to Metropolitan State College of Denver for my sabbatical leave to complete this project, and to (LAS) Dean Joan Foster and (English) Chair Bill Hamilton for being so kind and supportive as I struggled through it. Special thanks go, of course, to Chris Carter and the writers, directors, actors, and entire production company of *The X-Files*. Fantasy, even dark fantasy, almost always has an element of lightness and play, but, for me, imaginative works need to be something more than mere whimsy or fancy. In order to draw me in and hold me, the fantastic in fiction must also have three attributes: 1) a rich and textured world combined with an original concept; 2) a world that interpenetrates with ours and has relevance for human beings; 3) a world which has a life-or-death edge, an aspect that predisposes it to darkness rather than sweetness and light. *The X-Files* offers all of these qualities, as well as a very knowledgeable respect for the traditions which it borrows, interrogates and revives. Thank you again, *X-Files*. "It's been nice working with you."

I.
PARAMETERS
OF THE STUDY

Chapter One

The X-Files:
Mythos, Vision and Persona

Recently I saw an episode where Agents Mulder and Scully were chasing around after this really disgusting slimy sewer-dwelling creature caused, of course, by atomic radiation — that was partly human and partly lung fluke. This creature reproduced by bit- ing a sewer worker (whatever we are paying our sewer workers, it is not enough) and putting a larva inside him; later on, the sewer worker coughed up a baby fluke creature in a shower scene that I will never forget as long as I live. ... The episode climaxed with Agent Mulder fighting the creature IN A SEWER, and I recall thinking, as I watched them splash in the slime, that if the government is going to take my money, this is EXACTLY the kind of program I want it to be used for.[1]

Since it entered the pantheon of popular television programs in the fall of 1993, *The X-Files* has been a curious and provocative phenomenon. It appeared in the midst of the usual cop shows and situation comedies just as *Star Trek: The Next Generation* was preparing to abandon regular production and move into a series of films. At that point, dramatic shows with a specu- lative flavor seemed to he disappearing from the screen, leaving only televi- sion's peculiar notion of Real Life ("Real TV") and hyperbolic fictional humor or violence. Yet the waning of the calm, hierarchically ordered and morally unambiguous Star Trek universe made room for other visions, perhaps darker and more anarchic than the worlds of science fiction television had yet pro- duced.

Author Stephen King remembers that the most traumatic moment of his childhood was the launching of the Russian spacecraft Sputnik. In contrast, Chris Carter, *The X-Files'* creator and executive producer, claims to have been less affected by the space race and "much more affected by the big bang of my moral universe, which was Watergate." By early 1996 he had yet to see a *Star Trek* episode, admitting that he'd never been a science fiction fan. He says that he resisted a science fiction label for *The X-Files* because he believed that the show belonged "more in the realm of the extremely possible."[2] Opening *The X-Files'* fictional universe to the concept of "extreme possibility" allowed for inclusion of the symbolically and mythically powerful motifs of traditional horror fiction and a range of fringe experiences that included the psychic, the occult and the paranormal, not to mention a welter of ancient and contemporary fears, both conscious and unconscious.

The Mythos

Odd and frightening current events, folklore and urban legends combine with time-honored elements from mystery and horror fiction to supply premises and content for most of the 20-25 new episodes produced each season. This rich fictive resource contributes both variety and resonance to the show. It supplies the material for the roughly 80 percent of the episodes that are "free," that is, free-standing, what director Kim Manners has called the "monster of the week shows."[3] These episodes are free of direct narrative connection to the "bound" episodes which combine UFOs, alien visitations, contactees/abductees, cloning and the families/histories of the two protagonists with an overall conspiratorial worldview. The bound episodes are in a loosely serialized format, part of an evolving mythos, a story arc that provides an ongoing narrative frame for the series. Within this frame, the plots of free episodes may feature secondary protagonists, contain explanatory gaps and offer open-ended resolutions without diminishing overall narrative momentum. The free episodes also allow the main protagonists, FBI agents Mulder and Scully, to go through changes and have interactions that are unexpected, even contradictory. Thus both free and bound episodes make important contributions to the series-as-text. However, seeing the mythic frame in its entirety is indispensable for understanding *The X-Files* both as a structured narrative — that is, how it is put together — and as a cumulative, ongoing story.

Through the fifth season (1997-98), the bound episodes were roughly as listed below. (I have adopted the numbering system used by Lowry, with the first number in the parentheses designating the season and the second indicating that episode's place in the progression of that season's shows.)

UFOs/Alien(s)	Primarily Family
Pilot	Beyond the Sea (1X12)
Deep Throat (1X01)	Miracle Man (1X17)
Conduit (1X03)	One Breath (2X08)
Fallen Angel (1X09)	Colony (2X16)
EBE (1X16)	End Game (2X17)
Erlenmeyer Flask (1X23)	Anasazi (2X25)
Little Green Men (2X01)	The Blessing Way (3X01)
Duane Barry (2X05)	Paper Clip (3X02)
Ascension (2X06)	Piper Maru (3X15)
One Breath (2X08)	Apocrypha (3X16)
Colony (2X16)	Talitha Cumi (3X23)
Endgame *(2X17)*	Herrenvolk (4X01)
Anasazi (2X25)	The Musings of a Cigarette
The Blessing Way (3X01)	Smoking Man (4X07)
Paper Clip (3X02)	Memento Mori (4X15)
Nisei (3X09)	Gesthemene (4X24)
731 (3X10)	Redux I (5X02)
Piper Maru (3X15)	Redux II (5X03)
Apocrypha (3X16)	Christmas Carol (5X05)
Jose Chung's *From*	Emily (5X07)
Outer Space (3X20)	Travelers (5X15)
Talitha Cumi (3X23)	
Herrenvolk (4X01)	
Memento Mori (4X15)	
Gesthemene (4X24)	
Patient X (5X13)	
The Red and the Black (5X14)	

The above list indicates that an overlap exists between the episodes which contain major reference to the families of the main characters and those which deal with a content related to extraterrestrial visitations. The melding of the two themes begins in earnest (note underlined titles) after the first season, with "One Breath," in which Scully is found alive after a suspected alien abduction. In this installment Dana's (Scully's) sister Melissa is introduced, and in an opening sequence her mother tells the family story of young Dana shooting a snake and trying to heal it. A pertinent illustration of the subtle interconnections between free and bound episodes occurs in the fourth season's "Never Again," when Scully gets a tattoo in the form of an ouroboros, a snake with its tail in its mouth. A number of the early UFO episodes deal little, if at all, with the family story arc. Even so, the family drama, a scattered sequence of approximately 20 episodes through season five, is the emotional and narrative glue, as it were, that holds the series together. By the end of the fifth season, the family history has developed as follows:

Dr. Dana Scully was raised in a Catholic family, the daughter of a career naval officer and a loving and seemingly intuitive mother. She has three siblings — an older brother and sister and a younger brother. She earned her medical degree with a residency in forensic pathology, joined the FBI directly from medical school, and then taught two years at Quantico Academy before being recruited to the X-Files section, where she was placed by higher-ups to keep under scrutiny the unorthodox work of Special Agent Fox Mulder.

Fox Mulder's family consists of his father, who works for the State Department, his mother (they are divorced) and his younger sister Samantha, who Fox believes was abducted by aliens when he was twelve and she was eight years old. During the first five years of the series, several different versions of this event, recalled by Fox in flashback, have been shown. The loss of his sister was a singularly traumatic experience for him and serves as the key unifying mythological strand (one *X-Files* director has called it the series' "holy grail"), providing the motive for Mulder's obsessive search to solve the mystery of Samantha's disappearance and perhaps to determine what counts for truth in the world. Samantha seems to return in "Colony," but in "End Game" this manifestation proves to be an alien clone. Other cloned images of Samantha, this time of approximately the same age she was when abducted, turn up in "Herrenvolk," during the fourth season, and in "Redux II," in which she reappears again as an adult for a single short visit with Fox. In the first season's "Duane Barry," Scully herself experiences an alien abduction, after which she is found alive but in a comatose condition, and is hospitalized. During her coma, her father, who has died, appears to her, and her mother keeps a vigil at her side. Melissa Scully contacts Mulder and asks him to go to Dana; as a result, he is beside her bed when she wakes, and she tells him that she owes her survival to the strength of his beliefs.

A recurring doppelganger (or "doubling") motif comes into play in the following season in "The Blessing Way," when Melissa is shot, and later dies, because she has been mistaken for Dana. Moreover, in the first season ("Beyond the Sea"), Dana Scully's father (Bill) dies suddenly of a heart attack, and at the end of season two ("Anasazi"), Fox Mulder's father (William) is shot and also dies. Like the doubling of the fathers' names, the doubles of shifting identities, cloning, twins, psychic connectedness, mirrored images — these appear throughout the series, and not only in the family episodes. Three other father figures emerge to act as mythic helpers for Mulder in his quest for the truth, but two are murdered and one betrays him in Season Six (Senator Matheson in "SR 819"). To complicate matters, for several seasons it was hinted that a primary dark presence on the series, the Cigarette Smoking Man, might be Mulder's true father, and although that misdirection did not eventuate, he still remains a shadow-father in Mulder's life. With the proliferation of failed father images, it is hard to miss the psychological and mythic significance of the search for the absent father on the part of both protagonists, an element which is examined further in Chapters Two through Five.

"Anasazi" brings to light a closer connection between Bill Mulder and that mysterious unnamed operative known as the Cigarette Smoking Man (CSM), and sometimes referred to by other less flattering epithets. (In this study I usually refer to him as the Smoking Man or CSM.) Before his death, the elder Mulder asks CSM to conceal the father's involvement in a clandestine government experiment, and to protect his son Fox. CSM indicates vaguely and duplicitously that he will. Just before he is killed, William Mulder prepares to tell his son about his secret work in the State Department. In a continuation of the CSM/William Mulder plot line, the third season episode "Apocrypha" begins in 1953 with two young government agents questioning an injured man in a naval hospital. They are a young William Mulder and Smoking Man, establishing a long professional connection between the two. In this same episode, Scully corners the man who shot her sister and doesn't kill him, but turns him over to the police.

In "Paper Clip," Mulder and Scully find a hidden storage facility containing cabinets full of medical files, including one for Scully and one with Fox's sister Samantha's name pasted over his. A member of the "Shadowy Syndicate" or Cabal tells Mulder that when his father had threatened to expose a project that would create alien/human hybrids, Samantha was kidnapped to ensure his silence. Mulder's mother admits to him that his father had asked her to choose which child would be taken, but says that she refused. His father made the choice, and she hated him for it. The last episode of Season Three ("Talitha Cumi") shows Mulder's mother and the Smoking Man talking outside the Mulder family's old summer home. The dialogue suggests a previous intimate connection between the two, but they begin to argue and later the mother has a stroke and is hospitalized. In the next episode, the first in Season Four, an alien assassin revives Mulder's mother at the insistence of the Smoking Man.

In the final episode of the fourth season, "Gesthemane," a Defense Department official tells Mulder and Scully a version of Mulder's activities over the past four years that differs greatly from Mulder's own view of his life and work. The official, a man named Kritschgau, says that Mulder is the victim of an elaborate hoax that the government has perpetrated — the lie that human beings have been in contact with intelligent alien life forms. When Kritschgau worked at the Department of Defense, he had watched "a military/industrial complex that operated unbridled and unchecked during the Cold War create a diversion of attention from itself and its continued misdeeds" by concocting a smoke screen of false evidence that true believers like Mulder would be apt to accept. Kritschgau had run the DOD's agitprop division for more than ten years, and he tells Mulder that he knew about records of disinformation that went back to the Korean War. The only way to cover up the mountains of military, corporate, and governmental deception was to create something more incredible.

Finally, Kritschgau calls into question Mulder's intelligence, his principles, his autonomy and his quest for the truth: "They invented you — your regression hypnosis, the story of your sister's abduction, the lies they fed your father. You wanted to believe so badly. No one could have blamed you." Mulder is being accused of being unconscious, non-individuated (see note 12, Chapter 1) — and the last two sentences add the insult of being pitied for it. In terms of the philosophical matrix established by the show so far, a lack of consciousness on the part of the questing hero would destroy the moral center of *The X-Files* universe. The series narrative is Mulder's life story, and that life is invested in the validity of his quest. Anyone who has ever been accused of being duped when defending cherished socio-political or spiritual ideals could easily empathize with the shock and anger that Mulder displays. On a meta-textual level, however, this is just one more turn of the screw, and it is fascinating to re-view early episodes through Kritschgau's explanatory filter. Deep Throat, Mulder's first informant and mythic "helper," seen as a disinformation specialist, becomes an operative assigned to Mulder to *keep him* from learning the truth. One also begins to see alternative motives for the often puzzling actions of Deep Throat's successor, Mr. X.

The first intimation that Scully may have contracted cancer as a result of her abduction came in the third season episode "Nisei," when she meets with an abductee support group, one of whose members is dying of cancer. They recognize her as "one of them." She has her implanted chip removed and analyzed and finds it to be a device for replicating memory and thought processes. Further on, in Season Four, Scully discovers that she does indeed have cancer and enters the hospital for treatment ("Memento Mori"). But she finally decides to go back to work and pursue leads that may produce explanations and a cure. In Season Five, in the episode "Redux II," Mulder locates a second computer chip, which, when it is implanted as the first one had been, causes Scully's cancer to go into remission. This is the kind of cross-episode sequencing that delivers dramatic coherence over the years to the series' plot or action code.

Continuing from the last episode of Season Four, most of "Gethsemane" is told in flashback. The frame is an official hearing at which Scully is about to present her accumulated findings regarding Mulder and his work. She tells the hearing board that she lost a family member because of her allegiance to her partner, and that she had also contacted a fatal disease, given to her by those who had deceived Mulder. We learn that Scully's cancer has spread, and that she does not have long to live. At that point, Agent Mulder has apparently committed suicide and Scully tells the committee that she intends to expose the falsehoods that had ensnared her partner and tainted his work. In

Season Five, then, Mulder, who has survived his apparent suicide, begins to think that the space alien stories he had believed were promoted by the military to distract the attention of citizens from its development of an arsenal of biological weapons. From "Tunguska" and "Terma" on, however, and into the fifth season (and the *X-Files* movie *Fear the Future*), other plotlines give viewers a reason to doubt or to wonder about Mulder's defection. A race for a vaccine against the black oil virus and a scheme to use bees to deliver a lethal mutant strain of smallpox engage the shadowy Cabal and possibly their alien conspirators. The Smoking Man makes contact with a long-lost son, FBI Agent Spender, whose mother is an abductee, but the younger man seems to have little affection for either of his parents. Both Mulder and Scully have been taken off their X-Files assignment by the beginning of Season Six, and Agent Spender becomes one of their replacements. Then in the Season Six two-parter "Two Fathers" and "One Son," the Cabal is suddenly and radically terminated, and, although some possibilities are gone, this termination places viewers at the threshold of new and expanded mystery.

Whereas it is fairly easy to trace the family history through the approximately 120 episodes of five seasons of *The X-Files*, it is much more difficult to outline the development of the UFO plot line in the same clear way. As with the subplot of Mulder and Scully's partnership/relationship, the UFO plot lacks a clear forward direction. UFO episodes sometimes offer tentative or temporary resolutions, but more often they reveal mystery after mystery and twist after turn, continually postponing any clear understanding or definitive conclusion, never answering the obvious question: If the truth is out there, as Mulder says and believes that it is, *what* is out there? Are we any closer to knowing who is hiding what and to what purpose at the end of "Gethsemane" than we were when we were introduced to Deep Throat in the second episode? The complex and highly self-reflexive "Jose Chung's *From Outer Space*" reminds us that *The X-Files* plot has not progressed in the traditional sense, but has been exposed, layer by layer, as one peels an onion, without ever reaching a center and certainly without coming to a rationally explainable conclusion. The visual motif of the X-Files itself provides an image for the ineffable mystery that the series sets out not to solve but to complicate and perpetuate.

X the Unknown

Two matched sequences, one at the beginning and another at the end of the first season, set up the title concept for the show. At the conclusion of that season's final episode, "The Erlenmeyer Flask," a figure detaches itself from deep shadow, rounds a corner and begins walking forward, a man wearing a dark suit and tie. It is the Smoking Man. He proceeds down a narrow aisle between tiers of shelves that hold cardboard boxes. A unpleasant throbbing hum pervades the atmosphere. In a high-angle long shot, we see that the shelves and their orderly rows of boxes rise to the ceiling above, a gloomy void dotted with round faint bulbs, spaced apart, which give off a dim and insufficient glow. As he walks forward with unhurried deliberation, the man's face lies mostly in shadow. The boxes he passes, left and right, seem to have identification labels, but in the faint illumination, none are distinct enough to read. The man does not look at the labels. He knows where he's going.

He comes to a halt and pulls out a box with his left hand. At the same time, his right hand raises a stoppered glass specimen jar. In closeup, we see that a pale embryonic creature floats inside. With its small fetal body and oversized triangular head, it looks almost but not quite human. The man gazes intently at the jar, deposits it in the storage box and pushes the box back into place. He resumes his steady pace down the shadowed aisle to a blue door, through which he exits. There is a sign on the door's exterior — one of those "YOU ARE HERE" maps in red-and-white of a five-sided area with maze-like divisions. The man closes the door, locks it and moves away, exposing the words beneath the diagram: "PENTAGON EMERGENCY PROCEDURES" and "KNOW YOUR EXITS."

This sequence mirrors an almost identically shot scene which occurs at the end of the first show, the series pilot: The Smoking Man deposits a mysterious alien monitoring device in the same huge Pentagon storeroom, but in another file box. Because they bookend the first season, these two scenes serve to link the varying concepts and plots presented so far under the rubric of pervasive official secrecy and duplicity. At the same time, this setting alludes to the horror icon of the vault, a tradition in British Gothic and in American horror literature, from Edgar Allan Poe to H. P. Lovecraft to EC Comics' *The Vault of Horror* and beyond, to the present day. This vast shadowed, silent chamber with its soaring yet confining diagonal lines and vaguely disturbing background noise, its nameless occupant, and even the institutionally colored accents of door and sign provide visual cues that evoke imprisonment, claustrophobia, the truth being buried alive — an echo of the horrors of the nineteenth century.

The sensation of being closed in or trapped is communicated often throughout the series and is thematically significant, suggesting the entrapment of human beings in structures of control beyond their understanding or their power to resist. (The motif has further emotional and psychological power related to the universal trauma of the birth experience.) In "The Erlenmeyer Flask," the vault functions as a burial ground for another motif that recurs in the horror genre: arcane and forbidden knowledge that it would be "best not to know." Consider H. P. Lovecraft's famous (and fictitious) book of horrors, *The Necronomicon,* and the disturbing records detailing the Overlook Hotel's evil history that Jack finds hidden in the basement in Stephen King's *The Shining,* discussed in Chapter Six.

The Paranoid Climate

In the over 200-year development of the horror genre in literature, each new version of the form has symbolically expressed culturally determined, largely unacknowledged fears. Any horror literature, be it print, movie or television drama, also has as its special province to reveal in coded form our most distressing intuitions about human nature and the human condition. *The X-Files*, solidly in this tradition, depicts our cultural uneasiness by combining elements of supernatural horror with a uniquely 1990s distrust and fear of institutional power and secrecy. In fact, what has distinguished this series most clearly from other television entertainments from the beginning is its thesis of public and private conspiracy.

One of several references for the X in *The X-Files* is the symbol used for crossing out, denying or negating a piece of information, and, mathematically, X designates an unknown quantity. Although only 20 percent of the series, the bound episodes, deal directly with the shadow government and its layers of deceit and control, the motifs of the free episodes play effectively against this mythic background too, since all physical evidence of paranormal phenomena investigated by Agents Mulder and Scully are — like the alien embryo and monitoring device — deposited in this Pentagon vault, in the X files. Denied. Crossed out. Negated. Designated as unknown. By the end of the fifth season, the records of X-Files cases kept in filing cabinets in Fox Mulder's office have become a symbol for the larger repository. And in "The End" (5X20), some conspirator, probably CSM, burns these, destroying Mulder's own record of his story, the only independent, non-official versions of the truth.

Some observers find the paranoia of the late twentieth century distressing, even if at least partially justified. Former Senator Howard Baker, a Republican on the Senate committee that investigated the Watergate break-in and cover-up, commented that the Watergate scandal "was the beginning of a new era and an unfortunate one.... I don't know how long it's going to take us to get out of it, this era of cynicism and distrust of not only the government, but institutions." Government secrecy, a legacy of the Cold War of the '50s, has increased that distrust. By 1997, unofficial estimates of documents "hidden in government vaults" ranged from two billion to ten billion pages and these were being added to at the rate of about 10,000 new items a day. A 1997 Senate study disclosed that more than half of the documents are being classified secret by the Pentagon, with the CIA adding 30 percent, the Justice Department 10 percent and the State Department 3 percent. The chair of the Senate study, Democrat Daniel Moynihan, commented, "This is not a good situation. If everything's secret, then people think, 'What are they keeping from us?'"[4]

A First Amendment expert at the Freedom Forum in Virginia sees official secrecy as a root cause of public paranoia, declaring that "the government's obsession with secrecy creates a citizen's obsession with conspiracy." Many of the so-called "secrets" which have been released are mundane, but some are not, such as the "1947 letter from an official at the old Atomic Energy Commission demand[ing] that 'no document be released which refers to experiments with humans and might have adverse effect on public opinion or result in legal suits.'"[5] In light of subsequent disclosures about the Tuskegee experiments on black men and government-sponsored radiation experiments on human beings, it seems odd indeed that one television watchdog group (the conservative Media Research Center) would rate *The X-Files* "unsuitable" for children, not for its explicit or implied violence or its sometimes shocking and repulsive special effects, but "for its bizarre conspiracy theories alleging outrageous government atrocities."[6]

Of course, many of *The X-Files'* relatively young viewing audience were born recently enough to avoid the disenchantment of the McCarthy hearings or Sputnik or Watergate, yet they still "trust no one," a show motto. And they, too, have their reasons. A researcher who found that college students today were profoundly disturbed by the *Challenger* space shuttle disaster comments, "This is a generation of kids who distrust every social institution in the country, particularly politics, and *Challenger* was their first encounter with institutional failure." A college freshman recently observed that after the *Challenger* explosion it was no longer an automatic assumption that "you are going to come home and sleep in your bed. ... I never really took things for granted from then on."[7] Originally some Fox Network managers opposed *The X-Files'* central premise of "widespread covert activity to prevent the public from learning about the existence of UFOs." However, the network tested the idea with focus groups, and Carter remarks that "the thing that was amazing to me was that ... everyone believed that the government was conspiring. ... No one even questioned the notion."[8]

The fears expressed by this series apparently operate across political and ideological boundaries. In many ways the show reflects a scenario compatible with that offered by Northern Michigan Militia members who (as humorously reported by Al Franken) blamed the Oklahoma City bombing on "a band of rogue CIA and FBI agents working for the Japanese ... in revenge for the Tokyo subway gas attack by U.S. Army agents who were retaliating for the Japanese bugging of White House communications."[9] The current climate is one in which the ATF attack on the Waco Branch Davidian compound is viewed askance by individuals of varying political persuasions and in which a sympathetic "Ballad of Ruby Ridge" can be sung by a contemporary folk composer on public radio's *Prairie Home Companion* and receive a lusty round of applause. Older viewers who have known the disenchantments of Cold War "witch hunts," multiple political assassinations, the Vietnam War and Watergate are now considering the possibility of economic, ecological and even millennialist catastrophe.

Identifying herself as one of those more mature viewers of *The X-Files*, Ruth Rosen, a professor of history at the University of California at Davis, reviewed FBI files on the American women's movement after these were released by the Freedom of Information Act. She was amazed to find that feminist groups of the '60s and '70s had been infiltrated by FBI informants. She describes the correspondence between these women informants and FBI director J. Edgar Hoover. One informant wrote that the women's grievances seemed perfectly legitimate. At home, their husbands burdened them with the childcare and housework; at work, they confronted discrimination and harassment. In a letter to the director of the FBI, the informant suggested that she end her surveillance. Hoover vehemently disagreed and reminded her that her information was essential for "national security." Another informant wrote that the group she had infiltrated simply was reading literature and posed no threat. Once again, Hoover dashed off a letter in which he reminded the young woman that her work was necessary to the security of the nation. Rosen declares that her study of history leads her to believe that skepticism and a measure of suspicion is probably endemic to the American spirit, yet she also thinks that "abiding distrust of our government ... has been powerfully reinforced during the past three decades."[10]

Allison Graham suggests convincingly that in terms of the *X-Files* mythos, this period of increasing distrust extends back even further — five decades, in fact — to the year 1947, with the start of the Cold War, Richard Nixon's first term in Congress, the House UnAmerican Activities Committee's (HUAC) investigations of alleged Communist influence in the media, the passage of the National Security Act (creating the National Security State) and the occurrence of what many believe to have been a UFO crash in Roswell, New Mexico. Graham points out that in *The X-Files*' ongoing plotline, 1947 was the year "when the Jersey Devil first appeared, when alien tissues were first collected by the government, and when the governments of the United States, the Soviet Union, China, both Germanies, Britain and France secretly agreed to 'exterminate' any alien retrieved from a UFO crash."[11]

It is of some interest, I believe, that two European social and literary theorists, Michel Foucault and Mikhail Bakhtin, seem to have anticipated *The X-Files*, not by venturing into the fictional twilit zone of conspiracy and paranoia, but by conceiving of contemporary societies as controlling systems. While every citizen may not feel that he or she is directly affected by societal restrictions or secrecy, many people apprehend to some extent the limits that the socio-political system places upon their thoughts and their behavior."[12] Michel Foucault's *Discipline and Punish: The Birth of the Prison* describes the evolution of systemic control of human behavior: the modern disciplinary society — an invisible layered web of thought and action whose discourses penetrate and regulate almost all aspects of our lives.[13] The influential institutions of the system — think of science, medicine, psychology, business/

economics, the military, the law — each of these structures has its own specific language or code which establishes its expertise and its control over one area of human life. Much of this control is achieved by talk — schooling, indoctrination, behavior modification, psychoanalysis, "official explanations," expert advice, legal judgments and so forth — but if talk (and various kinds of drug "therapy") fails, the back-up mode is incarceration, not to punish, Foucault assures us, but to make sure that we are under control.

The X-Files from a Foucauldian perspective is a social myth, in that it both responds to and resists those sites of power that structure (and violate) our daily lives. However, The X-Files itself is also a symptom of cultural conditions. It is a reflection of the fears and anxieties of a cross-section of individuals who sense the presence of controlling structures, the ambiguous nature of the truth, and the absence of certainty; and who also doubt the good will, good character and good sense of the leaders of government, business, the military, the legal system, the medical system and so forth.[14]

Intertextuality and Verisimilitude

The X-Files' position as a dramatic series on commercial television makes it a piece of popular literature, and the plot structures of its episodes show its close affinity to the mystery/detective genre. Yet it is also a typically postmodern text, playing with pastiche and allusions and drawing upon a range of historical and current sources. Chris Carter claims to have been inspired by The Night Stalker, three films, and a short-lived television series of the 1970s that featured supernatural events and a detective-like hero. The X-Files also shows an intertextual relationship to other movies produced in troubled times, such as Universal Studios' classic horror cycle during the Depression and the atomic monster films of the Cold War 1950s. While the main characters of The X-Files are both FBI agents and in some ways related to previous television and film FBI operatives, Mulder, an independent spirit, is also reminiscent of such figures as Sherlock Holmes, Algernon Blackwood's psychic detective John Silence and a succession of '40s and '50s film noir private eyes. His partner Scully, the female scientist, descends from the woman-scientist-protagonist of 1950s monster films and has of course been compared to Clarice Starling, the FBI agent protagonist of The Silence of the Lambs. Among other recent references are the series' resemblance to the weird, threatening ambiance and fantastic elements of David Lynch's Twin Peaks and a clear contrast, previously noted, to the well-lit universe of the three Star Trek series still seen by audiences in many TV markets during the late 1990s.

Like us, Mulder and Scully are trapped in a world whose power structures and their overlapping and conflicting discourses render "the truth" essentially unknowable. Every week these two icons of our intertextual past confront our present and inherited fears. It is by the traits they bring to this confrontation — Mulder's persistence, honor and sensitivity and Scully's intelligence, expertise and strength — that existential horror is both communicated and consistently held at bay. The two protagonists' dedication to truth leads some to claim that *The X-Files* is not a postmodern text at all. Even though it demonstrates such characteristics of postmodernism as intertextuality and self-reflexivity, several commentators have seen the series as anti-postmodern or post-postmodern. "The Truth Is Out There" (the most frequently used of the show's mottoes), they assert, "runs counter to postmodernism's doctrine of disbelief. Together, the hermeneutics of faith practiced by Mulder and the hermeneutics of suspicion practiced by Scully provide a bifocal outlook on unexplained phenomenon [*sic*] that is characterized by a sincerity that stands in stark contrast to the mockeries of *Twin Peaks, Mystery Science Theater 3000* and *Beavis and Butthead.*"[15] It may be that *The X-Files* possesses attributes of more than one cultural or literary period, reflecting, for instance, modernism's expression of alienation and its stream of consciousness techniques as well as the blurred boundaries and intertextuality found in postmodern texts.

According to Keith Neilson, since World War II four new factors have entered horror literature: paranoid world views, the reworking of traditional figures and motifs, the combining of irony and humor with horror, and a "realistic depiction of everyday contemporary life."[16] *The X-Files* consistently displays all of these characteristics. However, in the forty-few minutes allotted to each episode, the series cannot portray the minutiae of daily existence as fully as do, for example, the teeming, sprawling novels of Stephen King. In *The X-Files*, immediacy and verisimilitude are achieved through the use of selective scenic detail and the foregrounding of realities that viewers recognize as emblematic of life in the 1990s, such as Mulder and Scully's omnipresent cell phones and computers.

The contemporary referents are varied and numerous, but they often relate to the paranoid subtext. One occurs when, in the first-season episode "Beyond the Sea" (1X12), the names of two serial killers bring to mind the name of one actual killer, Henry Lee Lucas. In "Darkness Falls" (1X19), loggers are cutting down old growth forests, generating a conflict between loggers and environmentalists. In the second season, we have "The Host" (02), featuring a mutant from a Russian ship that is dumping Chernobyl waste in the ocean, and "F. Emasculata" (22) and "Red Museum" (10), picturing instances of secret experiments being conducted on captive or unaware live populations. In the third season's "Nisei" (09), Scully scoffs at "that hokey alien autopsy film shown on the Fox Network," and in "Jose Chung's *From Outer Space*" (20), she performs an autopsy on an alien who turns out to be a disguised human being. When she views a videotape of this autopsy later, she is appalled at how it has been manipulated to distort the truth.

Episodes have touched or focused on video games, tattooing, meeting dates online, the disappearance of frog populations worldwide, plastic surgery, organ harvesting, cancer, prison brutality, shootings in fast-food restaurants, shootings by postal employees, domestic terrorism, Haitian refugee camps, mysterious airliner crashes, gated communities and — in one of the most provocative hours of the first five seasons — revisionist assassination theories. In the fourth season's "The Musings of a Cigarette Smoking Man" (07), the character from the vault sequence in "The Erlenmeyer Flask" listens to an audio tape which details his supposed history (shown in flashbacks) as a multiple assassin and perhaps the biggest conspirator of all. In a humanizing subplot, he stops and starts smoking, writes and tries to publish a novel.

In addition to referencing familiar topics of the late 1990s, series plots often originate in news stories that support a paranoid world view. For the episode "Blood," for instance, two current events sources provided the inspiration. The writers "began with a single note, 'Postal Workers,' that they subsequently combined with the hubbub in Southern California over malathion spraying. Authorities had released the pesticide from helicopters to eradicate fruit flies, alarming some local residents, who weren't entirely convinced by assurances that the substance was harmless to humans while being told that it might damage the paint on their ears."[17] "Wetwired" (3X23), which had as its premise a mind control device attached to cable television connections, was based on the general debate about television violence but also the writer's desire to explore the physical and psychological effects that TV has on viewers.[18] "The War of the Coprophages" (3X12) originated both in stories about mass hysteria and information about an artificial-intelligence researcher at MIT who had constructed insect-shaped robots. The writer of "Ice" (1X07) read an article in *Science News* about an item 250,000 years old that had been dug out of the ice in Greenland. (The episode, however, was set in Alaska to justify FBI involvement.)[19]

Against premises thus grounded in reality, the show depicts a range of shadowy helpers and mysterious antagonists interested in the X-Files. These characters are a shifting background that unseats the locus of the action and creates a disturbing, uncertain environment. Although the time and place is recognizably current, the people and organizations offer no solid ground. Mikhail Bakhtin, Russian theorist and critic, coined the term "chronotope" to refer to those spatial-temporal factors in fiction that "evoke the existence of a life-world independent of the text and its representations." Bakhtin, like Foucault, is concerned about power, but more particularly how power is represented in fiction. He maintains that the chronotope "mediates between experience and discourse, providing fictional environments in which historically specific constellations of power are made visible."[20]

In *The X-Files*, however, the constellations of power are clandestine, invisible. Some loci of control — the medical and psychiatric professions, the prison system — are shown in set locales, but usually power is being wielded by institutions and groups that are either not specified or not physically and temporally grounded. The show's FBI protagonists pursue the unknown, and perhaps the unknowable, in a range of places — an Arkansas town, an Indian reservation, the Arctic. But the fact that most episodes take place in the continental United States suggests that whatever disturbing questions are raised by the series' atmosphere of anxiety and unsettling ambiguity are homegrown questions. Locations are identified on-screen by white computer printout lettering. While this device communicates setting quickly, it also gives the effect of an official report. Whose report? To what agency or organization? Another shadowy locus of control.

The Expressionistic Vision

The settings, costumes and visual detail of the series-as-text generally conform to the typically realistic mode of most film or television dramas. Yet along with its "realism," the show concurrently employs a noir or expressionistic style in order to communicate pervasive anxious uncertainty. Blurred images, blinding light, silhouettes, shadows and darkness: the artistic vision of *The X-Files* is arguably one of its most compelling features, distinctive enough to be recognizable in parody.[21] Its dark and contemporary *mise-en-scène* not only links this television series to the genre of popular horror, but also to the characteristic style, primarily visual, of American film noir mysteries and German expressionism. These two film traditions also mirrored the anxieties of their historical context, and their intertextual echoes may be seen in *X-Files'* chiaroscuro lighting, claustrophobic spaces, arbitrary and heightened use of light and color, distorted sound, iconography of costume and appearance and other devices employed solely to engender or intensify emotional effect. Chapter Four examines specific expressionistic aspects in more detail, but for now, a brief overview will serve to indicate the similarities between the environment of the 1990s and the conditions which prevailed in the historical periods that lend their iconography to the expressionistic style that *The X-Files* has adopted.

Film expressionism flourished in Germany after that nation suffered its ignominious defeat in World War I and the ensuing disastrous economic consequences. Thereafter, according to Siegfried Kracauer, "the army, the bureaucracy, the big-estate owners and moneyed classes … continued to govern … [and] leading German industrialists and financiers … unrestrainedly upheld inflation, impoverishing the old middle class."[22] Next came a period of foreign investment which was very advantageous to big business but had the effect of destroying the middle class and democracy while bringing about mass unemployment. This extreme social instability engendered a radical artistic response: expressionism.

The expressionist style in films actually grew out of the expressionist movement in painting and the graphic arts that developed in Europe after the turn of the century. In motion pictures, the aim of this style was to achieve a heightened emotional effect by distorted lighting, intersecting diagonal/vertical/curvilinear planes, and nonrealistic costuming and acting styles. Later, expressionism developed a more realistic psychological style with the films of Murnau, but the early efforts *The Cabinet of Dr. Caligari, Nosferatu, The Golem* and others which took on fantastic or horrific subjects were most characteristic of the type. The nightmare world of *The X-Files* is comparable to that created for *The Cabinet of Dr. Caligari*, produced in 1919. The original intent of the film script's two young authors (Carl Mayer and Hans Janowitz) was to articulate a strong critique of traditional power structures, particularly the kind of political and military authority that sent a generation of young men to be killed on the brutal battlefields of the first world war. The *Caligari* sets combined painterly abstraction and scenic distortion with the express purpose of creating what Lotte H. Eisner calls an ambiance of "anxiety and terror."[23]

During the 1920s and '30s, facing economic hardships and the rise of fascism, many German directors, writers and technicians accepted offers from Hollywood and brought their "language of heightened expression" with them. Their artistic influence was felt especially in the classic horror films of the 1930s but also could be seen in Depression-era gangster movies. In the pre-World War II period, detective mysteries like *The Maltese Falcon*, crime films like *This Gun for Hire* and one notable "art film," *Citizen Kane*, showed a direction for expressionism in films of the future.

American film noir originated in another unsettled post-war environment. J. P. Telotte observes that, after the U.S. had defeated its foreign enemies in World War II, American life itself began to be viewed as the "locus of various long-disguised, almost invisible violations of our individual and cultural dreams," possibly because of "the unsatisfying return to normalcy that the war's conclusion brought to America, a return punctuated by rampant inflation, unemployment, labor strife, shifting social patterns and the rapidly growing anxieties of the Cold War." Writing about the Hollywood crime movies made after World War II, Kracauer comments that they reflect the kind of fear generated by the Nazi regime in which "sinister conspiracies incubate next door, within the world considered normal — any trusted neighbor may turn into a demon." Noir films "show the uncertainties Americans had begun to feel about their own system and its ability to cope with problems the war had uncovered; on the other hand, they evoke a larger sense of fear and anxiety that increasingly seemed to be accepted as inevitable and almost inscrutable."[24]

In detective, mystery and crime films of the classic noir style from the early '40s to the late '50s, not only the settings but also the characters and their physical presentation are iconically significant. In a portrait of the noir protagonist that could apply equally to *X-Files*' Agent Mulder, Terry Curtis Fox points out that the noir hero as detective is not disinterested and objective. His "every descriptive sentence carries an emotional and moral judgment on the matter at hand." Moreover, as Telotte observes, the hero's stance "at times seems nearly pointless, given the pervasive criminality, and at other times self destructive, because of the dangers it involves. But that stance is finally crucial to the attraction of these tales, for the moral center it fashions reassures us that, individually, man can cling to some human values, even as he is faced by corruption on all sides."[25]

Fox Mulder, like the noir heroes who preceded him, gives viewers privileged access to an unknown world. Unfortunately, as it was for his predecessors, this world is a corrupt, dangerous and impenetrable maze. Like the postwar noir detective, Mulder wants a say in and about the truth of the world, and he doesn't just want to find the truth or know it. He wants, as he states in the episode "F. Emasculata" (2X22), to reveal the truth, to tell people about it. Interestingly enough, the combined discourse, or discursive formation, of all of the *X-Files*' accumulating episodes becomes the "Truth" that "Is Out There" for series viewers. As one viewer comments, "I constantly have to remind myself: 'This is just somebody's creative mind at work'"[26]— in other words, that the show is fantasy and not reality.

Graham points out that scenic and character cues suggest that The Truth, rather than being Out There, may instead be In There. She cites the repeated instances of buried or concealed information or objects (related to the motif of the vault mentioned previously) but sees the depths of Fox Mulder's memory as the crucial manifestation of this motif: "The series is, in fact, premised upon the persistence of [his] memory."[27] In the episode "Little Green Men" (2X01), Mulder has a flashback in the parking basement of the Watergate Hotel in which he re-visits the scene of his sister's abduction. In this version of his recovered memory, Fox and Samantha are watching television on the evening of November 27, 1973, as a news report discusses the 18–minute-plus gap found in the Nixon tapes. The two are arguing about what to watch; Samantha changes channels and Fox keeps turning back to the news story. Then the lights go off. Fox is stunned by a blinding flash and Samantha levitates through an open window surrounded by an intensely glowing aura.

What Mulder has recovered is "both the memory of erasure (Nixon's) and the erasure of memory (his own). His 'undeleted file' of childhood memory stands in contrast to the 'deleted file' of official misconduct." Later (in "E.B.E.," 1X16), Deep Throat confesses to committing horrible crimes in conjunction with his government position. His hope is that he can atone for what he has done by assisting Mulder in his search for the truth. "In this transference of guilt, Mulder becomes the custodian of America's secret postwar history. He is now the haunted one, the living 'memory bank' of officially denied images...."[28] In acquiescing to this role of atonement, Mulder acknowledges and begins a life-or-death struggle with what psychologist Carl Jung would call our collective Shadow. His is a psychologically and mythically (in the larger sense) resonant quest in ways that will be discussed in more detail in succeeding chapters.

Although *The X-Files* features believable characters and realistic locations, its primary sources of verisimilitude are, I think, more oriented to mind than to matter. The first source is the ideology of conspiracy that it shares with many of its viewers, and the second is that it consistently quotes earlier texts and artistic styles to achieve a potent intertextual reality.[29] Viewers perceive these quoted elements as the "truth," not because they have any experiential connections with what is being depicted, but because they themselves swim in a sea of language forms and images created by literary and artistic texts, both popular and elite, and these imaginative constructions, perhaps more than any real-seeming small-town bungalow or recognizable urban landmark, not only promote believability, but also foster a pleasant reflexive response, a feeling of *deja vu* or that one is "in on the joke," a form of dramatic irony which is repeatedly exploited by the show's producers.

An exemplary case in point is the third season episode "Jose Chung's *From Outer Space*" (3X20), which offers the audience a wide range of often contradictory explanatory frames for the action of its convoluted story line. Each of these frames derives either from a story-within-a-story device or from reference to familiar film or TV conventions. In one sequence a pair of teenagers trade blandly romantic dialogue as they drive down a deserted country road at night. Since viewers have just been shown what seems to be a UFO flyover in a brief preceding shot, many will connect these isolated teens with similar innocent couples facing the unknown in 1950s science fiction movies. We expect them to have a dangerous, but not necessarily fatal, confrontation with space aliens, so when this confrontation does seem to occur, it is credible to us. Subsequently, after several disturbing anomalies that undercut the 1950s interpretive frame, we learn that the two teens had had sex before their encounter with extraterrestrials (or are those creatures extraterrestrials?) and we are suddenly and unexpectedly thrown into another textual referent: no, these are not two innocent dating teenagers from *Happy Days* after all. We begin to see them as the lusty, passion-driven teens of 1980s slasher films, victims-to-be whose sexual activity is speedily and horribly punished by Jason or one of his serial killer clones. While "Jose Chung" is unusual in its profusion of conflicting textual references, the episode calls ironic attention to the way fictional sources set viewer expectations and what audiences will accept as possible or "real" or "The Truth." Quoted plot conventions, though, are only part of the perceived realness of *The X-Files*. Its visual style and iconography also help to determine both its believability and its emotional impact.

The costuming of both main characters not only evokes an authentic world, but also intensifies emotional content in the expressionistic tradition. So seldom are Mulder or Scully out of "uniform"—suits and tie for him; jacket, blouse, skirt or labcoat for her—that showing either of them dressed differently has both impact and meaning. When Scully is being pursued wearing a jogging outfit, she seems especially defenseless and vulnerable, just as Mulder appears to be when he is shaving, stripped to the waist, and is visited by a beautiful vampire. The effect of the two scenes is totally different, one terrifying, the other erotic, but the departure from costume-type creates much of the emotion generated. In addition to their professional attire, both characters often wear trenchcoats or overcoats in outdoor or public locations. (Trenchcoats, telephones and the striped shadows thrown by Venetian blinds are part of the essential iconography of noir films.) These unisex coats are usually dark and loose-fitting, seeming almost too large for their slight bodies, and suggest the wintry chill that pervades their world (and ours) while giving the protagonists a "hand-me-down" look that invests them with childlike innocence and charisma. They're in over their heads. Like we are. They're smart and they're tough and they're young and sensitive. But they don't know what they're up against.

Mulder and Scully are Hansel and Gretel in a moonless nighttime forest or Alices in a very dark wonderland. No wonder they speak softly and express very little emotion. They seldom smile, almost never laugh. Yet in ironic juxtaposition to the show's gloomy humorlessness, both protagonists (and some other characters) persistently make deadpan, witty comments reminiscent of the repartee of the more sophisticated noir detective films. In the episode "Dod Kalm" (2X19), for instance, on a becalmed death ship, a drastically and prematurely aged Mulder is about to slip into a near-death coma when he croaks to Scully, "I always thought that when I grew older I'd take a cruise somewhere. This isn't exactly what I had in mind. The service on this ship is terrible...." These "Mulderisms" and "Scullyisms," as fans call them, undercut the seriousness of the fictional situation in a reflexive way that makes the viewer conscious of it as fiction, as entertainment, as imaginative play. However serious the protagonists or their predicaments seem to be, the trickster is never far below the surface of the narrative.

Another factor that distances the narrative, and complicates and enriches the audience involvement provoked by expressionistic techniques, is that both protagonists call into question media and genre conventions, most especially in the area of gender. Dana Scully has a classically pale and lovely face, but her red hair is styled in an unfashionable '50s noir-type page boy. Moreover, her clothes are not glamorous, and she is often less expressive and emotional, more calm and logical, than her male counterpart. Fox Mulder's first name links him with a feminine kind of sex appeal. He is slender, with a boyish face, full lips, a slightly oversize nose and a chin that cannot be described as strong. His soft light-brown hair, in a longish and wispy cut, suggests the waif, the urchin, androgynous and tentative rather than macho, confident and aggressive. His Internet fans extol his "radiant vulnerability."

Even though he violates macho genre stereotypes, there is no doubt whatever that Fox Mulder and his story dominate the ongoing narrative and that Scully is cast in a subordinate and supportive role. Generally noir films present a dichotomous image of women. The female protagonist is either the Bad Girl (the strong, sexy, duplicitous and destructive "Spider Woman") or the Good Girl (the soft and yielding, passive and forgiving nurturer). From the first episode forward, Scully has straddled these images by incorporating seemingly contradictory traits, much as Mulder does. She is beautiful and has even been called "hot" on at least one occasion. She is a strong woman, but her strength does not reside in the manipulation of her sexuality but in her expertise and her questioning mind. By virtue of writing reports on Mulder for the FBI hierarchy, Scully has some control of the story or the prevailing notion of reality, but her voiceover segments typically appear at the conclusion of episodes and do not represent her own experiences primarily (certain episodes, like "Memento Mori" [4X15] depart from this pattern). She functions to some extent as the mythic hero's scribe, the one who celebrates his deeds and tells his story. As such, hers could be compared to the role of Dr. Watson to Mulder's Sherlock Holmes: The story indubitably belongs to Holmes. Due to her FBI assignment and her own personal inclination toward scientific analysis and verifiable, objective truth, Scully occupies an adversarial position in the investigations the two perform, giving Mulder a chance to show his intuition and his empathy, as well as his superior deductive powers, since she continually challenges him to defend or explain his ideas and actions.

These two characters, because they paradoxically both conform to and interrogate prior film and literary conventions, suggest alternative social constructs and value systems. So do the indescribably familiar-yet-strange Vancouver, B.C., locales of the first five seasons, with their chilly, overcast exteriors and their neat but somehow cluttered, almost European-looking interiors. The regular use of Canadian supporting actors further estranges the action from our normal everyday entertainment experiences. The center of this distancing, however, is to be found in the series' protagonists. With their self-referential or reflexive humor, their defiance of gender stereotypes, and their echoes of intertextual sources, these two figures suggest the possibility of personal autonomy. They manage to see the unseeable, escaping the invisible web of controlling and conflicting discourses that surround them (and us), if only briefly and in a limited way. All in all, *The X-Files* benefits both artistically and thematically from taking a bold step into the labyrinth of intertextuality, ensuring a rich multiplicity of explanatory frames. The series constitutes a unique television experiment in presenting a drama that connects with the life of the imagination in codes that viewers of today — confused and apprehensive, angry or cynical — can appreciate and understand.

Some of the pleasures we get from this engaging, complex drama lie in its handling of plot and narrative techniques, characters and characterization, and stylistic devices which consistently deliver intense emotional and sensory impact. The three chapters in the section titled "Text," which follow, examine the features of structure, content, character, style and theme in more detail. The chapters in the "Context" section explore some additional historical and cultural connections between *The X-Files* and popular literature, vernacular stories, speculative nonfiction, psychology, mythology, philosophy, history and concerns about the future.

The Persona of the Text: A Hermeneutic[30] View

Any popular television series takes on a personality for its audience, and as long as that personality appeals, viewers tune in regularly, often loyally, appreciating the experience and learning what to expect from this mediated companion. The "family fun" hijinks of *The Brady Bunch* and its sitcom ilk, the wryly humorous camaraderie of *Mash*, the interwoven sentimental/gritty human interest tales of cop and doctor and lawyer shows, the desultory, laid-back "pointlessness" of *Seinfeld*— each television series achieves a persona of its own, even though each may share conventional features with other shows of a similar type or the same genre.

That the persona of *The X-Files* is complex and distinctive can be seen by what people say they *dislike* about the program. Those who don't like it characterize the *X-Files* personality as "depressing," "too serious," "too complicated — difficult to 'get into'" (a comparable human acquaintance might be judged as "hard to know"). Even talk show host Rosie O'Donnell, a self-identified fan of the show, complains that it "can be so dense and confusing you almost need Cliffs Notes to figure it out."[31] And the humorist Dave Barry describes the show's two main characters as "lugubrious," implying a self-indulgent gloominess that infuses the text overall with the same trait. Some people who don't watch the show have told me that just living nowadays presents too many serious issues, not to mention moral darkness and horror, for them to seek these out on the TV screen.

Also, to some, the horror genre itself is repellent. Over the past several centuries, the literary genres of horror and pornography have received the most public opprobrium of any and have been accorded the least academic respectability and attention. Chris Carter appears to acknowledge the cultural disapproval that connects these two genres by giving *X-Files* hero Fox Mulder a taste for pornography. However, overt sexuality did not become a strong component of modern horror texts until the British Hammer Films of the 1950s and '60s, and it is not foregrounded in *X-Files* plots. Nor is the violence of the show excessive or explicit, notwithstanding the occasional frozen human head that shatters on the linoleum or the suicidal patient who lowers himself into a boiling hospital water therapy tub. Such potent sensory moments, probably as much as its regular display of aliens, ghosts and monsters makes *The X-Files*, for some, a disturbing and unwelcome TV visitor.

On the other hand, the series consistently combines wide-ranging subjects, high-quality production values, surprising twists and sensory shocks in a way that appeals to its regular viewers. Liken it to a friend who's been around, who's had wild and unexplainable adventures, and can always pull an exciting tale out of the hat. In literary terms, a text (like a friend) that does this can help us "defamiliarize" our perceptions of reality. Over time, the way we see the world tends to become automatic and deadened, so one of the most important functions of art is to jolt us, so to speak, out of being victims of habit, to help us "recover excitement about life and to see familiar things in new ways."[32]

Imagine a friend who has gained considerable arcane and practical knowledge over a lifetime, not only as an educated person, but also as an indefatigably curious, bold, and active one. Imagine that you have accompanied this same friend on a number of exploits and have seen the world through this person's eyes. This friend has great empathy for the world's victims, the sad, the mad, and the "different" (the quotidian monsters that roam the *X-Files* landscape). Yet the persona of this friend, this dramatic series, is not *only* dark, not *only* serious; it is also clever and sassy and, well, subtly sexy. It subscribes to scientific truths and pursues practical probabilities without dogma, with flexibility and imagination. It is willing to consider the mystical and spiritual sides of existence. It is also willing to speculate — even wildly — and it knows how to be satisfied with mysteries that cannot be solved or stories that are unbelievable or don't follow a clear causal progression to complete closure.

That sketch describes my impression of *The X-Files* and the personal relationship I have had with the series over the past six years. It is the connection that has led me to investigate this TV series as a literary text — an extended piece of popular genre fiction — and as a cultural phenomenon, hoping to produce something like a portrait in words of a complicated and fascinating organism in its setting. While I am aware that the series has a genesis, a multifaceted point of origin, that it is the collaborative product of an exceptionally skilled group of creative artists and artisans, I only attempt to describe it in its fully developed state as I have experienced it. This means that the picture which follows seldom credits any individual contributors or their artistic contributions directly. Instead, I have concentrated on portraying the text and its relationship to our world as accurately, and with as much insight, as I can.

My intent is to help novice viewers see it as a comprehensible unified entity and regular viewers see it strange and whole through someone else's eyes.

Why Study Popular Literature?

Consideration of the sometimes lurid and sensational subject matter that is typical of *X-Files* episodes may raise a preliminary question: Are texts from popular genres, no matter how well-received or inventive, worthy of the kind of critical attention customarily devoted to "the classics"? Michael Kamman, for instance, argues that American popular culture in the twentieth century can best be summed up "in a single phrase: sentimental modernism," *modernism* being a world view and a literary position prevalent during the first half of the twentieth century. The modernist way of looking at things sees the human condition as one of conflict, irony, incoherence, existential alienation and meaninglessness. *Sentimental*, on the other hand, refers to the tendency of contemporary cultural products to move constantly toward outcomes that are sweeter, more satisfying, but, Kamman implies, less realistic or artistic. "Ultimately," he says, "Americans prefer cultural media that contain suspense and yet deliver, in the end, happy closure rather than distress. The sentimental ends justify the modernistic means."[33]

The suggestion here is that pure (unsentimental) modernism is a superior or more truthful way of seeing the world. Yet some might consider that point of view to be an elitist academic prejudice which considers certain texts to be more valuable because they are not only bleakly realistic, but also indirect and difficult. Lacking immediate appeal and accessibility, such works need to be taught and explained. "The classics," in fact, do require more of what scholars, teachers and critics know how to do best, that is, close reading — the process of studying a text to unearth ideas, connections, and significations which are not immediately apparent. "Once you give priority to close reading," observes Peter Rabinowitz, "you implicitly favor figurative writing over realistic writing, indirect expression over direct expression, deep meaning over surface meaning, form over content, and the elite over the popular. In the realm of [fiction], that means giving preference ... to symbolism and psychology over plot."[34] Consequently, the works of literature that are read and studied in high schools and colleges are seldom those read for pleasure by real people in real life. The novels, poetry and plays of Franz Kafka, James Joyce, T. S. Eliot, Sophocles and Shakespeare require guidance and training to comprehend and to appreciate, and the complexity, indirection and cultural remoteness of these texts justifies the expertise of those who teach them.

Yet, while most readers of popular novels or viewers of motion pictures and television probably don't discuss their personal reading or viewing choices with others in a very thoughtful way, the critical consciousness of popular audiences may now be at a higher level than at any time in human history. Internet chat rooms and bulletin boards encourage viewers to share ideas about popular texts, to discover agreements and to thrash out disagreements. Dialogue among participants, especially for those movies and television shows having "cult" status like *The X-Files*, makes it clear that faithful or repeat viewers can be observant and insightful.

As an example, consider an interpretive dialogue that occurred in September 1998 on the official *X-Files* Fan Forum. It followed the showing of "Detour" (04) a fifth season episode in which Mulder and Scully are stranded at night in a forest where they are at the mercy of invisible adversaries. They huddle together for warmth and agree to keep watch. Mulder asks Scully to sing to him to show him she hasn't fallen asleep. She protests that she can't sing, but finally gives in and sings the first verse and chorus of "Joy to the World" by Three Dog Night.

Scully doesn't sing the second verse. In it, the singer declares that if he were the king of the world, he'd "make sweet love to you." On the Fan Forum, Isabelle quotes verse 2 and asks her fellow X-Philes, "Did you notice the second verse? If Scully were the king of the world? Any other thoughts?"[35]

Several fans responded, including "Clyde Chung," who commented,

> That Scully would pick "Joy to the World" is so fitting. I agree with Alcott when she said that it represents Scully's willingness to go along on Mulder's quest even if she doesn't really see things from his point of view. I believe, however, that the song has an additional meaning. It says that M&S may not communicate well with spoken words ... but that it doesn't matter because it's the unspoken communication between them (represented by the "unsung" second stanza) that really counts. That's why Mulder never asked Scully to sing the second stanza. He already knew what she was saying without her having to say it out loud.[36]

X-Files fans (X-Philes), regularly become involved in such interpretive exchanges, building on each other's ideas, asking and answering questions, probing past occurrences and actions, speculating — and even giving advice — about future developments. The kind of active observation and interpretation being practiced is almost indistinguishable from the "close reading" that is taught and practiced in university literature classes, with one important exception. In fan discussions, no expert intervenes, as so often happens in classrooms, to tell participants who has the best ideas or what the text *really* means. Internet contributors express themselves in freewheeling, idiosyncratic ways. In this wider conversational environment, a study like this one cannot claim to be the only or the "correct" perspective on *The X-Files*. It can, however, contribute to the continuing public dialogue in two ways: (1) by showing how certain literary features and techniques contribute to the text as a comprehensive, integrated work, and (2) by providing historical and social background that relates the text both to the past and to its own particular cultural moment.

And some teachers and commentators do see value in popular texts. Tony Magistrale, who teaches the novels of Stephen King to university-level students, contends that "'popular' does not necessarily mean 'sub-literary.' Many authors who are now well-entrenched in the literary canon — Charles Dickens and Edgar Allan Poe, to name just two — were once considered beneath scholarly attention." Magistrale directs particular attention to aspects of Stephen King's fictional universe that are coincidentally shared by *The X-Files*, one of which is "a profound awareness of the most emotional and deep-seated American anxieties. No less than Hawthorne was a century earlier, King is a moralist for our era, concerned with telling cautionary tales about a nation on the verge of destroying itself from within." He argues that King's landmark novel *The Shining* "is disturbing not only because of its Gothic trappings, but also because it forces the careful reader to confront archetypal childhood phobias about parental discord, devouring mother and father figures, and child abuse. It reminds the reader that when a family unravels, no individual member is spared."[37]

To extrapolate from Rabinowitz then, popular literature is not usually respected or studied for the reason that it is easily understandable and puts more emphasis on exterior experience than on internal experience, which means, on plot rather than ideas. It is more concerned with what happens than with what those happenings represent artistically or intellectually. In addition to being unchallenging and superficial much of the time, I would suggest that popular entertainments have a far more insidious quality: They are ideological commodities that promote selfish, antisocial dreams and artificial needs. That is, popular television shows and novels project action, ideas and images of reality that are hegemonic in representing the interests of the ruling class and the market system. These mass-produced stories are one way those in control convince the rest of us that their truth is our truth and that our cultural situation is natural, incapable of being questioned or changed.

This ideological component explains why many studies of popular texts take a sociological or socio-cultural position, "reading" television shows or comic books or magazine fiction, for example, "against the grain" to show what such cultural products tell us about Americans and their beliefs. And it's easy to see that movie Westerns, soap operas and TV talk shows would reveal much about matters of ideology. Even *The X-Files* cannot escape being involved in the pervasive hegemonic system of representation, one obvious case in point being the fact that its admirable and charismatic protagonists are federal agents, agents who are allowed a fictional autonomy that would be, let us say, rare in the law enforcement establishment. However, with this text, I think it is safe to approach analysis from a literary as well as a cultural-historical-political perspective because *The X-Files* interrogates its hegemonic discourse through literary strategies: in its structure, content, character, style and theme.

It mixes generic forms and plays self-consciously with conventions, motifs and symbolic meanings. In thought, it maintains an overall focus on government and corporate malfeasance, and its underlying premise is that the truth, or truths, that are being withheld from us must be learned and told. Its subject matter interrogates consensus reality. Its textual gaps, contradictions and silences, detailed for viewers in such books as Michael French's *The Mixtake Files* and *The Nitpicker's Guide for X-Philes* by Phil Farrand, struggle against the mental closure of the formula plotline.[38] And its reflexive intertextuality and ongoing strand of wry humor, encourages an ironic, questioning stance on the part of viewers, while they at the same time immerse themselves in a story which is undoubtedly, in the popular tradition, sentimental, sensational and escapist.

II.
THE TEXT
OF *THE X-FILES*

Chapter Two

The *X-Files* Plot:
The Artistry of Escape

> A proper work of popular fiction appeals, ideally, to a whole
> populace, rather than to a coterie or an elite. It cuts across lines
> of class, occupation and education. It is formed by the fears and
> desires that keep a populace together, rather than by those that
> keep special interest groups apart. It is our equivalent of the
> tales our ancestors told around the cave fire. ... The formulas,
> or conventions, of our popular genres are shaped by the same
> forces that shape our national character.[1]

Popular, so-called "escapist" fiction like *The X-Files* is often considered
an inferior, lowbrow type of elite literary art. However, since the popular
forms described by John Cawelti in *Adventure, Mystery, and Romance* are
enjoyed by individuals at all intellectual and social levels, he contends that
popular narratives branded as "escapist" represent a true artistic type which
arises from the basic human ability to use the imagination and to experience
alternative worlds. Such imaginary experiences, he claims, have certain characteristics in common that allow us to judge them on their own aesthetic
terms. This "artistry of escape" is rooted in a central paradox. As human
beings, we desire security, but we also have a hankering, even a need, for risk
and change. We are "torn between a quest for order and a flight from ennui."[2]

So we seek intense experiences in popular fiction, stimulation that is
strong enough to break the ties to our everyday, normal lives. To accommodate our contradictory desires for safety and for danger, plot formulas give us
sequences that are familiar and predictable, but the stories themselves are full

of threat, confusion, violence, free-wheeling romance and sex (the proportions depend on the genre and the text in question). We can indulge in these "moral fantasies," as Cawelti calls them, because we can experience them from within the safety of an imaginary world. A moral fantasy is a melodrama, complicated in plot and character, that depicts a multiplicity of actions in a "real" world full of violence and tragedy, but ultimately affirms the moral rightness of the world order. Obviously, *The X-Files* occupies an ambiguous position regarding the essential morality of the world, or the universe. True, its protagonists do survive every episode, and they attract some supporters as well as enemies. But because they never really overcome or expose all of the diabolical forces arrayed against them, the benevolence of the universe remains uncertain, or at least its proof indefinitely postponed. However, Cawelti reminds us that "within basic limits of plausibility and audience acceptance, the more realistic, tragic and overpowering the evil plots, the more satisfying the ultimate triumph of the good."[3] And he agrees with Stade that formulas enable the members of a group to share the same fantasies. Formula fictions flourish in pluralistic societies, he suggests, because they serve four important cultural functions: They...

1. Affirm existing interests and attitudes by reflecting the same ones in the imaginary world;

2. Resolve the tensions that result from conflicting group interests or values;

3. Allow readers/viewers to explore the boundaries between the permitted and the forbidden in their imaginations and in a carefully controlled way;

4. Provide cultural continuity by assimilating changes in values into traditional stories.[4]

With his final point, Cawelti sees that popular fictions have the potential, not simply to reinforce a hegemonic system, but to prepare the way for cultural and ideological change.

Some Useful Terminology

Before taking a close look at the forms and techniques that *The X-Files* uses to tell its ongoing story, and how the weekly installments develop that story, some pertinent concepts should be defined and explained. Any reader who is conversant with terms ordinarily used in literary analysis should skip this part and move on to the section *Conventions and Inventions of the X-Files Plot* on page 40.

To begin, this piece of writing that I'm doing (and you're reading) is called a *critical study*, "critical" not in the everyday sense of seeking out flaws, but in the sense of taking a close look at a creative product of some kind. With literature, and that includes popular literature and popular dramatic literature like *The X-Files*, criticism means classifying the work in terms of its genre; interpreting its meaning; analyzing its structure, style and other literary features; showing its relation to other works; appraising its possible effect on readers; describing it in terms of the general principles that can be applied to all literary works; and, if appropriate, defending it against censorship or other negative judgments.[5] Most individuals who write modern critical studies assume that the texts that they choose to discuss are worth the effort of careful and thoughtful examination. A *text*, in this sense, refers to a complete work that may be analyzed and interpreted. It might be a novel, a short story, an individual episode of *The X-Files* like "Irresistible" or "Tempus Fugit." Or it could be the entire *X-Files* series as an ongoing and accumulating whole, the series-as-text. This larger text is the subject here.

A text can be popular or fine/serious/classical/elite literature. Each of these qualifiers means something a little different, but usually they refer to a work generally regarded as "literary art," one that is respected by experts and has outlived the period in which it was written. A text may also be either fiction or non-fiction, and it may be found in many types of media and genres. A magazine advertisement can be considered a text. So can a television commercial or a rock video. The term *media* refers to how the text is communicated to its audience, usually through print, electronically (including broadcast and recording) or by live performance. *Genre* refers to categories of texts that we somehow recognize as being the same type or belonging to the same group because of their form or content.

Genre can be a confusing term because generic categories overlap and combine, and are not mutually exclusive. Traditional literary forms, on one level of genre divisions, can be separated out into either poetry or prose fiction. To study a particular text, however, it is useful to work from more specific genre categories, such as novel/short story/play/ poem/essay. Popular genres are often identified as to both their subject matter and the medium in which they are presented: a television drama or series, a situation comedy (usually assumed to be a TV form) or a horror movie. Knowledge about the history and characteristics of a work's genre can enhance comprehension and enjoyment. That is, someone who has seen and read many detective stories, old and new, can better appreciate how well a particular movie uses the conventions of the detective genre and, additionally, what new and original elements have been added in this text to surprise and delight the viewer. As pointed out previously, audiences like the comforting repetition of a familiar story or form but also find enjoyment in unexpected and creative variations on the basic generic conventions, formulas and stereotypes.

In addition to the idea of a piece of writing or cultural product as a text, a few other concepts need defining and clarifying for use in the discussion that follows, among them, *narrative, story* and *plot*. A narrative is a sequence of actions or events told in chronological order. An historical narrative would be a sequence of supposedly real happenings and a fictional narrative a sequence of imagined happenings. Whereas *narrative* is a rather general term, *story* and *plot* tend to refer more specifically to literary, and especially fictional, texts, including drama. The story of any one episode of *The X-Files* or of the series as a whole may not precisely reflect the way occurrences unfold on the television screen. Such techniques as flashbacks or montage editing or cross-cutting between two different lines of action are not a part of the story; neither are the specific arrangement of scenes or dialogue sequences. These are features of the plot, which has been defined as being (especially for drama) the structure of the action — how the author has arranged the materials of the story to achieve the most effective presentation. The so-called "plot summaries" of the first three seasons of *The X-Files* contained in *The Truth Is Out There* (Seasons One and Two) and *Trust No One* (Season Three) are more a summary of the story of each episode, rather than its plot, but the book devoted to the fourth season (*I Want to Believe*) contains descriptions of episodes which include considerable dialogue and accurately reflect the way the action unfolds on screen. Detail and faithfulness to the sequence of action makes them closer to true plot summaries or synopses, but they certainly are not *brief* synopses.

The plot is of primary importance to any dramatic form because a playwright or scriptwriter cannot speak directly to the audience. The story must be told by means of what characters say and what they do, the two forms of action. Writers of prose fiction and nonfiction are not only free to provide ongoing commentary on the action, but are also able to tell us what people are thinking. Communicating a person's thoughts in drama is more difficult. In *Hamlet,* Shakespeare uses soliloquies to show the inner turmoil Prince Hamlet is suffering and some of the reasons (or rationalizations) for his behavior. Playwrights have also experimented with other devices to communicate what a character is thinking, such as brief asides to the audience, or the use of masks to indicate the character's social persona, and unmasking when he or she reveals true thoughts and feelings. Film noir detective dramas made heavy use of the "voiceover," a device which allows a character, in this instance usually the detective protagonist, to narrate the story as it unfolds. In this running monologue, the character explains events, makes plans, engages in logical deduction, gives the audience new information, reacts to characters and situations and expresses his feelings. We have an intimate connection to the viewpoint of the detective, and his voice takes on some of the characteristics of the author's voice in prose fiction. *The X-Files* also uses voiceover commentary from time to time, but not in this traditional way. Patterns and instances will be discussed in future chapters, especially Chapter Four.

The genres of popular fiction consistently and obviously follow the pattern of formula plots, conventional actions and events (such as a car chase in an action film or a shoot-out in a Western) and stereotypical characters, with these standard elements altered or added to creatively. In Internet discussions and in reviews, the genres most associated with *The X-Files* are fantasy, science fiction and horror. As a result of previous experiences with film and TV and even print versions of these fictional types, fans and critics have formed expectations for them. And *X-Files* episodes, partly because of the four obligatory commercial breaks during the one-hour time slot, have a strongly formulaic and repeated plot pattern. Each individual episode, however, offers within this pattern new characters, settings, dialogue, events and interactions, and, in some cases, developments in the overall story sequence of the series (the mythology or mythos or mythological arc). Cawelti likens formulaic plot patterns to the rules of a game. This comparison points up the fact that dramatic shows like *The X-Files* have something in common with the sporting events and game shows that are also a staple of television entertainment.

However, unlike such TV dramas as police and hospital and lawyer shows, *The X-Files* is not limited to the conventions and formulas of one genre. It draws from a number of them — traditional (print) horror fiction, folk tales/urban legends, science fiction film and television dramas, "paranoid" movie thrillers, crime/detective/FBI stories across media, social melodramas like popular novels and soap operas, and so forth. Thus, while the series is somewhat limited in its choice of plot patterns, it can choose from a wide range of *motifs*, which makes for some structural flexibility. A motif is a plot component, a unit of action or dialogue or some other artistic feature that is recognizable and original. Vampire stories are so familiar to us that the traditional powers of and rules for vampires are common knowledge. These are conventions of both vampiric folklore and the literary vampire tale. While observing some of these elements, though, *The X-Files* devises motifs of its own, which affect both the content and structure of episodes. In the case of a vampire affiliated with the decadent urban blood-sport subculture ("3," 2X07) or a vampire who gains access to his victims as a pizza delivery boy and lives in an RV vampire community ("Bad Blood," 5X12), these content variations also allow for some modifications in structural conventions. How will the investigation proceed? How will this new kind of vampire defend itself? How will its victims try to defend themselves? Will the climactic scene involve a ritual staking? In "3," one vampire is properly destroyed by the rays of the sun, but is later — and less conventionally — revived. In "Bad Blood," vampires are said to be obsessive-compulsive (definitely a new idea), having an irresistible urge to untie shoe laces and pick up scattered sunflower seeds. The employment of an original motif like a fat-sucking vampire named Virgil Incanto, who makes his living translating Italian literature, would certainly affect plot structure, and does, as when the central figure stalks his plump and vulnerable victims through chat rooms on the Internet ("2Shy," 3X06).

Conventions and Inventions of the X-Files Plot

The October 1997 issue of *Focus* magazine (UK) gave would-be script-writers these tongue-in-cheek instructions for putting together their own *X-Files* episode: "Just string these 10 plot clichés together" —

Step One: The core of your story should be an idea "as paranoid and off-the-wall as possible," and the best place to locate such an idea is in urban legends or by scanning magazines devoted to the paranormal and para-politics or by using news events or people in them with a "paranoid twist."

Step Two: In the first scene it is advisable to kill a US government employee ("as bizarrely as possible") in order to give the FBI jurisdiction in the case.

Step Three: Scully proposes a rational explanation of what happened to the victim ("which is obviously completely barking [up the wrong tree] otherwise you've got no show").

Step Four: Mulder responds with a solution involving aliens, government cover-ups or "obscure psychic experiments." Local law enforcement officials react in disbelief.

Step Five: The agents investigate separately, keeping in touch with their ever-present mobile phones.

Step Six: Either or both agents investigate a dark, threatening area carrying "their extremely bright yet poorly illuminating" flashlights.

Step Seven: "Mulder gets beaten up."

Step Eight: "Scully gets kidnapped yet again."

Step Nine: "Explaining it all to [FBI Assistant Director] Skinner."

Step Ten: "Getting rid of the evidence. ... Incriminating files and other evidence of the paranormal must end up back underneath the Pentagon or go up in smoke."[6]

None of the above advice gives the aspiring *X-Files* scriptwriter much help in plot construction, but the steps do point to some important elements that mark *The X-Files*' unique mix of convention and invention. *Step One* points to a thematic element — our fear of the structures of power and those who wield it — which is not only an *X-Files* "invention," but also qualifies as a "convention," in that it served as the central premise of a small genre of "conspiracy films" made in the 1970s. This idea also crops up as the defining feature of an immense outpouring of conspiracy and exposé literature (usually nonfiction books and magazines) published from the 1960s to the present day, and has been notably present in many forms of popular fiction during the same period. *X-Files* producer Chris Carter sees it this way: "The show's original spirit has become kind of the spirit of the country — if not the world. ... There is a growing paranoia, because as somebody once said, there are no easy villains any more. ... The world is run by selfish people whose motives are selfish — and as we all buy into the money culture, it is only going to get worse."[7] In conjunction with its paranoid premise, the series focuses on two thematic questions: "What is the truth?" and "What are the possibilities and parameters of trust and distrust among human beings, given the kind of world in which we now live?"

A third crucial thematic factor is the grafting of its prevailing conspiratorial world view onto a more traditional fear of the unknown. In the '90s, perhaps due to the approach of the millennium, public fancy seemed more willing to be skeptical about science and to consider and accept the existence of the paranormal—such phenomena as prophecies and precognition; angels and ghosts and near-death experiences; vampires, werewolves and demons; alternative realities, channeling, reincarnation and a variety of nonconformist religious or mystical beliefs. In a move that seems as logical as it is inspired, *The X-Files* combines two kinds of fear: socio-political paranoia and the ancient, numinous dread of the supernatural and unexplained.

Step Two refers to the opening act of each episode, a plot feature that is also somewhat conventional in that it is more than a "teaser"; it's a "grabber." Usually it depicts, in the most kinetic and intense manner possible, the inception of the mystery that will proceed to dominate the show. Starting in the middle of an action is a common technique in short stories, where every word counts, and in TV genres that must capture viewers' attention in the first few minutes. Such quick starts are a common convention of action genres especially. The rationale for FBI involvement in the case is almost never given in Act One, but emerges in Act Two, if at all. The suggested "killing a government employee" may be a useful convention for FBI dramas in general, but many times the validity of Mulder and Scully's assignment to cases seems more tenuous. Sometimes "crossing state lines" provides justification, as does "this seemed like an X-Files matter." Not surprisingly, "possible terrorism" gained some ground in Season Five, and in the *X-Files* film *Fear the Future*. Occasionally the agents just happen to be in the vicinity, as in "Chinga" (5X10), when Scully, on vacation in New England, encounters mayhem in a small town supermarket, or in "Detour" (5X04), when a roadblock on a Florida highway lures Mulder away from an FBI Team Building weekend that he and Scully are expecting to attend. At base, fuzzy rationales for involvement in cases are consistent with the indeterminacy at work in *The X-Files* world in general, a world "full of intriguing, frustrating, compelling, tantalizing, and sometimes murderous ambiguities."[8]

Another *X-Files* motif noted by *Focus* is the ongoing oppositional dialogue between the two protagonists. As in *Steps Three* and *Four* above, Scully offers rational explanations and Mulder counters with paranormal alternatives in what could be called a dialectic of belief and disbelief. This dialogic action is equally as important as physical action in forwarding the plot and leading to its outcome. Local law enforcement officials not only "react in surprise," to Mulder's theories, they are often openly hostile to the efforts of Agents Scully and Mulder to solve their cases for them. This adversarial situation is a convention of detective fictions, in which the private investigator and the detective or police officer/chief quite frequently spar verbally and compete with each other. On The X-Files, however, the conflicts are more general and arise among crime-fighting agencies and agents at all levels: an internal "war of one against all."

As Focus notes in Steps Five and Six, mobile telephones and "bright yet poorly illuminating" flashlights do indeed occur frequently, and may be among the most crucial of The X-Files' recurring inventions. Contact by cell phone forwards the action and adds to drama and immediacy. This form of communication instantly lets each partner know what the other is doing. When either cannot be reached by phone, a crisis may be in the making, as at the conclusion of "Nisei" (3X09) when Mulder is on the track of what he believes is an alien that is being transported in a secret government train car. He receives a call from Scully who has been in contact with Mr. X, one of Mulder's informants. X has warned her that it would be too dangerous for Mulder to board the train, and that he should give up the effort. By phone, Mulder tells Scully that he can't give up, and at that moment he jumps from an overpass to the top of the moving train, "losing his cell phone — and thus his lifeline to Scully — in the process."[9]

The cell phone is not only literally his connection to Scully; it is a sign of that connection. Their constant communication across the distances and situations that separate them represents their physical dependence on one another as partners as well as their emotional tie to each other. And on a more abstract symbolic level, their ability to make instant contact indicates their narrative position as a two-person protagonist, a duality within whom doubt and faith, suspicion and trust, intuition and factual certainty perform an unending dance. This dynamic tension between Scully and Mulder constructs their dual identity as a richly complex one, similar to that of a well-developed character in literary art, whose contradictory traits and conflicting loyalties and beliefs make the individual seem more believably human. Although complexity is not a quality usually associated with the protagonists of popular fiction, it has been argued that the same kind of doubled, actually quadrupled, main character (the captain as the man of action, the first officer — Spock — as thought or intelligence, the doctor as emotion, the engineer as professional competence) is the true protagonist of the original Star Trek series.

The searching beams of flashlights against the darkness is another symbolic construct, a motif that carries through episode after episode, becoming, as its mention in the Focus article suggests, a signature element of the X-Files visual style. Again, it is more than that. Light represents the ability to see the truth, to be enlightened or attain enlightenment, the light of reason. And "a light in the darkness" extends the metaphor into an expression of hope, as well. The fact that Mulder and Scully are so often thrust into places and situations obscured by shadow, and the fact that their lights do not appear to be very effective, makes their courage and persistence seem that much more poignant, Mulder's search for the truth that much more perilous. The light-in-darkness motif comes into play through actions that are plot features, and the light/darkness motif is also a continuing reminder of the underlying thematic concerns of the series as text.

Scully's kidnappings are actually few and far between, but the next "cliché guideline" (*Step Seven*) reminds us that Scully, usually portrayed as strong and competent, can also play the stereotyped role of female victim, a horror or thriller tradition. In her case, the surface features of characterization (intelligent, self-reliant) are denied, complicated and interrogated by genre conventions (being an object, being vulnerable) which makes her a more nuanced character. Again, the cliché of Mulder being beaten up (*Step Eight*) happens only occasionally, but is included in the article, I believe, because the writer has latched onto a staple convention of another genre — the hard-boiled detective novel or film. Actually, Mulder is more typically subjected to outright torture or to various psychic or emotional disturbances. Since he has the same passionate and personal involvement in his cases as the hard-boiled detective does, it makes sense that Mulder's dedication would be tested in a comparable way. However, he is not often subjected to beatings, which would be out of character with his persona and his class origins. He is an educated professional member of the upper-middle-class, not a tough, hip man of the streets, as the private eye usually is. In that way he more closely resembles the figure of the classical detective as sleuth.

Even though *X-Files* episodes are usually brought to a provisionally satisfying conclusion, *Step Ten* above is a reminder that resistance to total closure is one of the defining characteristics of the series.

The Rules of the Game

The formula plot, along with its conventional and inventive elements, carries us into the imaginative world of the story, providing the desired shocks and surprises and leading, in the end, to a sense of fulfillment and completion. Typically, any popular narrative moves from an unstable situation in which there are many possibilities through a progression of behaviors and happenings that narrow these possibilities to a more limited array of probable developments and then to a conclusion that could be said to be "necessary," a stable state and a closure that is logically and emotionally satisfying.

This traditional closed plot line is often conceived as a skewed bell-shaped curve, with the long slope to the left representing the rising action of approximately the first ¾ to ⁹⁄₁₀ of a narrative. Longer works usually give proportionately more time to the concluding section, the falling action or denouement. In the rising action, escalating interactions and conflicts bring about increasing tension and suspense until they reach the climactic moment, the high point of the action coming at the highest point of the curve. The right side of the curve then drops more or less precipitously back to baseline, representing the solution of the mystery, the wrapping up of the threads of the story, the answering of questions and the falling-off of tension. This plot format is called a "closed" structure because it wraps everything up by means of its "necessary," but often paradoxically surprising, conclusion — the clincher or the twist. This is the general format that *The X-Files* follows in its weekly episodes, both bound and free. First we'll take a look at the typical *X-Files* plot with examples, concentrating on the free episodes, before examining the more intricate and multi-leveled structure of the bound episode "Anasazi" (2X25) to see how the narrative codes of action, interpretation, symbolism, and so forth, function in the bound plot variants. The focus will then turn briefly to methods *The X-Files* employs to enhance suspense, thereby enhancing its "artistry of escape."

The *X-Files* plot format outlined below generally follows a mystery/action formula strongly influenced by the time constraints of the television medium. The duration noted per segment is approximate and variable, totaling out to about 45 minutes for each one-hour segment. Formula expectations and time requirements set the structural parameters for episode plots. As in sports and other games, the rules remain the same, but the possibilities for play, for invention, within the structure are infinite.

ACT ONE

About 5 minutes. The X-Files production staff calls this act the teaser. The scene is set, usually moving from a quiet beginning quickly into shock and suspense, introducing the incident that precipitates the investigation or will come to play within the action that follows. In "Avatar" (3X21), for instance, Assistant Director Skinner, after refusing to sign divorce papers, goes to a hotel room with a woman he meets in a bar, wakes up after a nightmare and finds that his female companion is dead. Subsequent action involves solving the mystery of the murdered woman and several other related killings that occur along the way. In the second part of the cliffhanger episodes bridging Seasons Three and Four, "Herrenvolk" (4X01) begins with a telephone lineman working peacefully in a rural daytime setting. He is stung by a bee and dies, watched calmly by five strange young teenage boys who look exactly alike. This beginning is followed by a brief reprise of the main events of the final episode of Season Three ("Talitha Cumi," 3X24), and the rural scene is not picked up again until well into the second act. Very occasionally, the first act is or introduces a flashback, especially in Season Five, which has a retrospective feel throughout. "Unusual Suspects" (5X1) starts with the Lone Gunmen being cornered and captured by a SWAT team in Baltimore in 1989 and "Travelers" (5X15) begins in Caledonia, Wisconsin, in 1990 and then, in Act Three, retreats even further into the past to the 1950s McCarthy era, as retired agent Arthur Dales proceeds to tell the story in voiceover narration. A clever device is employed at the beginning of "Tunguska" in Season Four (09), where the appearance of Agent Scully before a Senate committee gives structural reinforcement to the government conspiracy subtext and also introduces a flashback that continues the whole episode. When screen time catches up with "real" time in the second half of this two-parter ("Terma," 4X10), the Senate scene is reprised and the episode concludes in the fictional present.

ACT TWO

Ten to fifteen minutes. In this act, story parameters are established, Mulder and Scully are drawn in, rhythmic repetitions[10] (if any) are initiated, and theories (sometimes mistaken on the part of both agents) are forwarded. Often the scene shifts to FBI headquarters before it moves out again to the Act One location and others. Especially in Act Two, Mulder gives background or historical information about the phenomena being investigated. This is entirely consistent with his role as the repository of cultural memory mentioned in Chapter One, an aspect of his nature which is set in the first season in the sequence of "Shapes" (1X18), "Darkness Falls" (1X19) and "Tooms" (1X20). In "Shapes," Mulder informs Scully that J. Edgar Hoover opened the first X-File in 1946 concerning a case just like the one they are investigating. In "Darkness Falls," he mentions that there had been a previous incident in the same location 60 years before. And "Tooms," by reviving a "monster" from earlier in the first season, is dealing in *The X-Files'* memory as well as the history of the 100-year pattern of violent murders recounted by Mulder and investigated by Scully as the episode proceeds.

ACT THREE

Ten to fifteen minutes. Mulder and Scully's theories continue, questions are raised and, as their investigation proceeds, the partners pursue different aspects of the case on their own, doubling the possibilities for variety in setting and locations. Evidence (including autopsy, laboratory, electronic and historical) is found and considered. Although the range of narrative possibilities is beginning to narrow, the action and mysteries escalate and often more violence occurs, which helps to keep suspense high. The series frequently employs a suspense technique similar to the "red herring" of mystery stories, in which distracting or irrelevant "evidence" comes to light. In *The X-Files*, these distractions are usually not physical clues, but deduction by both Scully and Mulder in the form of theories and hypotheses that are based on some kind of stored information and are forwarded to explain the developing mystery or mysteries. Not infrequently, these explanations either go nowhere or are dead wrong. Viewers play the game by trying to figure out which suppositions and interpretations will turn out to be the correct ones. In the second act of "Eve" (1X10), a man has died from extreme blood loss and puncture wounds in the neck. While the viewer might think that these clues suggest vampirism, Mulder relates them to cattle mutilations as a feature of alien abductions. In Act Three, Mulder and Scully discuss the possibility that the doctor who cloned the daughters of two murdered men might have been responsible for their fathers' murders. This matter remains unresolved until the end of the fourth act, with Mulder still thinking that the doctor and an accomplice murdered the fathers. When it turns out that the girls themselves are the killers, it is clear that their powers of extrasensory perception ("I just knew") allowed them simply to tell Mulder what he already believed at every point in the evolving mystery.

ACT FOUR

Five to ten minutes. Suspense and physical action build to a crescendo, ordinarily producing a cliffhanger moment at the end of the act. But also, certain quiet sequences are most likely to occur during this act, sequences that feature relatively serious private conversations between Mulder and Scully. These moments of relaxed tension work to heighten the impact of the more intense climactic action that follows, and are generally in line with the *tension/release/accelerated tension* pattern especially characteristic of the horror or thriller plot. The episodes "Quagmire" (3X22) and "Detour" (5X04) both have obvious examples of this narrative technique. "Detour" features the scene, discussed by Internet fans and previously described, in which Scully sings "Joy to the World" to Mulder in an intimate Hansel-and-Gretel moment when they are stranded in a dark forest.

Such scenes often do more than create suspense. In "Quagmire," an intimate scene not only checks the rush of events, but also connects the relationship between Mulder and Scully to one strand of the *X-Files'* symbolic narrative code. After the agents' rented boat sinks in a lake, they are left stranded on a rock in the pitch black darkness. Scully is still disturbed at the loss of her newly acquired little dog to an unspecified predator, and she mentions that his name, "Queequeg," came from the novel *Moby Dick*. They discuss the novel, and Scully points out to Mulder how much his "megalomaniacal" quest resembles that of *Moby Dick*'s main character, Captain Ahab. The series has established that as she was growing up, Scully would call her father, a naval officer, "'Ahab' after the stern captain of the doomed *Pequod*; in turn, he called her 'Starbuck' after Ahab's upright and trusted lieutenant."[11] Thus this personal interlude both defines the nature of their working relationship and suggests a more deep-seated connection to, among other things, the Freudian "family romance." This connection recurs in a later episode ("Never Again," 4X13), when Scully tells Ed Jerse about the "other fathers" in her life and we suspect that she is including Mulder among them.

ACT FIVE

About five minutes. In this segment, the climax of the action occurs, precipitating a return to a stable situation; and there may also be one last explanation or revelation. Endings of *X-Files* episodes tend toward as much open-endedness and ambiguity as possible in the mystery genre, a genre that prefers to explain everything in the end, and these indeterminate conclusions and frequent narrative lacunae and silences show the close relationship of *The X-Files* to the horror form or genre. In some, like "Fresh Bones" (2X15), only the viewer, and not the agents or any other character, knows the outcome; in that episode, the corrupt commander of a Haitian refugee camp is seen in a final shot, buried alive and screaming in his coffin. In a similar closing — one of my personal favorites — scientist Chester Banton is shown strapped into restraints and electronic monitoring devices, being subjected to extreme, disorienting bursts of light and sound in a government lab while one experimenter remarks to the other that Banton will surely be a subject of study for a long time to come ("Soft Light," 2X23). "Avatar" (3X21) leaves both viewers and Mulder in the dark as Skinner refuses to divulge how he knew to arrive just in time to shoot the real killer, saving the life of the killer's intended victim. To enhance a sense of closure, sometimes a verbal tag or quip that has run through the show will be repeated here, as in "Syzygy," (3X13) when Mulder repeats, at the conclusion, his own version of the tagline that Scully has used throughout the episode — "Sure. Okay. Whatever." And in "Eve" (1X10), when the scientist who created the Eve/clones asks the girls, whom she is visiting in detention, how they knew she would come for them and they reply, "We just knew." The tag line "I just knew" is then used in other episodes to imply a psychic or intuitive mental connection.

The Mythological Trajectory

Both myths and fairy tales, earlier forms of popular fiction, transmute individual dreams into communal dreams that are shared by an entire culture. The mythic hero, as described by Joseph Campbell and others, leaves his immediate home and community in pursuit of adventure or a goal and faces a series of ritual encounters and ordeals that initiate him into a larger sphere of knowledge. When he returns to the society from which he came, he brings back a gift in the form of the knowledge he has gained. However, his community may not accept him because it views his new knowledge as deluded or dangerous. David Duchovny, the actor who portrays Fox Mulder, describes *The X-Files'* mythic quest in terms of his own character's "archetypal journey: starting from a position of innocence, which is one of trusting his father — the elders, in mythology — being a good boy and a good son, to being an outcast, feeling like his father is Darth Vader, then going to almost as innocent a phase, in which he believes that everyone's a liar, and everyone's out to get him, then maturing to a kind of enlightened cynicism."[12]

Although both protagonists have their own particular history within the X-Files story, Campbell's mythic storyline can be seen as a general template for the ongoing narrative. Mulder and Scully, acting as a dual protagonist, enter the mysterious realm of the unknown and the unexplained, signaled by "X," the X-Files cases, where they fight monsters, face disdain and treachery, and endure a multiplicity of threats to themselves and those they love. But the goal, or truth, they hope to find and communicate to the larger society keeps retreating before them like a mirage. The quest is unending. And given that they discover the truth, if that truth is not pragmatic and scientific, but miraculous or mystical, will the community at large accept or reject their gift?

When the Cigarette Smoking Man interrogates the benevolent alien Jeremiah Smith ("Talitha Cumi," 3X 24), he suggests that a spiritual truth would be rejected. He tells his captive that human beings are weak and venal, that they want to follow authority mindlessly, so they are satisfied with science and require "no greater explanation." This attitude, he says, is just what is required for the success of the Syndicate and its (conspiratorial) "project." Significantly, this negative point of view is expressed by a man whom viewers know to be a liar and a murderer — we are even reminded of his crimes in this scene when Jeremiah Smith morphs into Deep Throat and Fox Mulder's father, two of CSM's victims. Since we know that he cannot be trusted, we can then continue to believe in the moral fantasy that "the truth is out there"— and that we would be willing to accept it even if it required an intuitive leap of faith into a strange, uncertain world.

Whereas each *X-Files* episode achieves some temporary sense of completeness at the end, the overall resolution of the narrative action of the series, which would certainly involve more than the maturing of a single protagonist and would more likely entail the enlightenment of the entire human community, remains a goal as ineffable as the quest for the Holy Grail. Accordingly, the serial format of *The X-Files*, while allowing for small terminal satisfactions, prolongs the ultimate outcome of acceptance or rejection of the truth indefinitely. The mythic element is important, yet Mulder and Scully's activities are not regularly devoted to the larger story of the series, to family history, alien intervention or overt metaphysical speculation. Only occasionally are Scully's religious beliefs tested or Mulder's philosophical concerns addressed. Each episode, through its story, depicts answers to questions about the nature of power, of evil, of the universe and the human role in it; the meaning of "good," "real," "trust," "the truth." Some of the free episodes, like "The Field Where I Died" (4X05) or "Never Again" (4X13), have more significance to one partner than the other, and some episodes, most often the two- and three-parters, provide more information about the story-line of the series as a whole, but most plots show the main characters in the dailiness of their working lives — even though, admittedly, the routine happenings that S/M encounter in their working experience are spiced up with the "extreme possibilities" of fantasy.

There is both rational appeal and psychological satisfaction in following two separate yet interrelated lives (with their memories, true or false) which are engaged once in awhile by matters of principle, belief and personal relationships, but most of the time are just doing a job that has to be done. Most of our lives are like that. Those periods in which we are "just doing our jobs" are the times when we are most apt to be, not "the heroes of our own lives," but actors in someone else's story. This position is the traditional role of the detective, who investigates and solves puzzles that do not involve him or her personally. And the typical plot structure of *X-Files* episodes, both bound and free, is basically that of mystery/solution with variations, very closely related to detective stories, especially paranoid motion picture thrillers like *Chinatown* or *The Parallax View*.

The nesting of stand-alone episodes within an ongoing mythic story arc has been crucial to *The X-Files'* success as a popular fantasy. Similar series have not always been able to solve the problem of either too much or too little ongoing narrative structure. *Twin Peaks* is strangled by its time-bound connecting story; its episodes have to be viewed in chronological order, and once the central mystery of who killed Laura Palmer is solved, narrative momentum quickly fades. In contrast, an omnibus television series like *The Twilight Zone* or *The Outer Limits*, with their free-standing installments, lack the overall cohesion and appeal of characters developing in an evolving story. *Star Trek* and its several clones achieve shows that can be played in almost any order but also have some evolving elements over time, like *The Next Generation* romance between Troi and Riker or the conflict between the *Enterprise* and the Borg Empire. But for the purpose of capturing and holding viewers, *The X-Files* improves upon *Star Trek* by sustaining a tantalizing unconsummated romance and a continuing mystery, while at the same time offering a preponderance of episodes, themselves mysteries, that can clearly stand alone.

Mythos Episodes and
the Structure of "Anasazi"

Rarely does a mythology episode stand alone as "Beyond the Sea" (1X12) does in the middle of Season One. As previously noted, the myth usually develops in two- or three-part sequences that either bridge two seasons or are shown consecutively during a given season. The episode "Anasazi" (2X25) was shown as a cliffhanger at the end of the second season. The story then carries over into the third season with "The Blessing Way" and "Paper Clip." Because of this narrative position, "Anasazi" is developed principally through physical action designed to stimulate viewer involvement and excitement. While there are several verbal revelations, the story largely ignores the conflictive possibilities of dialogue and dialectic. Scully and Mulder do not parry questions, advance or dispute theories, or have quiet, intimate, revealing conversations. Act by act, the episode skillfully orchestrates suspense and shock by engaging the physical action potential of the generic formula plot and downplaying verbal correlatives. Thus, in fact, does every *X-Files* episode mix up its own particular brew of the generic elements described in the preceding section. In "Anasazi," the plot schematic could look something like this:

Act	Structural Component	Episode Description
I	Stable to unstable; Introduction of (one) mystery.	Rural chronotope (isolated, placid) Dessicated corpse exposed.
II	Mulder, Scully drawn into other mysteries and complications increase.	Urban chronotope (complex, anxious), CSM drawn in by Syndicate; Mulder drawn in by Three Gunmen; Scully drawn in by Mulder; Mulder becomes inexplicably violent.
III	Partners separate as mystery, violence escalates.	Scully investigates, encounters danger. CSM and Mulder's father have meeting. Mulder witnesses father's death. Scully becomes most active investigator.
IV	Increasing suspense to end-of-act cliffhanger.	Mulder finds father's killer. Scully shoots Mulder.
V	Final confrontation or exposure; loose closure.	Rural chronotope (as Act One); Confrontation between CSM and Mulder (unseen). Dramatic conflagration; Mulder's fate unknown.

This episode contains unexpected, shocking actions, like the killing of Mulder's father and Scully's wounding of her partner. It downplays such possible components as repeated verbal tags and ironic humor, background explanations, theoretical disagreements and extended intimate conversations. However, it does not follow that the narrative, being highly physical, is therefore shallow or aesthetically uninteresting. In fact, it is an excellent example of the artistry of escape, as the narrative codes it develops connect it to the ongoing mythos and interact to create cohesion and layers of meaning within a complex structural pattern that the preceding plot outline only suggests.

I am borrowing the notion of narrative codes — codes of action, interpretation, characterization/description, realism and symbolism — from Russian and French structuralist critics, but using the term *code* in a loose and informal rather than formal and abstract manner.[13] Here, *code* refers to an implicit or explicit strand of meaning or representation that unifies and complicates a single episode, the two- or three-part series of which the episode is an installment, and the family mythos that is the ongoing chronological "glue" of the series. Since the codes of action and interpretation operate chronologically and the codes of characterization, realism, and symbolism ordinarily do not, the latter are less essential to plot development *per se*, which is the essential concern of this chapter. Instead, the codes of character, reality and symbol tend to enrich and to be enriched by sequentially developing events, actions, logical inferences, explanations, relationships, patterns of suspense and mystery, descriptive elements and such literary tropes as metaphor, metonymy, irony and hyperbole.

"ANASAZI": ACT I

As discussed earlier, an *X-Files* first act typically begins in an unfamiliar area with unknown characters, and ends in some kind of a shock. "Anasazi" starts with an earth tremor during the night that awakens a young Indian man on a Navajo reservation in New Mexico. The next morning, three generations of Native American men sit around the breakfast table — a grandfather, a father and the son (the young man from the previous scene). Contrasting with the sunlit rural tranquillity of this setting, an iconic disturbance occurs at the end of the Act. The young boy discovers skeletal remains that look vaguely extraterrestrial; they have been exposed by the earthquake of the night before. He brings them back home to show his father, grandfather and friends, establishing the discovery and sharing of secrets as the basic repeating elements of the action code of this episode.

The code of realism in Act One places viewers in a recognizable but relatively exotic location, reminding them that earthquake activity can take place in the U.S. southwest desert. These regions are generally known to be earmarked for underground disposal of atomic waste. Yet the hazards of atomic radiation are not depicted or dealt with as part of the action code in "Anasazi" as they are in other *X-Files* episodes.[14] Here, the threat is simply a symbolic overtone connected to the overall conspiratorial premise of the series. Instability in these regions, then, is linked to death by the skeleton as we see it, shot from above, filling the screen and bathed in the ominous clarity of the morning sunlight. Across the narrative space of this brief introductory act are juxtaposed the iconic representation of survival — of the Navajo family (grandfather, father, son) — and of mortality (the skeleton). The spiritual dimensions of Native American experience are introduced through the interpretive code when the grandfather tells his grandson that the desiccated remains should be taken back because, he prophesies, "they" will arrive soon. The ambiguity of the pronoun "they" creates a mystery, demands an inference — the aim of the interpretive code. Who will be coming? Land owners? The killers? Archaeologists? Law enforcement officers? The military? Government agents? Or perhaps other aliens (remembering Deep Throat's comment from Season One that "'they' have been here for a long, long time").

Played against the warm, placid desert setting, the unearthing and exposure of the mysterious corpse also references a recurring interpretation-code element in the series: Dangerous secrets lurk behind the curtain of ordinary life and our conventional unexamined beliefs. These are secrets that "they" know and wish to keep hidden. Both individuals and the body politic must unearth these passive and active deceptions in order to achieve psychic health. By consciously accepting "the truth," then we will know what the world — the universe — is really like and what kind of reasoning and actions will work in it. This is, of course, Mulder's quest, the inferential linchpin of the entire series as text.

"ANASAZI": ACT II

This act introduces the two other strands of the action code, each with its own secrets, which will eventually interweave with or find their way back to the original Native American context. This context represents, in both spiritual and historical terms, a nature-centered life source in polar opposition to the artificial, hierarchical and repressive U.S., Western, and global culture, a culture depicted as essentially deceptive and malevolent at its highest levels. The scene shifts into a pocket of resistance in this larger culture, to a room on the east coast of the United States where a computer hacker accesses another secret. Thus the action code of both the first and second acts centers around the previously mentioned *discovery of a secret*. As the three-part mythos sequence progresses, each discovery is eventually worked out, with its consequences, and other secrets are "brought to light." As he sits in front of his computer reading a book (*Greatest Conspiracies*), the hacker is amazed to find that he has actually succeeded in breaking into highly classified files in the Defense Department computer system. When he begins to copy the files, the action code moves into its next phase (as in bringing the skeleton home in the preceding act) of *appropriating the secret* and the reality code extends into the world community, depicting (in the metonymic image of "secret files") the forces which are the polar opposites of the higher consciousness and way of life represented by the Navajo. We know from the reiteration of the action pattern *discovering the secret* that now "'they' will come."

Next, the reality code projects us into three offices in the U.N. Building in New York City, in a montage sequence of three telephone calls from and to officials sitting at desks in well-appointed offices. Each speaks a different language: Italian, Japanese and German (the WWII Axis powers). Subtitles indicate that they are passing along the information that MJ documents have been compromised.[15] What this montage represents is the World of the Father, which is also the World of the Symbolic. These men have ultimate power over language and the information it disseminates. The scene features dominant world languages spoken in settings that clearly reference a global power network. Subsequently, an alternative language system (Navajo) will be shown to exert a subversive power to counteract the hegemony of dominant language systems. As the montage continues, the last call brings the scope of the action down to the realm of familiar antagonists. The German official calls the Smoking Man, who responds in German, suggesting his link to the international syndicate he either belongs to or serves. CSM comments that this was the call he never wanted to get. Again, the interpretation code is activated, as viewers are led to wonder how, when, and in what way the eventuality of such a call was considered by CSM and his nameless cohorts.

In the next scene, Mulder answers the door of his apartment and opens it to the three "Lone Gunmen," who tell him that a hacker called The Thinker has accessed top secret Defense Department files and now wants to meet with Mulder. This information initiates the next step in the action pertaining to secrets: *sharing the secret.* Two other pieces of information emerge in this scene: Mulder has not been sleeping and is not feeling well, and the wife of a long-married couple in a nearby apartment has just shot her husband. With this scene, three strands of the action code are in place: the Native American strand, the syndicate cover-up strand, and the investigative strand, represented by Mulder and including his mysterious ailment and his coming involvement with the MJ files. Significantly, too, the site of the action has moved to Mulder's personal space — his apartment — and involves his immediate neighbors. Thus the code of reality shows the outside world moving inside, the threat invading his haven, the political becoming personal, or suggesting that, as the '60s slogan would transpose it, "the personal *is* political."

"ANASAZI": ACT III

One aspect of the action code has not yet been established. But it has been prepared for in the family mythos episodes up to this point — the involvement of William Mulder, Fox's father, in a seemingly related but larger mystery, which may connect to the unsolved disappearance of Fox's sister Samantha. Drawing in this element, in Act Three, CSM contacts Bill Mulder and suggests that the copied Defense Department files will expose his involvement in government crimes. Inserting Mulder, Sr., into the plotline of this episode has the effect of linking the action and symbolic code of this particular show to other installments of the mythos which have occurred in the past and will happen in the future. While the interconnected action codes of "Anasazi" are being established, other narrative codes also continue, as I have indicated by references to both interpretation and symbolism in the discussion of Acts One and Two.

Codes of characterization will be explored more fully in Chapter Three; however, one example of evolving character traits will show how such information is woven into the evolving series action code. In the encounter between CSM and Bill Mulder, Fox's father is pouring a drink with a shaky hand, implying problems with alcohol. CSM tells him that his son has the MJ files, and Mulder is dismayed: Fox might learn about his father's part in what the files reveal. As CSM leaves the now visibly ill and distraught Mulder, Sr., he blandly mouths clichés that demonstrate his familiarity with lying while also suggesting his coldness and his capacity for dark irony. He tells "Bill" that it's good to see him again, and observes that he is "looking well." Evidence is presented in the later (flashback) episode "Musings of a Cigarette Smoking Man" (4X07), that Mulder's father and CSM were army buddies at the time Fox was born. This information retroactively illuminates the way these two men have dealt with the need to make decisions that had no right choices and take actions that offered no good alternatives. Mulder's father was evidently weakened, broken by the experience, while CSM became cold, hardened and cynical. Although he professes a belief in the shadowy cause he serves, he is a lone figure, smoking himself to a slow death.

During this scene with CSM, Mulder's father asks if the other will protect Fox and CSM replies by saying that he always has, hasn't he? The relationship between father and child is one continuing strand of the symbolic code of the series. The search for the father, as depicted in *The Odyssey* when the goddess Athena tells Telemachus, son of Odysseus, to find his father, represents the quest for one's place in the World of the Father. Both Mulder and Scully participate in such a quest through the adventures they have and the decisions they make. In other episodes, Scully worries about whether or not her father had been proud of her before his death. In "Anasazi," Mulder's sick, guilty, untruthful father and his violent death, which comes at the end of this act, stand in full contrast to the grandfather/father/son continuity and spiritual connectedness depicted in the Navajo reservation scenes. This juxtaposition symbolically underscores the extreme difficulty of finding an honorable position within a repressive, deceitful and exploitative system.

While Act One ends with the opening of a mystery — "they will come" —
Acts Two, Three and Four all close with outbursts of violence that not only
disrupt personal space but also temporarily deny viewer preconceptions about
normal family and working relationships. The startling impact of each of these
climactic scenes within a broader (mystical/paranormal and conspiratorial)
plot framework shows careful manipulation of the action code. Each incident
not only forwards the sequence of actions in an intensely dramatic way, it also
asks questions related to the interpretation code and ties the close of each act
to the overall action-strand of discovering, keeping and sharing secrets. It
should be mentioned at this point that in episode after episode similar
instances of careful, workmanlike plotting show *The X-Files* to have an uncom-
mon mastery of this crucial element of the artistry of escape.

"ANASAZI": ACTS IV AND V

At the end of Act Two, Assistant Director Skinner asks Mulder a seemingly legitimate question about whether or not he has an illicit copy of the MJ
files, and Mulder hits him. Act Three, then, begins with the FBI reaction to
his striking his superior — an official hearing to assess Mulder's mental condition and his ability to continue as an agent. At the close of the third Act,
Bill Mulder has asked his son to visit him after the Smoking Man departs. Mulder, Sr., is prepared to tell Fox of his past (secret) work at the State Department, but before beginning, steps out of the room and is shot by hidden
assailant Alex Krycek. Fox rushes in as his father, dying, asks for his forgiveness. The next Act (Four) begins as Fox, still at his father's house, phones
Scully and she warns him to leave the scene immediately. The fourth act ends
with Mulder holding his father's killer Krycek at gunpoint, apparently about
to shoot him, when, instead, Scully shoots her partner to prevent it. In the
first scene of Act Five, then, a bandaged Mulder is resting in a room in Farm-
ington, New Mexico, the location of Act One.

Scully has solved the mystery of (or uncovered the secret behind) Mulder's aberrant behavior earlier in the episode and has also engaged the Indian
patriarch introduced in the first act, Albert Holsteen, to translate the taped
Defense Department files, which are encrypted in the Navajo language. The
figure of Albert is a point at which the code of character and symbol intersect. According to Elizabeth Kubek, he "represents an epistomology that the
dominant Order has repressed. As a Native American, Albert represents an
Other who has come to be very important in the cultural Imaginary — the
spiritual man."[16] At this juncture, he also enters the code of reality as a liminal figure, one that occupies the border between the real and the Imaginary.
In both our world and the fictional world, secret WWII military documents
were translated into Navajo because it was an encryption system that the
Japanese could not break. At this point in the plot viewers might conclude

that long-kept official secrets are about to be revealed, completing the action code of *discovering and sharing secrets, or repressed knowledge*. However, in the next episode, "The Blessing Way," we learn that "The Thinker," the hacker who uncovered these secrets has been found murdered, adding another and possibly fatal step to the *secrets* sequence: *paying the price*.

And there is yet another secret beyond the MJ files that remains to be dealt with in this episode, the desiccated skeleton that was unearthed in Act One. In Act Five, Albert Holsteen asks Mulder if he is willing to sacrifice himself for the truth (as The Thinker has?), and Albert's grandson takes the agent to the buried boxcar where he had found the alien corpse. Meanwhile the Smoking Man contacts Mulder by cell phone and warns him that exposing anything would mean exposing his father.[17] But Mulder proceeds to investigate what appears to be a buried train refrigeration car which contains a mass of similar corpses, at least one of which — he reports to Scully by phone — has a smallpox vaccination, a mystery to be carried on to succeeding episodes. Scully tells her partner that the documents that Albert Holsteen is translating indicate that WWII Axis scientists were imported to the U.S. after the war to continue their human experiments. CSM arrives with soldiers and orders them to destroy the buried boxcar that now also holds Mulder, an ironic link to Bill Mulder's request that CSM protect his son. The burning of this repository of secrets and Mulder with them concludes the sequence of four end-of-act climactic moments in which the agent slugs his boss, witnesses his father's death, is shot by his partner and is possibly immolated himself. To add to its symbolic resonance, the conflagration of this last scene suggests a mythic comparison: Mulder's desire to expose secrets, to give people the truth, can be likened to Prometheus' gift of fire to human beings, an act which was also punished by "the gods." This connection has been suggested in an earlier episode by the fact that Mulder admits to having a phobic fear of fire.

Even though it is the first of three parts, in itself "Anasazi" clearly reflects what Cawelti calls "the artistry of escape" by balancing mimesis, or recognizable reality, with characteristics of escapist imaginative experience. It respects the game-like rules of an action/mystery plot formula but introduces playlike variations in its family, conspiracy and paranormal elements. Since plotting is the essential core of this aesthetic, the way "Anasazi" develops four highly climactic sequences within its five-act structure, all the while maintaining an array of symbolic, interpretive and other narrative codes, makes it something of a popular *tour de force*. The suspense that is such a significant aspect of adventure, mystery and horror plots, especially, is often tied to the fate of a character we care about. In the case of "Anasazi," each of the four most intense and shocking moments of action involve Agent Mulder as a central figure. Not surprisingly, this episode was voted the fans' favorite during season four (tying with another mythology episode, "Duane Barry," 2X05). It offers "intense but temporary emotional effects like suspense, surprise, and horror," gives opportunities to identify with appealing, admirable characters, and allows viewers to live for awhile in a familiar yet strange imaginary world.[18] In the next two episodes, which were aired at the beginning of the third season, some four or five months later, Mulder is literally brought back to life by means of a Navajo ritual, during which time he is visited by the spirits of Deep Throat, an early mentor, and his own father, both victims of the system they had served. The connections among two- and three-part episodes not only create unity in that sequence, but also contribute to the overall coherence of the series story.

Plotting for Suspense

Cawelti's study of popular narratives maintains that the most artistic method of achieving suspense is to extend audience anticipation and dread from small units of action (like, what's around the next corner or lurking in the basement) into larger and more believable ones, more believable because the less constricted the suspense techniques are, the less contrived and artificial they seem. It would follow then that the most powerful extensions of suspense in *The X-Files* are those which connect all of the bound episodes and are part of the interpretation code. These can be stated as questions in the mind of the viewer: Are there aliens? If so, who are they and why are they here? What is the Syndicate? And are there other shadowy conspiratorial organizations? What are these groups? What are their aims? What is the interface between our government and these organizations? What happened to Samantha Mulder? Are the Cigarette Smoking Man, Walter Skinner, Bill Mulder and Bill Scully, Jr., good guys or bad guys?

Certain lines of suspense, like Scully's cancer (what caused it? will she recover?), may extend over a full season or more of the bound episodes. The more spectacular, but not necessarily more artful extensions of suspense occur within between-season cliffhangers like the "Anasazi" sequence or "Gethsemane" (4X24) and "Redux I and II" (5X02 & 5X03), a narrative sequence discussed in Chapter One, in which Scully identifies Mulder's body and he is assumed to have committed suicide. Connected episodes are not always bound to the mythic arc of the series, so their suspense may be tied to the fate of characters we care about. In "Fallen Angel" (1X09), viewers meet Max Fenig — charming, kooky UFO buff extraordinaire — and he reappears posthumously in "Max" (4X18) and "Tempus Fugit," (4X17) where we wonder what happened to him and the airplane he had boarded. And why? In fact, the suspense that is such a significant aspect of adventure, mystery and horror plots, especially, often depends on our identification with a threatened character, as in "Anasazi," where each of the four most intense and shocking moments of action involve Agent Mulder as a central figure.

One of the most artful means of extending suspense is for the text to appear to be departing from the conventions of its genre. Cawelti holds that the threat of such a departure is a "terrifying and complex experience of considerable artistic power."[19] Several illustrations from the horror film genre come to mind: *Night of the Living Dead* (1968) deviated from other film texts of its period by not being stylishly and romantically Gothic in the manner of Universal (1930s) and Hammer Studios (1960s) productions. It is gritty in its realism, kills off its appealing young lovers, and features a black man as hero—and he does not survive. The first *Nightmare on Elm Street* (1984) violated a traditional generic feature of the oral horror story by refusing to end with "and then I woke up." Its teenage characters are chased and brutalized through many levels of nightmare. And *Hellraiser* (1987), arguably one of the most potent supernatural thrillers of the 1980s, linked Sadean sado-masochism with interdimensional bogeymen in such a way as to suggest a linkage between inner and cosmic depravity. Only *Ghostbusters* (1984) before it had succeeded in capturing a numinous Lovecraftian sense of a universe permeated with evil, and, since *Ghostbusters* was a comedy, our generic expectations were not so fixed.

Because *The X-Files* is a liminal text, drawing on conventions of the thriller, horror, action, and detection forms, among others, it seldom seems to violate generic boundaries, only to stretch them. Its most successful stretching of these limits comes in sequences of reflexive humor, primarily banter between the two protagonists and serious-but-funny interludes or remarks put in the mouths of guest actors or other less significant characters. One random example that comes to mind is the very stoned pair of teenagers that Mulder and Scully interview in a restaurant in "Deep Throat" (1X01), where the young couple wolf down food and giggle at just about everything, casting doubt on their testimony. Among the 119 episodes aired in the first five seasons of the series, there are a handful that are reflexive throughout. One is "Jose Chung's From Outer Space," partially described in Chapter One. Other such episodes include "Clyde Bruckman's Final Repose" (3X04), "Humbug" (2X20) and, to a greater or lesser degree, "Home" (4X03), "Small Potatoes" (4X20), and "Bad Blood" (5X12). To show that X-Philes are definitely in on the joke, four of these six shows have been voted fan favorites of the seasons in which they appear: "Jose Chung," "Home" (runner-up), "Small Potatoes," and "Bad Blood." While these episodes stray from the grim life-or-death intensity that marks horror literature in general, they are consistent with the overall spirit of the show and acknowledge the close relationship between the grotesque and the humorous. They also recall movie spoofs of the genre, as in such 1940s and '50s productions as *Abbott and Costello Meet Frankenstein* and some of the Vincent Price versions of Edgar Allan Poe short stories. The large number of reflexive and openly satirical scripts aired in Season Six suggests that

The X-Files is at the self-conscious stage of its development as a genre. It has reached this stage not as part of a group of like genre products, but as a unique and singular generic phenomenon that is repeating a development which had previously taken place in the cinematic horror genre. These sixth season "*X-Files* Light" episodes, as one fan called them, in Season Six became the usual rather than the surprising exception in the series' offerings.

Another way that *The X-Files* has consistently built up suspense in individual episodes from the beginning is through the conventional use of repetitions, especially the Rule of Three. Three-part structures have a rhetorical meaning: an inherent sense of completion — beginning, middle, end; introduction, body, conclusion — giving the impression that the subject has been covered or that the range of experiences has been adequately sampled. This plot convention is a regular feature of folktales and fairy tales: The questing hero first encounters a dog with eyes as big as saucers, then as big as platters, then as big as mill-wheels. *The X-Files* regularly employs events, small and large, that are repeated three times: three attacks, three sightings, three murders, three repetitions of a tag line or, as in "Anasazi," three confrontations. Such patterns of threes set up a rhythm of iteration that creates expectation, and this expectation creates suspense. Although a three-part sequence fits well into the abbreviated television hourly slot and between the obligatory commercial periods that break it into five Acts, in some episodes the producers-writers play around with a busier schedule of repeats, each number having its own inherent "meaning." One very interesting example is the four-part structure of "Monday" (6X14). The rhetorical significance of four parts is comparable to that of a square, its four points touching on all possibilities, the four points on a compass, the four seasons, the completion of a cycle — making a circle of the square. In this episode, the repeated day actually happens 40 or 50 times, according to the only character who realizes that reality has been locked into a pattern of infinite regress. But on-screen, all we see are four repetitions. Act One introduces the crucial situation: Mulder and Scully are blown up by an explosion in a bank during a robbery. Then the second through the fifth Acts begin with Mulder waking up late and wet in a waterbed that has sprung a leak. This "bad day" recycles until the principal players "get it right." In Act Five, Mulder finally does.

It is clear that from the beginning the genre category identification of *The X-Files* was left open, so as not to lock the series into formulas and content that would limit its flexibility — and its longevity. The episode "Squeeze" (1X02) was the first to demonstrate a clear connection to the horror (not SF or UFO) genre and since then more than two-thirds of the episodes could be categorized as horror or thriller stories, following the character, content and stylistic conventions of these related forms, with plot structures, as described earlier in this chapter, that often or usually follow the pattern of mystery/

detection. The next chapter will continue this study by describing the elements of content and genre as they occur in both the free and bound episodes, but with an emphasis on the free-standing ones, because these horror/thriller stories make up the majority of shows aired and represent so many of the qualities that viewers recognize as being quintessentially *X-Files*

Chapter Three

Genre and Content

I'd rather live in a world surrounded by mystery than live in a
world so small that my mind could comprehend it all.[1]

The *X-Files* world is indeed surrounded by mystery. There are stories
devoted to various paranormal powers: prophetic dreaming, shape-shifting,
precognition, control of lightning and of fire, invisibility, distance seeing,
mind reading, and psychokinetic abilities, as well as various kinds of demonic
forces and possession — the dark side of the higher spiritual subtext that
attaches to Mulder and Scully. There are stories featuring monsters from the
tradition of supernatural horror and plots which involve paranormal abilities
that suggest an extension beyond the ordinary limits of the mind and body.
There are tales of demonic intrusions into human reality that suggest obsessive-compulsive behavior and other contemporary neuroses.

There are traditional literature or folktale figures and extrapolations or
permutations of these: a manitou (werewolf) that emerges on the boundary
between ranch and Indian reservation; several vampires — one related to an
urban "Goth" context and another to a small-town RV community; the Golem,
a Jewish folk figure featured in an expressionistic German film of the 1920s,
succubi, a sea serpent, an African air spirit, the chupacabra (Latin American
goat sucker), a Frankensteinian "creature," an evil doll and evil machines —
TVs, computers and household gadgets.

And there are mutant or beast humans ("bigfoot" women and fluke men),
scientifically altered humans, humans with paranormal powers, ghosts of
humans, evil children, demonic bosses, cancer eaters, fat-sucking parasites,
terrorists, serial killers and escalating death fetishists. Some less threatening

human types show Scully's connection to traditional religious beliefs or Mulder's attraction to nontraditional and non-religious ones. Stigmatics, faith healers and ill or misbegotten children are Scully's particular province, engendering her own particular kind of sensitivity. And Mulder's area of sensitive interaction often appears in connection with girls or women who are either victims of abuse or in some way powerless. These activate the spiritual natures, powers and insights of the two protagonists, forging a godlike connection between them and the other characters.

And there are also aliens (assassins, clones, MIBs, faceless rebels, Grays and drooling saurians) and alien ships, and wicked scientists, and abductions, and implants, and genetic hybridization procedures, as well as secret files and records, clandestine operating rooms, encoded documents, exploding vehicles, swarming SWAT and decon teams, labs and morgues, mysterious helpers and opponents, dark clubrooms and hearing rooms, bright, well-appointed government and corporate offices — and cover-up after cover-up after cover-up.

So with these content features, is *The X-Files* a fantasy, a thriller, a mystery, a horror or science fiction text, or something else?

The X-Files Genre: Science Fiction or Horror or What?

As we have seen, most *X-Files* episodes follow a mystery-detection plot pattern with a solution, not always clear-cut, at the end. However, having a mystery/solution structure is not the same as dealing with the content of unexplained mysteries or extreme possibilities. Somehow the series manages to present a world that is full of improbabilities of all kinds while still assuring its viewers that they can, in fact, know "the truth." This tricky maneuver is attempted by a handful of highly imaginative literary forms which picture the kind of mysterious universe that Shadow envisions. *Fantasy, science fiction, gothic literature, supernatural fiction, dark fantasy, horror,* and *magical realism*— all of these literary types feature content that deviates from our common-sense ideas about reality and so-called normality. While each type can be referred to as a "genre," they are difficult to package together into a neatly interrelated and integrated generic grouping. *Horror* and *science fiction* are not branches of the tree called *fantasy,* and the only defining characteristic of *horror* as a genre seems to be horror itself — the emotion that it aims to generate in the reader or viewer. The conventions we associate with horror fiction are more iconic (imagaic and sensory) than structural or formal. Dark enclosed spaces, monstrous beings and a handful of conventional situations and suspense techniques have carried over from the gothic stories of the 18th and 19th centuries. But horror does not have a characteristic plot line of its own. It does not even necessarily contain elements of fantasy. Readers and viewers have always known, and have been reminded by movies like *Psycho* and *The Silence of the Lambs*, that human insanity is just as horrific as ghosts or demons or other supernatural creatures. Chapter Five will explain more thoroughly the relationship of *The X-Files* to its gothic and horror fiction antecedents.

For now, I will simply "place" the series in terms of story types that many people are familiar with, and I'll begin with *science fiction*. *X-Files* producer Carter denies that his show is a science fiction text, and there are some good reasons to agree with him, and yet....

One dictionary of literary terms defines science fiction as "a popular modern branch of prose fiction that explores the probable consequences of some improbable or impossible transformation of the basic conditions of human ... existence."[2] This definition is general enough to cover *The X-Files* and it does not contradict Carter's claim that the series deals in extreme possibilities. For *The X-Files*, those "transformed grounds of existence" include such content features as paranormal events and entities, off-the-wall conspiracies and cover-ups, and alien visitations. Northrup Frye, Sheridan Baker and others put the emphasis on the science aspect, as "fiction in which new and futuristic scientific developments propel the plot."[3] This definition probably shows why Carter rejects the SF label. *The X-Files* teems with scientistic (a mixture of scientific and seemingly scientific) explanations and devices galore, but the storyline is propelled by human interaction and motives rather than "scientific developments." Gary Wolfe's *Critical Terms for Science Fiction and Fantasy* suggests that three elements are commonly included in most definitions of the SF form: scientific content, social extrapolation and some perceived link to the "real world."[4] Wolfe also lists a sampling of descriptions of science fiction by writers, critics and scholars, some of which are consistent with recognized features of the *X-Files* series.

Sam Moskovitz, for instance, calls science fiction "a branch of fantasy identifiable by the fact that it eases the 'willing suspension of disbelief' on the part of its readers by utilizing an atmosphere of scientific credibility for its imaginative speculations in physical science, space, time, social science, and philosophy." Harlan Ellison sees the form as "anything that deals in even the smallest extrapolative manner with the future of man and his societies, with the future of science and/or its effects on us, with fantasy as an interpretation of the realities with which we are forced to deal daily." Even though *The X-Files* lacks a futuristic component, it does speculate imaginatively, not about an unknown future, but about a fictional universe that is contiguous in time and space with our own. Brian Aldiss enlarges science fiction to a philosophical process, as "the search for a definition of man and his status in the universe which will stand in our advanced but confused state of knowledge (science) and is characteristically cast in the Gothic or post-Gothic mould."[5] *The X-Files*, then, could qualify as science fiction because it extrapolates from our known contemporary social and political reality, uses "science" to make credible its ventures into the imaginary, and definitely has the quality that Aldiss refers to as being "Gothic or post-Gothic." This gothic aspect is seen in content, in characters and in the series' expressionistic aural and visual style, which will be discussed more fully in the next chapter.

Perhaps the most powerful and oft-noted constituent of the series, however, is the way it captures the current world view and its concurrent fears, then projects these into a slightly skewed, but nonetheless compelling, version of a reality that viewers accept. In other words, it extrapolates from our present situation to a very similar but not identical parallel world. It shows us our fears, gives them force and faces, and engages them in ways we cannot in our everyday lives and surroundings. Traditional futuristic science fiction also extrapolates in this way, but from a more distant space-time perspective. Also like its science fiction cousins, *The X-Files* uses science or the appearance of science to make its fantasy elements more believable.[6] Theories and hypotheses, lab data, official records, formulas and discoveries, electronic gimmicks and gadgets in an unending stream are an integral part of every episode and this scientistic element finds its correlative in language, in the fact that Mulder's voice of intuition and imagination is almost always balanced, countered, or supported by Scully's voice of scientific knowledge and skepticism. This ongoing dialogue instantiates both the expressive and the intellectual as fundamental and desirable human capabilities, which are nevertheless often at odds while paradoxically incomplete alone.

Aldiss' comment that science fiction has ties to the gothic may be disputed by some, but is certainly historically correct. Pure gothic forms date back to the mid–1700s, but the gothic had undergone many changes by the late 19th century, evolving into detective, scientific, and romantic mystery-adventures, as well as the classic ghost story. And although early gothic tales often included a wide range of bizarre and shocking supernatural elements, these were not invariable components of the form, especially in its later developments. Nowadays, imaginative fiction may use such "gothic trappings" as an ancient castle or a vengeful ghost, but even stories with a heavy gothic ambiance — the novels of Anne Rice, for instance — are seldom categorized as gothic fiction. There are crossovers, of course. Joyce Carol Oates, a serious author in the gothic tradition, has seemingly transmuted the form to an acceptable literary level, and the label of "southern gothic" has been applied to the works of such respected writers as William Faulkner and Flannery O'Connor. Nonetheless, gothic romances, descendants of *Wuthering Heights* and *Jane Eyre* (Charlotte and Emily Bronte, mid–19th century) and many lesser works, have laid claim to and just about taken over the popular gothic designation today. Aldiss suggests that *gothic* is still sometimes used to refer to a look or a style that mimics early gothic features, but usually only to suggest an overall dark and foreboding atmosphere rather than taking place in the long-ago-and-far-away or having the medievalist features of early gothic fiction.

Whereas *gothic, fantasy, supernatural fiction* and *science fiction* are terms that refer to generic structures, the rubric of *horror*, as previously noted, refers to an affect (emotional content), and is applied to stories in which the protagonist has reason to be horrified, causing readers or viewers to feel that emotion as well. "Horror" is not alone in this mode of definition. At several points in this study I refer to *The X-Files* as being a "thriller," a term that also describes a popular literary type primarily in terms of its emotional content. Since horror on its own doesn't clearly designate a genre, some writers and critics have turned to the label of Dark Fantasy. However, both an encyclopedia of fantasy and Wolfe's *Critical Terms* disapprove of that use, pointing out that "in recent years many works have been called Dark Fantasy in order — for reasons of perceived prestige — *not* to call them Horror," which may be true.[7] These two sources prefer to use "Dark Fantasy" for works of literary fantasy which arouse a sense of horror. A literary fantasy as ordinarily defined refers only to those works which create an entirely separate alternate or secondary world; think of *Lord of the Rings* as a classic example. Since *The X-Files* does not do this, a more precise generic designation, and one that would suggest its gothic qualities, would be Supernatural Horror Fiction.

The fantastic encyclopedia holds that supernatural fiction is more closely related to science fiction than to pure fantasy. This is true of *The X-Files* as well. In supernatural horror, the real world encounters an invading supernatural element that threatens violations of the body (including conversion and seduction) and must therefore be destroyed or neutralized. Supernatural fiction developed from the gothic by way of the late 19th century ghost story. One compelling indication that *The X-Files* is linked to this tradition can be found in the way it uses explanatory language and dialogue as action: "Owing perhaps to the problematic relationship that tends to exist between the real world and the invading supernatural element, SFs [supernatural fictions] very frequently incorporate ongoing arguments meant to *explain* the invading element, often in a tone of elect knowingness."[8] Both Mulder and Scully argue and supply scientific and esoteric information in this tone, forwarding the narrative, just as the scientist Van Helsing does in the novel *Dracula*.

Another more respectable literary typology could be applied to *The X-Files*, but I am reluctant to use it because it traditionally refers to the literature of colonized cultures, usually of Central and South America: Magical Realism. In Latin America, literary artists employ magical realism techniques to reference the fragmented consciousness of tribal peoples who have had to adjust to the impact of cultural and economic imperialism. "The fantastic attributes given to characters in such novels — levitation, flight, telepathy, telekinesis — are among the means that magic realism adopts in order to encompass the often phantasmagorical political realities of the 20th century." Like supernatural fiction, magical realism combines the realistic with the fantastic, sometimes relying on extravagant and poetic language and using the familiar components of folklore and legend with creative embellishment. These elements are integrated into a "narrative that otherwise maintains the 'reliable' tone of objective realistic report...."[9] Perhaps for U.S. audiences, the most recent and familiar text of this type has been the book and the film of *Like Water for Chocolate*. It is true that *The X-Files* reflects the methods of magical realism in extrapolating from ordinary reality to a parallel world in which fears take on forms derived from myths and gothic traditions, urban legends and news events. But magical realism is not generally a popular form, is practiced primarily by such renowned and respected writers as Gabriel Garcia Marquez (*One Hundred Years of Solitude*) and Jorge Luis Borges, and does not concentrate on arousing horror. Magical realism speaks to the anxieties of exploitation and cultural disintegration, whereas American (and also British) popular horror fiction attempts to deal with our fear that — despite our prosperity, despite our many self-satisfactions — we are somehow wrong, somehow flawed and guilty, somehow monstrous. In her study of fantastic literature, Rosemary Jackson observes that "from about 1800 onwards, those fantasies produced within a capitalist economy express some of the debilitating psychological effects of inhabiting a materialistic culture. They are peculiarly violent and horrific."[10] Thus we could think of supernatural horror fiction as the magical realism of our particular political/economic context — corporate capitalism. The horror story allows us to face our own Shadow and to deal with socially derived fears in a socially approved way. I contend that the best stories do this by arousing two kinds of fear: aesthetic and visceral.

Aesthetic Fear: The Connection to Tragedy

Supernatural horror stories reach back to the oral tales of pre-history. They were also the first form of popular fiction in print and influenced the rapid growth of literacy in 18th and 19th century England. Middle- and even lower-class citizens wanted to become readers so that they too might partake of the frights found in the "penny dreadfuls" and "shilling shockers" that were the "pulp fiction" of the Victorian period. In *Danse Macabre*, Stephen King offers this reason for the undeniable appeal of horror fiction: It is a place where one can exchange one's many conscious and unconscious terrors for a substitute fear that can be worked out through the power of story. But how does "story" — in particular, the stories of *The X-Files* — achieve this transformative effect? One way is to extrapolate current fears or represent them symbolically, then to present them in a dramatic narrative that echoes the features of the earliest dramas, the classical Greek tragedies that Aristotle described in his *Poetics* some four centuries before the birth of Christ. Reviewers of *The X-Files* have commented not only on the fear, but also the pathos that characterizes *X-Files* episodes, and in his seminal work, Aristotle defined tragedy as being "the imitation of an action that is serious and complete, achieving a catharsis ... through incidents arousing pity and terror."[11] He maintained that the tragic effect depends on the central character of the drama having a respected position and admirable traits, so that his destruction arouses pity in the mind and heart of the spectator; this same pity resident in the work itself (the play) is the quality of pathos. The terror engendered by the hero's (or less frequently, heroine's) fate would lie in the fact that this person was not only worthy of our respect, but was also someone much like us.[12] The tragic hero falls due to a character flaw or an error of judgment on his or her part—again, something that could happen to us.

In the period of the British renaissance, the plays of Shakespeare and his Elizabethan contemporaries likewise featured tragic protagonists who were leaders, persons of noble birth—a Prince Hamlet or a King Lear—manifestly on a higher social level than audience members. Their position of leadership and power makes the characters' final drastic change in fortunes that much more moving because their actions affect the lives of all citizens, not just a few intimates. And the flaw or error—Hamlet's indecision or Lear's shortsightedness—allows audience members to identify imaginatively with characters of high station who have the same pathetic human frailties as you or I. The working out of the action code (to return to Barthes' terminology) of the drama arouses and then expunges the emotions of pity and fear. In the movement of the central character from good fortune to bad, the inevitable has taken place. Viewers have seen and experienced the worst—and survived. Moreover, the outcome is satisfying because the audience has been led to anticipate it through the devices of suspense and foreshadowing. This combination of identification and suspense practically ensures that audience members will find release from the grip of pity and fear at the conclusion of the drama—and with it, intense relief. Although this audience reaction is considered an aesthetic and intellectual one (and supernatural horror fiction is supposed to produce gross physical responses only), the formal qualities of tragedy are used to prime advantage in a number, maybe even a majority, of *X-Files* episodes, as we shall shortly see.

The free episodes of *The X-Files*, especially, arouse the emotions of pity and fear as we respond to the predicaments of their victim-monster protagonists. Also, the tightly climactic five-act form of the free episodes is roughly analogous to the form of renaissance tragedies (English and French) and to the serious realistic problem dramas of 19th century playwright Henrik Ibsen. Ibsen portrayed the tragic (or quasi-tragic) protagonist as a middle-class citizen, in line with emerging democratic ideals and changing social conditions. Audiences began to accept the innate worth of more ordinary central characters and became willing to identify with them. In most of the free episodes of *The X-Files*, the monster assumes the role of a subsidiary or stand-in protagonist for Mulder or Scully, who are usually featured in the mythos episodes.

Generally, the The X-Files' victim-monsters are human, human-like, or have been human at some time in the past, and they typically embody a problematic kind of behavior or behavioral principle, a fatal flaw, if you will. These aberrations can be seen as ways of losing control over the self: through reversion to a more primitive state, by obsessions or phobias, or by breaking an ancient, basic and powerful taboo. Such horror icons as sea monsters and horrible diseases may also represent an individual psyche under the control of one of these aberrations, but such non-human objects of fear obviously cannot serve as protagonists. Take for example, the episode "Firewalker" (2X09). The ancient volcanic organism that attacks a group of scientific investigators has been discovered and unleashed by a mechanical device called Firewalker, which is under the direction of Dr. Krepkos, leader of the expedition. The doctor, then, occupies the role of tragic protagonist rather than the lethal organism. Krepkos' Frankensteinian monomaniacal scientific quest is the shadow of Mulder's own search for the truth, and his character flaw is "hübris"—arrogance or, basically, in this context, valuing scientific knowledge over human ties. This fatal error propels the action and leads to the loss of his lover and the supernatural-horror equivalent of exile or banishment for Krepkos himself.

The feeling that one has lost control to either outer or subconscious forces violates a conventional but deeply felt American belief in the importance of individual freedom and dignity. A person dominated by an obsession or a phobia, or who is driven to violate a potent taboo, has lost or relinquished his or her conscious volition in order to follow the dictates of the repressed unconscious elements of the psyche. The outcome for such "monsters" illustrates the danger of unconscious contents to the integrity of one's persona. And because many people are capable of falling into comparable errors, even though they do not approve of the actions of this human monster, they do sense the pathos of his or her situation. In concluding scenes, the protagonist-for-a-day of the monster-of-the-week episode is often shown in a final physical confinement that is an extension of and a logical outcome for his or her actions. That is, whereas before the individual was a prisoner of instinct, subconscious drives, selfish motives or sociopathic impulses, in the end, that person is literally imprisoned.

The human monsters on The X-Files range along a continuum from sympathetic to unsympathetic, from obvious victims to just as obvious willful perpetrators of evil—but usually they are a combination of both, in line with the persistent liminality found in The X-Files narrative. The series explores the moral borderlands and interrogates the polarities of viewers' beliefs, continually searching for the truth and continually finding that truth is provisional, perplexing and paradoxical. The series itself, then, engages in a metatextual quest for the parameters of the truth which mirrors Agent Mulder's, and the "mixed" nature of the series' monsters helps deepen the tragic emotion of pathos that they evoke. It is the relative presence of "good" in a "bad" person or of mitigating circumstances in an evil act which determines how much pathos attaches to the outcome of any given episode. Although the amount of pity viewers feel will depend on their individual life experiences, beliefs and character, the amount of pathos inherent in the text itself depends primarily on how well it melds or encompasses contradictory and paradoxical truths. Let's take a look at a few cases in point.

The Victim-Monsters of The X-Files

CASE ONE

Scientist Dr. Chester Banton unwisely becomes his own test subject in an attempt to ascertain the nature of dark matter. The experiment causes his shadow to become fatal to anyone it touches. At the end of "Soft Light" (2X23), he sits strapped in a chair in a secret government laboratory, being bombarded with extreme, disorienting blasts of intense light and sound. One government scientist who is monitoring his agonized responses tells the other that Dr. Banton will be useful as an experimental subject for a very long time. Banton is positioned at the exact point where gothic and science fiction merge, the "Frankenstein point" that can be interpreted as either identical to or an instance of the tragic flaw. He goes too far. He commits hübris, attempting to usurp the prerogatives of the gods. (See also "Ghost in the Machine," 1X06, and "Synchrony," 4X19.) By pushing scientific experimentation beyond acceptable limits, Banton turns himself into an unintentional murderer who frantically warns his upcoming and unwitting victims, usually to no avail. In the end he becomes an object of pity and fear through his position as an experimental subject imprisoned by a soulless and heartless State.

CASE TWO

Oklahoma small-town teenager Darin Oswald sits alone in his jail cell after being arrested for murders he committed after being struck by lightning and attaining the power to direct lightning to his purposes at will. At the end of "D.P.O." (3X03), Mulder and Scully discuss his fate while the camera regards Darin through the barred window in his cell door. Without the benefit of a remote, he flips from channel to channel on a TV, staring blankly at the screen, and then he clicks the set off. The writer of this episode has stated that the motif of controlling lightning represents the destructive anger of a "disenfranchised adolescent."[13]

We see Darin as a not-very-bright kid who has one friend, an uncaring mother, a dead-end existence in a small town on the edge of nowhere, a talent for playing video games, and a hopeless crush on a beautiful teacher who has been kind to him. Typically, he's a trouble maker when he gets a chance (we've been there). Identification with this trickster aspect of his character can make him delightful, perhaps perversely. He zaps stoplights at a crossroads from his perch on a billboard ledge and giggles at the resulting chaos. He is also understandable and sympathetic in his adoration of the teacher — perhaps the only adult, certainly the only member of the "system," who has ever paid any attention to him. But the power he has been granted is far too much for his undeveloped morals and his overdeveloped resentments.

In the end, the society has restrained him, and his "readings are normal," but his kind of "fiery resentment" (see also the episode "Fire," 1X11) will always be dangerous to those for whom an acceptable place in the community, in life, is more or less assured. Thus at the end a little bit of his power remains. Darin is certainly responsible for his choices, as he must be for his story to have any meaning. But given a similar kind of power, would we ourselves make exemplary choices? He becomes a symbol of youthful destructiveness, thus an object of horror, at the same time that he arouses our pity and fear because his actions are both understandable and monstrous.

CASES THREE AND FOUR

B.J. Morrow ("Aubrey," 2X12) and Virgil Incanto ("2Shy," 3X06) are driven to murderous acts by compulsions beyond their control. Almost everyone who lives in a consumer culture understands at a gut level what it means to have an obsessive-compulsive disorder. As a society, we eat too much (Americans are now the fattest people on Earth), drink too much alcohol, shop impulsively and gamble excessively, run up massive credit card debts and go to "consumer counseling," develop dependencies on people and on prescription as well as recreational drugs, and suffer from a host of addiction-related physical ailments. Such out-of-control behaviors may be blamed to some extent on the inescapable, pervasive advertising culture which surrounds us. B.J. and Virgil, however, are predisposed to their compulsions by heredity or biological makeup (see also "Squeeze" 1X02, "Tooms" 1X20, "Leonard Betts" 4X14, and "Teliko" 4X04. Their fatal flaws are inherent, inescapable.

Unbeknownst to her, B.J. is the granddaughter of a 1940s serial killer and her genetic predilection for committing the same type of crime appears when she becomes pregnant with her lover's baby. Virgil's compulsion arises from his need to consume large quantities of human adipose tissue to make up for a congenital lack of essential fatty acids. He is forced to prey on others in order to survive. After B.J. finds and kills her grandfather, she tries to abort her baby — a son — and is put under suicide watch in prison. At the end we hear that her married lover, a local police detective, wants to adopt her baby, an ironic and chilling final note. In the closing scene of "2Shy," Virgil Incanto's skin is peeling from his face in fleshy gobs, signaling that his days are numbered, as he tells Scully that he realizes she thinks he is a monster, but that he was only taking what he needed to feed his hunger.

The compulsions of B.J. and Virgil stand for those of the viewer, reminding individuals that they should fear their own hungers and subconscious urges. B.J., some might think properly, eliminates her grandfather and tries to avoid giving birth to a baby who might pass along her "bad seed." Both Virgil's and B.J.'s predicaments contain elements of exculpation and blame. The complex interweaving of these encourages ambivalence and reflection and discourages black-and-white judgments or one-sided condemnations. Thus episodes like these lead away from categorical thinking while at the same time eliciting the emotions of pity and fear.

Visceral Fear: Personal, Collective, Liminal

> What makes *Psycho* immortal, when so many films are already half-forgotten as we leave the theater, is that it connects directly with our fears: our fears that we might impulsively commit a crime, our fears of the police, our fears of becoming the victim of a madman and, of course, our fears of disappointing our mothers.[14]

The mix of thinking and feeling that tragedy brings about is essentially an aesthetic response. But many responses to horror fiction involve fears that are more basic and visceral. These are the kinds of real-life fear that *The X-Files* plays upon to achieve the effects we expect from a work of supernatural horror. Like many others, Stephen King believes that our fear response as readers and viewers hinges upon the fundamental and universal fear of our own death. When reading and viewing, we connect our dread of our own particular death to the threats being depicted, causing us to feel that mixture of fascination and revulsion which is the base emotional response to horror texts. In his introduction to *Night Shift*, King declares that, metaphorically, his job as a writer is to show us the corpse stretched out on the table under the sheet and to make us touch it there ... and there ... and ... there. He sees the same kind of death-inspired fascination/revulsion at work in the apparently irresistible curiosity that makes people slow down to gawk at a nasty car wreck on the highway, and this seems reasonable. However, many people regard the desire to witness a scene of mayhem and destruction as purely perverse voyeurism. I have some reservations about that.

Some time ago I learned that psychologists studying soldiers who had fought in the first World War had discovered that those who were most susceptible to "shell shock"—called "battle fatigue" in World War II and "post-traumatic stress disorder" more recently—were those soldiers who had been least prepared for the bloody horrors of the battlefield, who had never experienced and had not anticipated the carnage or its effect on their psyche. (I also believe that a high guilt quotient was added during the Vietnam War and has carried over into more recent U.S. military actions, i.e., Panama.) The seemingly morbid urge to "slow down and look at the wreck" could be, in fact, a natural and even healthy reaction. We are preparing ourselves for the worst as best we can in a "civilized" society where very few of us have ever experienced first-hand the full-blown horrors of systematic torture, cataclysmic natural disasters, or even the kind of modern warfare that we (or our leaders) unleash from time to time on the people of countries like Grenada, Panama and Iraq. And, as the claustrophobic Mad Professor tells his intended victim in the Dutch film *The Vanishing*, "Death is not the worst thing." Death is frightening without a doubt. Through it we step into the always fearsome unknown. And it is inevitable and permanent. It is perhaps the ultimate fear, the final, inexorable thing we have to worry about. But there are many other fears that catch our breath and chill us to the bone. These flesh out, so to speak, the symbolic substructure of any supernatural horror text, and are built up from the fears of childhood and of humanity's more primitive phases.

To reprise these developments quickly, the very young child is afraid of heights, or more properly, falling, and of loud noises. From the age of about 18 months to five years, children begin to develop a fear of animals, and from the age of two on, they become most afraid of snakes. A fear of darkness develops after the child's first year, for obvious reasons: Human beings are very sight-oriented, and darkness curtails movement and stimulates the imagination. Like the fears of childhood, the fears of our primitive ancestors still populate our subconscious. These reflect two phases of development, rural and urban. People who live close to nature understandably fear its more extreme manifestations: droughts, floods, storms, earthquakes, volcanoes, predatory animals. It is also common for country dwellers of many regions to fear witches and ghosts, presumably because these stand for the shadow image of human relationships—witches have potential (magical) power over you, and ghosts represent any guilt you might be harboring about the misuse of your own power, your own mistreatment of relatives and other members of your tribe. Beliefs in supernatural beings or beings with paranormal powers grow from the terrifying prospect of weaknesses in human bonds, a very frightening possibility for those who absolutely depend on family and social ties for survival. These ancient fears have been put to use in gothic and modern supernatural fiction in the idea of the haunted house, a symbolic representation of the human psyche, in which the attic harbors ghosts, the persistence of guilt, and the cellar or underground crypt or vaults are associated with demonic elements or uncontrollable base instinctual drives. From very early on, the supernatural has symbolized human fears by attaching itself to related archetypes from our deepest racial memories.

Gradual urbanization in Europe and elsewhere generally improved safety and stability for many, and the town (as in medieval England) became a symbol of order in the middle of a lawless countryside. But the move to such urban centers brought with it new sources of fear: fire, mobs, noise (a childhood fear that suggests or threatens chaos) and pestilence-disease. These urban fears also account for some of the perennial tropes of the horror story. For instance, disease. The American granddaddy of the viruses, plagues and deadly funguses and parasites of *The X-Files* is Edgar Allan Poe's vision of a country devastated by plague, whose prince abandons his people and hides himself and his nobles away in a locked fortress to wait out the pestilence in luxury and safety — or so he thinks.[15] Skipping ahead to the 20th century, in Stephen King's novel *The Stand*, the U.S. government causes a fatal flu-like disease by sponsoring a research project which goes badly awry, releasing an infection that quickly wipes out most of the world's population.

Many Americans know that the government and its agencies have been blamed for the Tuskegee syphilis experiment on black men, on radiation experiments involving U.S. citizens, and even on biological warfare research that may have caused the Gulf War Syndrome and the AIDS epidemic. *The X-Files* ups the ante by extending guilt to an "octopus" of corporate, global and extraterrestrial entities. The U.S. government is just one of its agencies. In "F. Emasculata" (2X22), a pharmaceutical company secretly tests a gruesome and deadly plague on prison inmates, and in an ongoing plot strand of the series mythos, the government may be collaborating with aliens to develop a virus or a vaccine for possible use on U.S. citizens. Abduction by either aliens or a global syndicate operating through the U.S. government resulted in Scully's cancer and that of a number of other abductees. And where does Mulder locate the cure or antidote for his partner's cancer? In the same secret Pentagon vault (described in Chapter One) where the Smoking Man disposed of X-Files evidence twice during the show's first season. In this way, *The X-Files* attaches radical distrust of those in power to the primitive fear of rampant and uncontrollable disease in much the same way that Poe does in "The Masque of the Red Death."

The free episodes contain a subgrouping of plots devoted to various paranormal powers: prophetic dreaming, shape shifting, precognition, control of lightning and of fire, invisibility, distance viewing, mind reading, psychokinetic abilities, prophetic dreaming, as well as instances of demonic forces and possession. This latter subject echoes the primitive fear of "witches" and sorcerers, and it touches ancient sites of dread in the human psyche. The psychology of C.J. Jung, which has become one of the fundamental components of the thought matrix of the '90s, holds that all individuals participate in a "universal unconscious," almost as part of their genetic equipment, thus they possess deeply hidden memories inherited from the experiences of their ancestors. Even though we don't have access to those ancient memories on a conscious level, we resonate to them subconsciously. These fears also perform the structural function of rhythmic opposition — they are the iconic representations of the dark side, contrasting with the higher spiritual subtext associated with Mulder and Scully. As whole texts, "Die Hand Die Verletzt" (2X14) — crudely but effectively, and then more subtly, "Irresistible" (2X13), "The Calusari" (2X21) and "Grotesque" (3X14) with their literal or implied demons — can be contrasted with such episodes as "Born Again" (1X21), "Revelations" (3X11) and "All Souls" (5X17), with their sometimes quite complex statements about traditional religious beliefs. The latter episodes highlight Scully's connection to the tenets of her Catholic upbringing; her religious faith playing a narrative counterpoint to Mulder's faith in just about everything else that is similarly unproven or unscientific. Both have faith, and when Mulder begins to lose his faith in alien visitation in the fifth season, it has the quality of a religious experience, a "fall from grace."

The X-Files' paranormal episodes can be considered a subdivision of its monster stories, but episodes that most clearly merit the designation of supernatural come from the historical horror tradition. Such "old faithfuls" as zombies, werewolves, vampires, freaks, succubi, poltergeists and golems, as well as newer additions like Latin American chupacabras and African air spirits, reflect *The X-Files'* ancestry from its folk roots to the present. The plots which involve preternatural abilities, on the other hand, have deeper symbolic resonance. Not only do they contribute to a spiritual or metaphysical subtext, but they also reference a thematic strand of the series that has been mentioned previously — liminality. These episodes suggest the possibility of extending human experience beyond the ordinary limits of the mind and body.

As is the case with many post-modern texts, *The X-Files* continually questions or stretches such limits. Its plots and characters deal with the blurred boundaries between life/death, self/other, real/unreal, power/powerlessness. Its stories examine the polar oppositions that pervade both our world and our thinking. Settings thrust us physically into the borderlands beyond comfortable middle-class existence (an Asian ghetto in a large American city, a Haitian refugee camp, a migrant-worker border encampment and innumerable hospitals and prisons) — even old folks homes, factories, leper colonies and zoos. In *The X-Files,* the American small town is inevitably portrayed as a contested and destabilized site, and only the FBI offices in Washington and occasionally the homes of Scully and Mulder are firm ground. Of course, any categories of content for *X-Files* stories overlap and blend in the liminal fashion that characterizes the series' style and world view. As only one example, plots that are built around demonic intrusions into human reality can be seen to explore liminality, be related to the traditional demons of folk legends and horror stories, deal metaphorically with obsessive-compulsive behavior, and examine religious ideas about the nature and the source of evil.

"Sensation in All Its Glories"[16]

Seen alongside other television programs of the late '90s, *The X-Files'* content and style is unique, even compared to fantastic adventures like *Hercules, Xena,* and *Highlander* or the shows that have followed *The X-Files* into the realm of the dark supernatural like *Buffy the Vampire Slayer, Brimstone* or Chris Carter's own *Millennium*. In fact, a number of other series with supernatural premises were launched in the mid–1990s and soon disappeared. Yet in 1998 *The X-Files* moved into its sixth season, and also moved from being a cult series to a mainstream hit consistently in the top 20 shows of the week. By 1997 over 20 million viewers were watching its primetime weekly episodes, and its seven-day-a-week reruns consistently ranked first among hour-long shows in syndication, thereby reaching another ten million viewers. There are many reasons for this success. Commentators cite its big budget, excellent writing staff, charismatic lead actors and close attention to production detail. They less often mention its content — the raw materials of supernatural fiction — and the skillful way this content is handled.

One important aspect of *X-Files* subject matter is that more than any comparable show, it relies on an appeal to the senses. It places its characters — especially, but certainly not only, Mulder and Scully — in situations that make the viewer squirm from sheer visceral empathy. Nowadays we are seldom exposed to extreme sensory stimuli, and that's the way most people like it. Who wants to climb down into an old New Jersey sewer and wade hip-deep through the murky, stinking waters, or perhaps be dragged by something unknown down into the slimy depths, swallowing gunk and choking — even in the line of duty? Who wants to perform an autopsy on a decaying cadaver, or to stick one's hand into a nest of shredded newspaper and withdraw it smeared with human bile, or to sort through plastic-wrapped tumors and amputated body parts in a hospital's biohazard disposal bin? Radically unpleasant extremes of smell, touch and overall bodily sensation are suggested or graphically depicted in almost every episode, and one of the most common situations is one of enclosure or entrapment, probably because it is such a widespread phobia and has historically been a commonplace of horror stories. Crawling through ventilation ducts, being shut in a buried boxcar or stuck in a malfunctioning elevator (with an emphasis on the "mal"), being bound to a chair in a windowless basement, struggling up through the crawl space under an escalator (with something nasty right behind you), or lying in any number of places and positions: pinned down head to foot by chicken wire in a gulag, enclosed in a sealed coffin as the dirt is shoveled onto it, or restrained on all sides in a narrow crematorium chamber — such situations as these push the phobic button of almost any viewer.

An old book about surviving hazardous situations divides its advice into categories for quick recall in case of an emergency. *The X-Files* regularly presents sequences that fit such categories — too hot, too cold, too wet, too fast, too high, even too dry, as in the episode "Dod Kalm" (2X19), when Mulder and Scully dehydrate into the appearance of dried apples because the ship's water is catalyzing their bodies' chemicals and pickling them in sodium chloride. Scully scavenges some meager sources of uncontaminated water — fluid from a sardine can, a little lemon juice, liquid from a decorative snow globe. The ship lurches and the glass containing the precious mixture falls to the floor before either she or Mulder can take a drink. This scene combines a life-or-death situation with homely details that suggest taste, smell, feeling (touch), individual memory and visual associations. *The X-Files'* artistry of escape lies in its expert handling of such narrative materials to arouse involuntary sensory responses. Through the process of identification, viewers not only rehearse for possible real horror in their own lives, as was suggested earlier, but they also enjoy being made to *feel*. Actual intense physical sensation, when it occurs in contemporary "civilized" life, usually takes the form of pain that most people try to avoid or alleviate. Because they can deaden unpleasant sensations, citizens of the Western world experience a restricted range of sensory input on a regular basis. Yet people want to feel their bodies, and they probably need to do so, to exercise their senses as many — realizing the truth of the popular saying "use it or lose it"— consciously exercise their muscles. A large part of the appeal of spectator sports may come from this need to experience the reality of the body, vicariously if not actually, in a society that tends to suppress and vitiate the body's response ability.

An entire continuum of situations foreground sensory experience in *The X-Files*. At the lower, more subdued end of this continuum would be the sewer, the autopsy and the tight places previously mentioned. These are drawn-out experiences, designed to be entered into and savored (flinching perhaps). Situations at the high end of the continuum give viewers a sudden sensory jolt, are undeniably gruesome and often shocking. Stephen King has called this element in its more sickening, sense-oriented manifestations the "gross-out." He believes that it originates in "childish acts of anarchy," but that in fiction it requires an artistic link. *The X-Files'* plague episode "F. Emasculata" (2X22) features large, pulsing boil-like growths that explode onto bystanders, infecting them with the virulent disease. The artistic link would be that the plague results from a conspiracy to experiment on prison inmates without their knowledge or permission, such conspiracies being a thematic component of the series.

One of the episodes most redolent of "gross-out" is "The Host" (2X02), and it also offers a well-integrated aesthetic justification for its sensory assaults.

The story grows from the premise that atomic waste being dumped in the ocean from the Chernobyl disaster has produced an organism that is partly human and partly a parasitical liver-fluke (one of the many liminal or mixed creatures of *The X-Files*). A number of scenes take place in the sewer — some are referenced above — and these, while heightening the revulsion that is a requisite component of horror, take place mostly at the low-key end of the sensory continuum. However, the Dave Barry quote that begins Chapter One describes a scene from "The Host" that falls at the opposite end of that continuum — qualifying as a real gross-out. Toward the end of Act Two, a sewer worker who has been attacked by the fluke-man coughs up a baby fluke-creature in the shower.[17] But of all the episodes with a high gross-out level, perhaps the most terrifying and stomach-turning is "Sanguinarium" (4X06). It answers the question, What might a surgeon who is insane or in the thrall of black magic do to an anaesthetized patient on an operating table? Even the thought is chilling, and the episode conjures up situations and images that touch basic fears about entrapment and helplessness, as well as dread of power figures and controlling institutions.

Occasionally characters are attacked violently by an invisible force or will inflict violence upon themselves. The episode "Pusher" (3X17), as an example, presents a strong visual metaphor for the horror of not being in control or being controlled by someone else. In this case the controller is a would-be Ronin (a masterless Samurai) named Robert Modell, who has developed the ability to inflict his will upon others. Under Modell's (Pusher's) influence, a fireman unwillingly douses himself with gasoline and then, sobbing and protesting, lights a match and bursts into roaring flame. This moment is a shocker and a potent visualization of the dangers of powerlessness. Such jarring sequences take on added impact and significance because they are so seldom used. Oddly enough, even though the series occasionally employs shockingly violent scenes and a constant flow of low-key sensory gross-outs, *The X-Files* is usually restrained in its violence, at least in terms of direct murderous attacks on the physical body. While Mulder and Scully both carry firearms, they rarely use them. And when they do, it is often in a paradoxical way, as at the conclusion of "Pusher," when Mulder plays Russian roulette with Modell. By forcing Mulder to turn his gun on Scully, Modell "pushes" her to act against her partner in order to save herself. Her clever solution to this impasse does not involve the use of a firearm at all. This scene posits the idea that weapons are inherently untrustworthy, in that they can be turned against those who use them, and the situation also examines the notion of trust in general, an important theme of the series. As often happens in *X-Files* stories, what is graphically violent is in the end deflected toward thought and symbol.

Other popular entertainments, like TV or film action-adventure and cop shows, involve more crashes, explosions, gun fights and cases of individual assault than *The X-Files*. Most horror movies, supernatural or not, typically depict gore-splattered attacks by villains or monsters. Although this type of content especially marks Slasher and low budget exploitation films, it is also common in many of the motion pictures that have become "horror classics"— at least since the 1950s. Hammer's lush and lurid Technicolor remakes of traditional monster stories gave new meaning to the British epithet "bloody" during the '50s and '60s. These productions saw great popularity, not only in Britain, but in Europe and the U.S. as well. They also spawned Italian imitations that were even bloodier than *they* were. And the Hammer movies themselves were much more graphic than their U.S. predecessors, the Universal Pictures monster cycle of the 1930s and '40s. Rejecting both the Hammer and Universal traditions, a succession of original and sensation-oriented American movies emerged in the '60s, beginning with George Romero's *Night of the Living Dead* and evolving into the blended space-horror genre with the first *Alien* film, after which the sensory focus moved to Canada's David Cronenberg (*Scanners*) and back across the Atlantic, mutating into cosmic horror with the *Hellraiser* films of England's Clive Barker.

This lineage of relatively "adult" supernatural horror films conspicuously displays violence that is much more terrible and extreme than that of *The X-Files*, whose depiction of physical mayhem is often subtle, discriminating, and "off stage," in the manner of the Greek tragedies that it also resembles in other ways. *X-Files* stories tend to affirm the primacy of an individual's interior life, so the motives, emotions, and compulsions that drive external acts take on more importance than the violent acts themselves. This effect is heightened by occasionally giving either Scully or Mulder the opportunity to comment on a case as he or she prepares a final report. Their commentary tends to be reflective and philosophical rather than explanatory or instrumental. In this voiceover monologue, a kind of intellectual closure is imposed on the materials of supernatural horror without necessarily tying up all of the narrative threads.

The X-Files as a Serial Text

Being a cross-genre, postmodern narrative, *The X-Files* is a supernatural horror text that employs a mystery-detective plot format with content features and storytelling techniques borrowed from other literary forms, and some of these are related to the fact that it is a serial. Stories that are presented or published one installment at a time have similarities in content regardless of genre type and other features. Jennifer Hayward examines serial fiction from the novels of Charles Dickens published in newspapers in segments, to a popular Sunday comic strip of the 1940s, to a present-day television soap opera. She points out that certain narrative motifs are shared by all serials, such content features as "sudden returns from the dead, doubles, long-lost relatives, marginal or grotesque characters, fatal illness, dramatic accidents, romantic triangles, grim secrets, dramatic character transformations."[18] Hayward admits, however, that such devices are not unique to serial fictions and that, in fact, they go back to the Odyssey and to the Greek tragedies previously mentioned in this study.

Nevertheless, the seriation of a narrative over extended periods of time calls for extensive reliance on serial conventions to maintain continuity, interest and suspense. *The X-Files* is no exception, even though its serial element — the episodes bound together by the mythic arc — represents only about a fourth of its narrative space. Yet even the most casual *X-Files* viewer can find examples of every motif mentioned by Hayward in the *X-Files* story as it completes its sixth season:

Sudden returns from the dead	Deep Throat and William Mulder visit Fox in "The Blessing Way" (3X01)
	Melissa Scully calls Dana on the telephone in "Christmas Carol" (5X05)
	Fox claims to have been dead and risen again in "The Blessing Way" (3X01)
Doubles	Dana and Diana, partners for agents Mulder and Spender
	Fox's father William Mulder and Dana's father William Scully
	Clones of doctors (Gregor) and Samantha Mulder in several episodes
	A shape-shifting alien assassin who can be anyone's double
Long-lost relatives	Samantha reappears ... or does she?
	Agent Spender turns out to be the Smoking Man's son
	Cassandra, in "Patient X" (5X13) and "The Red the Black" (5X14), seems to be CSM's estranged wife
Marginal or grotesque characters	There are many of this motif because of *The X-Files'* affiliation with supernatural horror fiction
Fatal illness	Both Scully and Mulder's mothers have had a fatal illness, but were cured
Dramatic accidents	Scully's abduction in "Duane Barry" (2X05) and "Ascension"(2X06)
	Mulder caught at a Russian Gulag ("Tunguska," 4X09)

Romantic triangles	Scully, Mulder and Phoebe Green ("Fire," 1X11), Dr. Bambi Berenbaum ("War of the Coprophages," 3X12), Detective Angela White ("Syzygy," 3X13)
Grim secrets	Mulder's mother and father, about his past, his sister, and his father's work What does CSM know about the master plan? Are there aliens or are they a military disinformation project?
Dramatic character Transformations	Mulder becomes more cynical, ironic, rejects belief in aliens and UFOs for an equally far-out cover-up premise

The foregoing does not propose that *The X-Files* is some kind of paranormal soap opera on the order of *Dark Shadows,* but only aims to show that seriation in itself brings with it certain kinds of content which, in the *X-Files* case, have been incorporated into the narrative spine of the show. Serial elements create suspense by becoming part of a pattern of delayed closure, bringing forth mysteries that blossom, fade and are plowed under to bloom again later as other mysteries. It might be added that this kind of story-telling is related to a female TV aesthetic that finds its best expression in open-ended tales with continuing plot lines, strong and interesting female characters, room to question the central narrative voice — in this case, both Mulder's and the FBI's — and an emphasis on the process of the investigation rather than its outcome.[19]

Although a mention of character traits is jumping ahead somewhat, it seems apropos to point out here that traits associated with Mulder — his emotional sensitivity, his capacity for bonding with female victims and his belief in the paranormal — also place him within the parameters of a female aesthetic. Two critics observe that his sister's abduction has made Mulder a "male in crisis, ... open and vulnerable ... in a pattern that is typically gendered as female."[20] These critics quote Carol J. Clover's pertinent comment that "the man who is open to the occult is open to the feminine in his nature and to nature at large."[21] This connection is reinforced by Mulder's return to life as a result of a Native American ritual in "The Blessing Way" (3X01), and it is humorously interrogated in several "outdoor" episodes, namely "Quagmire" (3X22), in which Mulder searches for a sea serpent and finds an alligator, and "Detour" (5X04), in which he is wounded and spends a cold, miserable night in the forest sheltered in Scully's comforting arms. It is in "Quagmire" that Scully undercuts any Earth Goddess identification with nature on her part by telling Mulder that it's only when you get back to nature that you realize that everything is out to get you. But she *does* credit that comment to her father.

Playfulness, the
Unexplained and the Unexpected

The playfulness and reversals found in "Quagmire" and "Detour" are related to the wry humor and elements of the unexpected that are so characteristic of *The X-Files* and were established at the beginning of the series. From that point, humor and playfulness became not only a mode of communication between Mulder and Scully, but also a means to enrich the show's narrative texture, providing a contrast to high seriousness and high strangeness, as well as to the occasional melodramatic and sentimental moments of *X-Files* scripts. Mulder begins his *X-Files* role on a self-mocking note when Scully knocks on his office door in the pilot episode and he calls out that no one is there "but the FBI's most unwanted." A little later, as the two agents drive down a country road at night, the radio spits out noisy interference and Mulder stops the car, gets out, and draws a large X on the road behind them with red spray paint. When Scully asks him what that was all about, he responds, "Oh, you know. Probably nothing." Further on in Act Two, Mulder and Scully experience nine minutes of missing time at this spot. These negatives and losses — nobody, unwanted, nothing, (time) loss — establish early on Mulder's position in a discourse of opposition and subversion vis à vis the cultural mainstream. His continuing droll comments are not just comic relief. They are frequent reminders of his adversarial role, his role as a Trickster, where the status quo is concerned.

Playfulness in reflexive episodes begins with "Humbug" (2X20), a re-visioning of the premise of Tod Brownings's classic 1932 horror film *Freaks*, and moves on to "Clyde Bruckman's Final Repose" (3X04), "War of the Coprophages" (3X12), "Jose Chung's *From Outer Space*" (3X20), "Home" (4X03), "Small Potatoes" (4X20), "Post-Modern Prometheus" (5X06) and "Bad Blood" (5X12). These episodes explore the interface between the horrible, the grotesque and the ridiculous. This boundary is ever-shifting, as indicated by the fact that what scares one generation will probably only amuse the next. The reflexive episodes also expand the ironic tone of Mulder and Scully's one-liners and repartee to entire stories. Several such episodes take a more sober but equally imaginative view of the cultural position of the *X-Files* text, by proposing revisionist histories that involve the Smoking Man in the assassinations of JFK and Martin Luther King ("Musings of a Cigarette Smoking Man," 4X07) and show the all-but-forgotten terrors of the Communist witch-hunts conducted by Senator Joseph McCarthy during the Cold War ("Travelers," 5X15). These historical rewritings offer alternatives to the dominant version of history, a constructed record that is "ideologically-motivated ... the discourse of the Symbolic Order, the discourse of the Other," the discourse of the Fathers.[22] Not only are official histories the stories told by the winners, they are also merchandise, economic entities that are bought and sold — in books, in newspapers and on TV. Frederic Jameson observes that the "packaged past" as commodity does not know the "rich dialectic of the unique and the iterative."[23] Because works of the imagination have a propensity to be dialogic and idiosyncratic, they call into question standard versions of reality. Thus Rosemary Jackson has labeled all fantastic fiction, "the literature of subversion."

Imaginative fiction often allows or creates narrative gaps and unexplained story elements. These are common devices of supernatural horror, arousing numinous dread in readers and viewers that could be described as the dark side of religious awe and wonder. Numinous dread is the apotheosis of horror emotions. While it is sometimes made more intense by the tragic response of pity and fear, what triggers it is a sense of lack or loss caused by the absence of clarity or resolution in the text. Stephen King's *The Shining* contains an example of how a carefully constructed and placed scene can set up expectations that are never fulfilled in the action code but operate thematically, symbolically, subconsciously, opening up pockets of numinous dread. But they can also function concurrently as foreshadowing devices or some other constituent of the codes of action, interpretation or realism. The short scene described in the next paragraph opens a hole in the narrative and at the same time intimates the existence of a "providence" that will operate later in the book as "the shining," a telepathic connection among good, ordinary, honest people which can combat the (supernatural) monsters of greed, selfishness, perversity, hunger for power and possibly even "the sins of the fathers."

The scene occurs early in the novel. In a flashback, the protagonist Jack Torrance recalls the accident that caused him to quit drinking. He had been a passenger in a friend's Jaguar. It was late at night and both of them were very drunk as they rounded a curve going 70 miles per hour and saw a child's bicycle in the middle of the highway. Jack's drinking buddy Al stomped on the brakes but hit the bike at about 40 m.p.h. anyway and "something thumped underneath them as the tires passed over it." The two pulled off the highway and inspected the damaged Jaguar and the demolished bicycle. Then they spent two hours searching the sides of the road with a high-powered flashlight for a body. There wasn't one. Jack wonders if "some queer providence, bent on giving them both a last chance," had intervened. He could still remember "the squealing tires, the crash ... that single crushed wheel with its broken spokes pointing at the sky." This incident sets up a mystery: A riderless bicycle appears in the middle of a highway in the small morning hours. But the reader never learns how it happened or what "thumped" under the car as it passed over. Had there been a rider, and, if so, what happened to that person? It is the first supernatural occurrence in the story, but it is an incident without agency or resolution, and it just hangs there, waiting to be explained until the end. It never is.

In marked contrast to such horror stories as *The Shining*, stories of detection ordinarily supply a mass of information, including both real and false clues, and then set about sorting out all the puzzles and data and putting everything in its proper place. Supernatural horror, on the other hand, leaves the kind of disturbing gaps and unresolved questions described above. A British commentator points out:

> What defines *The X-Files* is the allure of unknowing: Instead of declaring a mystery and solving it by the end of the show, as Columbo or Father Dowling did, Carter has spent five years showing us everything except the truth. He is a high-concept tease who understands an essential psychological dynamic: The less you give, the more people want. Watching *The X-Files* is almost an interactive venture. It's incomplete enough to compel viewers to complete the blank parts of the narrative.[24]

A reader or viewer is typically left with the feeling that she doesn't have the whole story, that some decaying hand may still thrust itself out of the loose earth covering that recent grave site, grasp her ankle and drag her down. The text that leaves questions unanswered is a story that never ends. Rosemary Jackson locates the lack within the literary type itself— within "fantasy," in her more expanded sense of fantasy as non-realistic fiction. She argues that "the imaginary area which is intimated in fantastic literature suggests all that is other, all that is absent from the symbolic, outside rational discourse."[25] Examining fantastic texts within their cultural context, including Freudian psychology, Jackson finds that fantasy "characteristically attempts to compensate for a lack resulting from cultural constraints: It is a literature of desire, which seeks that which is experienced as absence and loss."[26]

Thus, in horror tales, the unexplained and the unaccounted-for express what we may lack or be losing as a result of living in the world of the Symbolic or the Father: awareness, autonomy, trustworthy love, spiritual fulfillment and so forth. When apprehended consciously, narrative gaps may seem random accidents or continuity errors. Who substitutes the dead dog for Private McAlpin's corpse in the episode "Fresh Bones" (2X15)? And why? What did the demon's first wife remember *but not tell* her husband in "Terms of Endearment" (6X07)? Who is conducting the experiment in subliminal suggestion along with chemical phobia enhancement in "Blood" (2X03)? Is Mulder's explanation really what's going on? One of the writers of "Blood" has commented that he "doesn't have the slightest clue who or what might have been transmitting the subliminal messages and doesn't really care, leaving such things for viewers to consider."[27] At the end of "The Calusari" (2X21), the demon-twin has been exorcised, but Mulder receives a warning which is not resolved in that program (or any other by the middle of Season Six). He is told that although the possession has been broken for the time being, he must be careful because *it* knows who he is. Questions about the nature of the alien presence, about the identity and purposes of the Global Conspirators, and about how supernatural phenomena are positioned vis à vis mundane reality — these are connected to the symbolic code of the series as a whole and remain persistent ongoing fissures in its narrative coherence and unity.

X-Files episode titles, or lack thereof, can be seen as metatextual manifestations of the textual quality of being open or fissured. Much to the annoyance of fans and casual viewers alike, titles are not displayed when the episode is aired, and the names given are usually too brief and not descriptive enough to give solid clues as to content. Some, of course, make an obvious reference to some aspect of the story: "Excelsius Dei" (2X11) is the name of the old folks home where the action occurs, "F. Emasculata" (2X22) is the parasite that carries a plague-like virus, and "2Shy" is Virgil Incanto's Internet chat room sobriquet; "Clyde Bruckman's Final Repose" (3X04), "Jose Chung's *From Outer Space*" (3X20) and "Musings of a Cigarette Smoking Man" (4X07) are long enough to get a handle on, but titles like "Herrenvolk," "Avatar," "Elegy," "Shadows," "Shapes," "Quagmire," "Schizogeny," "Teliko," "The End," "The Beginning" are abbreviated and cryptic, while others are only cryptic. "El Mundo Gira" (4X11) — "The World Turns" is about a UFO scare and a chupacabra visitation at a migrant worker's camp. Since the story is told by two Mexican-American females, the title could be an oblique reference, even an homage, to that other kind of serial, the soap opera, with "El Mundo Gira" being the borderline and nighttime version of the daytime drama *As the World Turns*. The lack of titles or their obscurity simply makes episodes a little harder to find and discuss, which, one must assume, adds to the mystique of "unknowability" that the show cultivates. Staff sources claim that the titles were never intended to describe episodes for viewers, anyway, but are simply applied as labels during the production process. Whatever their origin, nondefinitive and obscure titles blur the boundaries of the text, keep us from summing it up in a couple of words so that it can be separated clearly from our daily reality. Just as the visual quality of the *X-Files* title is blurred in the opening credits on the TV screen, the episode titles are missing, and when we do find them, they don't tell us much. Although they operate outside the text, they still reinforce the many instances of small mysteries — forms of word, name and number "magic" — that occur regularly within the text. When the show transforms and uses the names of real people, actual addresses and birth dates, and when it weaves literary, film and television allusions into its plot, it is drawing the outside world into the text, again breaking down the clear differentiation between story and reality.

The unexpected, or reversals of expectation, are a variation of the unexplained. These also break audience immersion in the story by questioning or denying either rational processes and logical suppositions or the conventions of the genre. One example in the movie slasher genre is the teens in the *Nightmare on Elm Street* movies who think they have awakened from a terrible dream — and so does the viewer — but find themselves in an even more terrible nightmare. A standard character in supernatural horror tales is the unbeliever, the scientist or smart aleck or patriarchal "voice of reason" who scoffs at the mention of supernatural entities or the paranormal. It is conventional for that character to get his comeuppance. Either he is eliminated or hurt badly by the forces whose existence he rejects, or he becomes a believer, like Luke, who, at the end of *The Haunting of Hill House* repudiates his former materialist position that the house is "valuable real estate" and declares that Hill House is evil, that it should be destroyed and "the ground sown with salt." If such a character were to survive the story with his disbelief and scorn intact, this would be an unexpected development and a reversal of most readers' or viewers' expectations. Although the question of belief in the supernatural is only incidental in the following two scenes, they both illustrate similarly adroit handling of expectation and surprise. The first is from a 19th century gothic (vampire) story and the second from a second season *X-Files* episode.

In Sheridan LeFanu's "Carmilla" (1872), a traveling mountebank offers to sell the heroine Laura and her companion Carmilla an amulet for protection against the vampire "which is going like a wolf ... through these woods." According to the peddler, the charm, a strip of vellum inscribed with cabalistic ciphers and diagrams, when pinned to the pillow at night, will protect the young ladies so that they "may laugh in his [the vampire's] face." ("His" seems to be the easily missed cue here.) Both Laura and Carmilla buy one immediately, and the result seems to be beneficial, but Carmilla will not accept any kind of supernatural explanation for its powers, saying that the charm acts only on the body and that "it is nothing magical, it is simply natural." In the end, the charm does not protect Laura at all; convinced to rely upon it by Carmilla, who is actually the vampire, she barely escapes with her life. The idea of a false protective charm links this horror tale incident to one that occurs in *The X-Files*. In "Fresh Bones" (2X15), when Mulder and Scully enter the processing center where Haitian refugees are being detained, a boy offers Scully a protective charm. She is not interested, but Mulder buys it for her. In Act Five, the two agents visit the municipal graveyard. Scully is not feeling well — possibly the result of being wounded in the hand by a branch of thorns earlier in the day. As she sits in the car staring at her hand, the wound expands and a couple of groping fingers emerge from the hole. She reaches up, tears the protective charm from the rear view mirror and throws it out the car window. At that point, her hand returns to normal.

Within the fictional context, magical charms would be a positive force if the source were trustworthy — a child, your partner, a knowledgeable tradesman, a trusted friend — so some of our expectations have been violated in these two sequences whether we realize it or not. Such techniques open up escapist narratives to doubt and speculation, and the entire array of ironic, playful and unexplained devices produces fissures in believability and coherence that give rise to "cracks in the imaginative façade ... lead[ing] us ever deeper into the labyrinth of meaning."[28]

Animals and Objects

In Barron's history of horror literature, Kurt Nielson cites "the realistic depiction of everyday life" as a significant post–WWII development in this genre. In a related development, commonplace natural or manufactured items, otherwise realistic, have very frequently become objects of horror, including the mechanical and electrical objects that people live and work with and the animal life with which they share the planet. The houses in *The Amityville Horror* and the *X-Files* episode "Home" are ordinary places compared to Hill House or Dracula's castle, but terrible things happen in these more mundane places too. Stephen King's "Mangler" and "Trucks," and his devil-car *Christine*, are unreasoning killers, as are the wasps that attack Danny in *The Shining* or the family pet turned savage in *Cujo*. Daphne du Maurer's understated story "The Birds" portrayed natural creatures intent on a mission of destruction relatively early in the post–WWII period (1952).[29] In this tale, the peaceful, settled life of a British seaside farming community becomes disrupted and then completely decimated by hordes of birds in a way that makes it easy to imaginatively extend this singular attack to other farms, villages, towns and even cities. In fact, the main character does this, conjuring up a mental picture of city dwellers who would be completely unable to cope with the birds' fierce, implacable saturation attacks. When the government sends aircraft up to combat them, the attackers fly in masses directly into the propellers of the airplanes, causing them to crash. The hero, Nat, a laconic farmer who had served in WWI, contemplates what the official response might be: "Maybe they'll try spraying us with gas, mustard gas. ...They'll have to be ruthless. Where the trouble's worst, they'll have to risk more lives. ...All the livestock, too, and the soil—all contaminated. ...People panicking, losing their heads." (The birds are not going after livestock or other animals, only people.)

The ecological dimension of birds joining forces across species and attacking human beings, for reasons unstated but easily guessed, may have been more a philosophical abstraction to readers of the '50s and '60s than it is today. In his 1975 study of the popular horror genre, Les Daniels refers to the story as "enigmatic," although "much was made of ... its possible philosophical implications."[30] As the story ends, Nat listens "to the tearing sound of splintering wood ... [wondering] how many million years of memory were stored in those little brains, behind the stabbing beaks, the piercing eyes, now giving them the instinct to destroy mankind with all the deft precision of machines." Few individuals in the '90s would be able to escape the environmental message here, although the story does not belabor it.

The X-Files offers relatively unnatural as well as natural organisms run amok. Among the former are the beasties in "Ice" (1X07), "Firewalker" (2X09) and "F. Emasculata" (2X22), previously discussed. The latter include the locusts that appear at the faith healer's trial in "Born Again" (1X21), the maggots that swarm over corpses in "Fresh Bones" (2X15), a huge python and a rain of toads in "Die Hand Die Verletzt" (2X14), rats and cats in "Teso dos Bichos" (3X18) and, of course, cockroaches in "War of the Coprophages" (3X12). The oddest horror icons finding their way into the *X-Files* menagerie thus far are bees, which in "Herrenvolk" (4X01) and "Zero Sum" (4X21) carry a deadly mutated form of the smallpox virus, linked to "the alien/syndicate conspiracy to monitor and control the earth's population via smallpox-based genetic markers."[31] The bee motif was also used by *The X-Files* movie released in the summer of 1998 after the completion of the show's fifth television season. In the promotional video clips *Inside The X-Files*, which were also aired in '98, Carter describes the bees as a colonizing force with a correlation to the mythology being developed on the show — the idea that aliens are taking over the globe. According to him, the bees may eventually be used in a surprising way. Actually, using bees as an agency of supernatural horror is a surprise in itself; somehow the bee image lacks the viciousness and potency of the image of, say, the wasps in *The Shining*. Although no one enjoys a bee sting, and some few allergic sting victims do die of anaphylactic shock, bees traditionally represent a positive and productive force of nature. This would seem to diminish their ability to arouse numinous dread.

Several links, though, might dispose viewers to accept bees as an icon of horror; two are derived from other popular texts — the monster movies of the 1950s and the seemingly immortal *Star Trek* series on film and TV. One link, however, grows out of a real-world association, the so-called "killer bees" from Africa that escaped from a Brazilian experimental laboratory in 1957, made their way inexorably toward U.S. borders, and have since arrived and begun to crossbreed with domestic bees. The "invasion" parallels the supernatural horror convention that the threatening and destabilizing element be foreign and exotic, like a Dracula who emerges out of darkest Transylvania, or the *X-File* aliens, who have appeared from God knows where in the universe. Although killer bees had a made-for-TV movie named after them in 1974, the strongest tradition of unnatural or evil natural creatures (usually altered by human malfeasance) comes from the "creature feature" movies of the '50s and '60s.

Indeed, the memory of these science fiction thrillers is so strong in the culture that when radioactive ants, flies and gnats were recently found at the Hanford Nuclear Complex in Washington state, the news article began with a reference to "those Cold War–era B horror movies in which giant, mutant insects are the awful price paid for mankind's entry into the atomic age." The article (titled "Mutant Insects: A Myth") goes on to assure readers that "the house-size ants of *Them!* are physical impossibilities," just in case citizens might be taking the monsters of supernatural fiction literally.[32] The enormous ants, spiders and tarantulas that appeared on movie screens of the '50s–'70s were huge because they represented the enormity of the problems posed by nuclear energy and perhaps the enormity of our national guilt in dropping nuclear bombs on the civilian population of Hiroshima and Nagasaki. The oversized atomic mutants who attacked our rural and urban communities in these films delivered appropriate retribution, and by defeating them, we reclaimed not only our clout, but also our innocence.

Obviously, the bee motif of the *X-Files* mythos does not portray its bees as giant bloodthirsty monsters. They are normal-sized insects being used as a tool by aliens and their human allies to implement an unspecified plan that requires (human) population tracking and control. Possibly, the textual impetus for using this particular species is connotative, the intention being to set up certain qualities of bees to function as signs or symbols. Considering *The X-Files'* intertextuality, one link could possibly be to a primary antagonist in the *Star Trek* series: the Borg, a collective race that conquers and assimilates members of other races, when it encounters them, into its so-called "hive mind," thereby eliminating all independence and diversity. The beings thus transformed are referred to as "drones," as are the cloned copies of young Samantha, Mulder's sister, in "Herrenvolk" (4X01). Americans generally place great store in freedom and individuality, even though these are mainly ideological constructs, and a very few attain the consciousness or autonomy needed to escape the conformist pressures of contemporary culture.

It may be that people pay vehement lip service to individual liberty and volition because they sense that these are an ideal rather than an actuality, like the Truth. If so, this inconsistency between inner and outer reality, between belief and truth, would create an area of psychic dissonance capable of being addressed by the Borg concept. The bees' "hive mind," like that of the Borg, functions as a sign suggesting mind control and powerlessness. The link is strengthened somewhat by the fact that both the *X-Files* aliens and their ruling class allies are occupied in cataloging and manipulating the human race. Paranoid individuals do not find that premise unbelievable. The bees — an non-individuated, unreasoning force — may simply be acting as a suggestive connotative image rather than an explicitly denotative one.

Aliens and the Conspiratorial Legacy

One of the most imaginative directions *The X-Files* has taken is to adopt the figure of the alien that has become so familiar since 1947's UFO incident in Roswell, New Mexico, and to make it a conflicted repository of fears, threats and even hope. Primarily it suggests invasion, genetic manipulation, government, military and corporate treachery, and so forth. The image of the Gray alien has certain physical characteristics that link it to other historical and popular culture phenomena. In the '90s, it arouses as much, probably more, cynical amusement as it does terror. Some conspiracy buffs will tell you that reducing the alien to a humorous figure is the result of a plot to make the creatures seem cozy and harmless — thus to allay our suspicion of their secret and nefarious purposes. Since at least the film *Close Encounters of the Third Kind*, one view of these little fellows is that they are harmless, even friendly. On the other hand, they are creatures of the imaginal, thus they represent the unknown and cannot help being vaguely disturbing.

As *The X-Files* presents them, they are nebulous, misty, indeterminate, suggesting the ghosts, wraiths and attenuated ectoplasmic spirits of the 19th century ghost story. Their bald heads and hairless bodies look suggestively skull-like and skeletal. They are small and sexless, like children, and, with their large dark eyes and unformed features, seem to lack emotion and individuality. In the UFO literature, their characteristics and nature vary depending on who is reporting or theorizing: Maybe they are bio-machines that function as the pilot system of bio-mechanical UFO craft; alien intruders whose abductions of human beings are aimed at producing a bi-racial cloned race that will inherit the earth; or a manufactured and soulless race of androids that serve the purposes of higher entities. Whichever of these, or other, scenarios seem most credible, *The X-Files* has not committed itself to any. The morphing assassin who first appears in "Colony" (2X16), the cloned doctors and "sisters" who may be maverick colonists; the inexplicable, cyclopean Lord Kimbote of "*Jose Chung*" (3X20); the faceless humanoids that attack the "experiencers" of "Patient X" (5X13) and "The Red and the Black" (5X14): these other, more concrete and physically threatening, alien entities assume roles in the action code of the series. The Gray generally does not. Earlier icons of gothic and horror fiction usually interacted with humanity, representing its most primitive and basic fears or its guilts and uncontrollable impulses. The image of the not-quite-human Gray is a new variation. As *The X-Files'* most omnipresent horror icon, its ghostly, indistinct image lurks at the borders of the free and bound episodes alike, haunting viewers with intimations of past official misconduct, conspiracies and future discontinuity and disaster.

The X-Files is certainly not the only popular text to work from a conspiratorial premise over the last several decades. In the aftermath of Watergate, a small subset of psychological thrillers, suspense and detective dramas adopted a decidedly paranoid world view, marking a significant change from the overt attitudes of the 1950s toward official power and institutions. Of course, in the '50s there was a vague malaise — suspicion and anxiety; there were noir detective films and dark problem dramas, like *Detective Story*, *Sweet Smell of Success* and *Ace in the Hole*; there were beatniks and angry young men and rebels without a cause. But whatever distrust and fear Americans were feeling was generally directed at the Red Menace and the nuclear threat.

The '60s changed all that. And a scattering of paranoid films made in the early '70s hammers home the premise that the truth, though perhaps desirable, can be exceedingly dangerous, the same premise that is echoed throughout *The X-Files*, especially as it applies Mulder's quest. These movies run the gamut from the intimate threat of *Klute* or *The Conversation* to the more public conspiracies of *Chinatown* and *The Parallax View*. *The X-Files* shares their atmosphere of impending doom, of a gradually unfolding and escalating threat that resists being pinned down to anyone, any reason, but is nonetheless implacable and often fatal. Generally films of this type are not either science fiction or horror (though this changed in the '80s and the '90s with *Blade Runner* and *Dark City*) and there is also a paranoid ambiance in some movies of the blended SF/horror genre, a couple of which are discussed in Chapter Six.

Of the several 1970s "conspiracy flicks" mentioned above, *Klute* is the most personal. The eponymous police detective hero is assigned to protect an expensive call girl, Bree, who has been receiving demented and threatening telephone calls. It is necessary to find the truth — the identity of the caller — in order to stop him and protect Bree, yet the closer Klute and Bree approach the truth about the caller's identity, the more dangerous he becomes. Although this sounds like the plot of many detective movies, what sets *Klute* apart from these others is its careful, artful style and the fact that the villain, Peter Cable, is a rich, powerful businessman and someone that Klute knows socially. Cable murders prostitutes and his business partner, but he has the prestige and clout to be almost above suspicion. One camera shot sums up his position, deliberately panning down the glass wall of the corporate skyscraper, floor by floor to the ground. This shows his place in the corporate hierarchy, as the killer sits in his posh office at the top of the building, listening to a tape of Bree's voice. Cable is identified with this modern structure, as the gothic villain who is such an integral part of the horror tradition is identified with his castle (think of Dracula) and the power over others it represents.

In a later scene on the roof of this edifice, Klute talks to Cable as helicopter noise fills the air. The copter then takes off, with Klute's face reflected in a window and Cable's face, behind the window, gradually consumed by thick shadow as the craft lifts off. Dread and unease is communicated by the film's fragmented viewpoint, many close-ups and tight medium shots, bodies cut off by the frame, people looking at the camera with eyes focused obliquely, away from the viewer. The workmanlike camera and elegant visual style are qualities that all of these films have, and one that is shared by *The X-Files*. This stylistic grace and power may be more apparent in the television show because so few TV dramas have such a carefully cultivated and dramatically effective visual style.

The actor who plays Peter Cable, Charles Cioffi, somewhat resembles President Richard Nixon, especially as his five o'clock shadow becomes darker and he appears progressively more tense and deranged. The same actor portrays FBI Section Chief Scott Blevins on *The X-Files*, appearing in the first episode as the person who assigns Scully as a partner to Agent Mulder for the purpose of reporting to those in command about Mulder's unorthodox methods and cases. In Seasons Four and Five, Blevins reappears as a mole who is also in the employ of Rausch, a multi-national pharmaceutical firm. When Mulder accuses him of a number of crimes against Scully and himself in an FBI investigative hearing, Blevins hurriedly leaves the room and is shot and killed by a mysterious colleague, referred to in the cast list only as the Senior Agent.

As a cultural aside, Alan Pakula, the director of what he called "my paranoid trilogy"—*Klute* (1971), *The Parallax View* (1974) and *All the President's Men* (1976)—died in November 1998 in a car accident that would qualify as a suspicious incident in the second of these films. A metal pipe lying on the Long Island Expressway was apparently kicked up by another car and crashed through the windshield of Pakula's car, which then veered off the highway and struck a fence. *The Parallax View*, the second film in his "trilogy," and Roman Polanski's *Chinatown* were both released in 1974 and both moved the conspiracy film concept further in the direction of public and corporate wrongdoing and political intrigue.

Adopting a classic Private Investigator plot and using the conventional icons and action units of a noir detective film, *Chinatown* enlarges that typically personal and small-focus genre by placing it in the larger public arena. *Chinatown* translates the black and white shadow palette of the noir style into a muted sunny yet sepia-toned Los Angeles of the 1930s. Behind the scenes of the noir murder mystery resides a truly horrendous entrepreneurial villain, Noah Cross. He is speculating on property in Los Angeles County, controlling the water supply and forcing farmers to sell at a loss and move out, so that he can make millions from development after a reservoir is constructed in the valley. In younger days, Cross sexually abused his daughter, producing another daughter (his granddaughter). In the end, J. J. Gittes, the private investigator, knows all of Cross' sordid past and unpunished crimes, personal and public, but can do nothing about any of it. Added verisimilitude resides in the fact that the corrupt land grab was an actual event in California history.

The Parallax View is probably the most chillingly conspiratorial motion picture ever made. Unlike *Klute* and *Chinatown*, the audience is never given *any* hope of finding out about one super-villain's sins or crimes—and then perhaps seeing him punished or brought to justice. *These* men don't have names *or* faces. The film begins with the assassination of a U.S. senator atop the Space Needle in Seattle and the almost immediate death of his apparent assassin. Within a short time, individuals who were in a strategic position to witness the event begin to die, seemingly from accidents or sudden, unrecognized health problems. Joe Frady (echoing the TV series *Dragnet*'s Joe Friday) is a rogue investigative reporter who goes undercover and follows leads to an organization called the Parallax Corporation, which seems to be in the business of recruiting assassins. However, the end of the movie indicates that this organization does not, or at least does not always, recruit assassins, but the patsies or fall guys who take the blame for assassinations, posthumously. Joe unwittingly becomes one of these. There is, however, another possibility. The intelligence forces of the Parallax Corporation may have been aware that Frady was investigating the group, and then simply set him up to be the fall guy for yet another political assassination.

Noir style comes into play throughout *The Parallax View* in intimate interior scenes, where black shadows obscure the background and mask the perimeters of characters' faces, and sometimes in shots where black silhouettes are shown against windows and bright exterior scenes. Horror film tricks with sound accentuate contrast: A scene with a dam pouring a deafening roar of water cuts suddenly to an absolutely silent country road; a telephone rings shrilly and over-loud in a quiet house. The musical theme of the film is so haunting and redolent of threat that it has been used repeatedly in *X-Files* episodes, almost becoming a melodic trademark of conspiracy and paranoia.

The Parallax View translates the black and white of noir stylistics into color by using combinations of red, white and blue throughout. This is its most consistently unifying visual element, and the artificiality of such color manipulation is scarcely noticed because of the subtle and artistic way it is done. Some of these devices are discussed in the next chapter, in conjunction with the style of *The X-Files*. Yet the television series also resembles this cinematic forerunner in its lack of closure, the number of questions it leaves open at the end. The final scene of the film reprises an early one in a suggestively cyclic fashion, with the implication that this outcome will be repeated again and again. The members of a federal investigative committee are seated in a row, raised above the line of sight, at some distance in front of the camera. They sit behind a low desk-like wood-paneled wall decorated with regularly placed official seals. The chair of the committee solemnly intones the findings of the group. They are the same as before, at the beginning of the story. This latest assassination has also been found to be the work of one disturbed man acting alone, and there is no evidence whatsoever of a wider conspiracy.

A significant feature of *The Parallax View* is that it does not have a single, identifiable villain — no crime boss, crazy serial killer, corrupt businessman or crooked politician. The villain is, instead, the system — or an outgrowth of it — a private corporation whose operatives do the dirty jobs that powerful, wealthy groups and individuals want done, but don't want to do themselves. The audience almost never sees anyone from the Corporation, only when assassins are glimpsed momentarily or when Joe Frady meets low-level anonymous contacts. The company has inherited its shadowy nature from the dark man or shadow archetype in gothic literature. This villainous prototype descends from being a fully rounded character (often, in early works, a nobleman or a feudal tyrant), to gradually becoming a less clearly defined evil presence as the horror genre proceeds into the twentieth century. The Parallax Corporation, like the malevolent entities in such modern prose fiction as *The Haunting of Hill House* and *The Shining,* is amorphous and hidden, almost invisible. It resides in a dark universe similar to that of *The X-Files,* in which nameless men, secret and dangerous organizations, and unknowable insidious forces surround and control us. *The X-Files'* environment, like that of *The Parallax View,* is the land of the Men in Black.

Chapter Four

Character, Style and Theme

"We tell interesting stories with interesting characters played by interesting actors."—Chris Carter, commenting on the secret of *The X-Files'* success[1]

William B. Davis, the actor who portrays the Cigarette Smoking Man, has claimed — one suspects facetiously — that his character is the real star of *The X-Files*, and certainly, CSM has increased steadily in importance since his original non-speaking turn in the first installment of the series. Remember that it was he who tucked the mysterious alien implant away in a Pentagon vault at the end of the Pilot episode and stashed the alien hybrid fetus in the same location at the end of the first season. In the overall scheme of things, CSM has become the primary antagonist of the series, attaining the level of a "worthy adversary" of the *X-Files* protagonists Agents Scully and Mulder. His status is affirmed by the level of complexity and the ability to affect the course of the action that his character has reached over the years. He is, in effect, the "king" of the MIBs (Men in Black), in the fictional chronotope that I have previously referred to as "the land of the MIB." Although he appears mostly in mythos episodes, his traits position him uniquely in terms of the *X-Files* cast hierarchy, the nature of which is primarily determined by the genre of the text.

In the array and treatment of their characters, a motion picture and an hour-long television drama resemble a piece of short fiction more than a novel. Shorter forms usually feature one central character, which explains why Fox Mulder is the focus of the action even though he and Scully in some ways make up a dual protagonist. This central character tends to be complex and interesting, while supporting roles are usually more simplified and stereotypical.

Time constraints alone demand that if some characters are explored fully, others must be sketched in quickly and in broad strokes. Since minor characters need to be easily "readable" at first glance, they should, first of all, look like what they are supposed to be.[2]

At the most basic level, characters have distinguishing biological traits: human or animal/ monster/ alien? Man or woman? With very minor characters, this is really all the viewer needs to know.[3] Interestingly enough, this is the level occupied by most of the Men in Black. They are not only unnamed. In many instances, their biological nature is also unclear (human or alien?— although they appear to be human). They are the pervasive background population of the story, and, as discussed briefly in Chapter One, their anonymity unseats the locus of the action. Their place is every place. In their implication of threat, they resemble the white-clad FEMA crews and black-clad SWAT teams and camouflage-clad military special forces. But MIBs operate singly or in limited numbers, and viewers are even more uncertain about their identity and intentions. At least the various official militias occupy set locations and answer to knowable organizations and chains of command.

The most memorable *X-Files* MIBs may be the humorous characters; in "Jose Chung's *From Outer Space*" (3X20), one is played by a professional wrestler and the other by a game show host. They reflect a slightly exaggerated version of the classic type, serving the intent of this episode to take an ironic look at the entire confused cosmography of the UFO universe. Agent Morris Fletcher in "Dreamland I and II" (6X04/5), is another reflexive version of a Man in Black. He is portrayed as a stereotypical and comically unpleasant individual, making him a remarkable reverse-image double of Agent Mulder. At one point, this doppelganger element is strikingly foregrounded when Mulder catches sight of his image as others see him — as Morris Fletcher — in Fletcher's bedroom mirror and goes through a series of ludicrous pantomimed moves which his double mimics exactly.

More serious and threatening MIBs appear in other episodes as a consistent *X-Files* feature. They are ordinarily identified in character lists by such descriptors as the Crew-cut Man, the Grey-haired Man, the Dark-suited Men, and the Dark Man. These types differ from the ones in "Jose Chung" and "Dreamland" in that they do not try to intimidate, nor are they funny. They have no developed dispositional or motivational traits, but take part in the action, usually as hitmen directed by some unnamed villainous force, human or alien. These more dramatically active MIBs appear in "Tempus Fugit" (4X17) and "Max" (4X18), one as the assassin whose job is to kill Max Fenig and retrieve the piece of alien technology he has carried aboard a commercial airliner. The other in the same two episodes is a character who is named in the cast list (Scott Garrett) but is never called that name in the episode. His purpose, though, resembles that of his nameless predecessor, for he tries to shoot an Air Force Reserve officer who knows the truth about the downed airliner and then attempts to take another artifact of alien technology from Mulder. Unexplained MIBs like Garrett are identical in dress and general appearance to alien MIBs and to the anonymous MIB operatives of the FBI, CIA, Parallax Corporation or other proto-military intelligence organizations.

Other minor characters are more than just biological entities. They attain more complexity by having distinctive physical traits, often visual — size, age, health, voice, "normality" or lack of it, even clothing and possessions. The middle-class women of the UFO support group Scully meets in Nisei (3X09) are characters that show who they are mainly by their appearance and their surroundings — the suburban living room in which they meet. Senator Matheson, one of Mulder's sometime helpers, is characterized by his attractive, gray-haired, dignified look and demeanor, as well as by his large, sumptuous and official-looking paneled office. Sean Pendrell, an eager young agent with an obvious crush on Agent Scully, seems mostly a physical presence designed to become a sad casualty in "Tempus Fugit/Max" (4X17/18). In addition to their biological and physical traits, some characters are portrayed in terms of their disposition or customary life attitude. The gentlemen of the Cabal, the Lone Gunmen, Mr. X and Deep Throat, Assistant Director Kersh, Mulder's mother (Teena) and Scully's father (Bill) — all have a consistent, coherent temperament that helps to provide optimum credibility for the individual and enhances the probability and unity of the ongoing series plot. Deep Throat has been described as "avuncular," for instance, and Frohike, of "The Lone Gunmen," can be depended upon to be a dorky and humorous rogue. Assistant Director Kersh is cold, even harsh, and businesslike. And so on.

The most interesting characters from the mythos not only have biological, physical and dispositional traits, but also go beyond these to demonstrate motivation, as well. Some, like Scully's sister Melissa and her brother Bill, are not seen frequently, but during their turns on the show they display a range of traits that indicate needs (instinct), desires (which are semi-conscious) and sentiments (conscious goals). The reasons for their actions are obvious — either spoken or implied — and their motivations are probable and clear, thus contributing to the crucial probability of the action and the entire text. Scully's mother and Mulder's father are also portrayed as having well-defined motives, as do Agent Jeffrey Spender, Assistant Director Skinner and Alex Krycek. And these latter have been regular participants in the action long enough to for viewers to accept them as having motives that sometimes change or conflict. Whereas the dispositional traits of even a well-rounded character are focused and few, more important characters exhibit a multiplicity of motives, some of them contrasting, even paradoxical. Because The X-Files is a popular genre text that is also a serial, characters with established attitudes and motives may well go through changes in personality, behaviors and belief. Serial genres typically involve large casts of characters of differing backgrounds and social classes, and there is time to explore the stories of many individuals and realize the full dramatic potential of even extreme character transformations.

Mulder, Scully, The Smoking Man and Skinner have all shown new or unexpected personality traits in individual episodes, and sometimes over a number of installments. While Mulder and Scully are the most fully realized characters on the series, the protagonists of the free-standing, single-story episodes — heroes like Max Fenig or monsters like Donny Pfaster or victim/monsters like Chester Banton or the Great Mutato — are all, like Scully and Mulder, developed to the point of having clear motivations and both deliberative and decisive traits. They make choices and those choices affect the action and the outcome of the plot. Usually, however, viewers do not see the free episode protagonists recognizing, considering, evaluating and weighing alternatives. The deliberations which go into decision-making are foregrounded more in the two central protagonists. Mulder and Scully discuss plans and procedures along with the nature of the case and the advisability of certain courses of action. Mulder is the one who most consistently faces moral choices, but Scully provides a sounding board, a foil to Mulder's character, and a way to externalize the process of expedient and ethical deliberations. She is his alter ego. Mulder doesn't need soliloquies to deliberate his actions the way, say, Hamlet does. He has Scully to talk to.

In *X-Files* stories, the antagonist or villain is either a personal or a collective figure. Later I'll examine the proposition that Dracula is us, that he represents our collective and individual Shadow. It is also likely that the *X-Files* monsters of the week picture our shadow selves as well, but on a more personal and individual level. The aristocratic villain in the gothic/horror tradition is the one with the power. He represents systemic structures that are overt, repressive and parasitical. It sometimes seems that fictional plots require that the inequities and abuses of a political or economic system be embodied in the figure of one villainous leader, someone the audience can both despise and slyly admire for awhile until this person (characteristically "he") receives his comeuppance. Genre fictions have destroyed this romanticized and glamorized villain again and again for centuries.

The X-Files rings significant changes on this pattern by creating a hydra-headed monster, a shadow syndicate. This organization embodies a Lovecraftian conception of evil which is pervasive and amorphous — a changeling without a single face, villainy unpersonified. When scripts humanize an interesting villain like the Smoking Man, just behind and above him stands the Well-Manicured Man and beyond him is a gathering, a mysterious organization fronted by a heavy-set man in a business suit who is decidedly non-ethnic but who seems vaguely Mafioso in appearance and manner. Even with the demise of many members of the Cabal in Season Six, other corporate, governmental, military and investigative organizations remain to orchestrate vile plots, with or without the collaboration of alien forces. Not necessarily above these entities, but beyond it, are interconnected, coexistent and hidden "interested parties"—various agencies of control that envelope a globe suddenly grown much smaller and its population much more vulnerable to the machinations of the mighty.

The most salient feature of a dramatic protagonist is that the outcome for that character is bound up with the outcome of the plot and connected to the overall theme. In the mythos episodes, Mulder and Scully are the central figures, and what happens to them is of primary importance. In the free episodes, the protagonists are usually the subjects of the mystery to be solved. In addition to the possession of the full range of traits—biological, physical, dispositional, motivational and deliberative/decisive—protagonists often display some, but not all, of the following characteristics:

- The story is obviously about them.
- They change the most or are most capable of change.
- They control the story, as being narrator or commentator on the action.
- They are the most rounded, the most active (rather than passive) and the most constantly "on stage" of all of the characters.
- They are the most complex, with conflicting needs, motives and passions.
- They are characters with whom the audience identifies (but does not always or necessarily like or admire).
- They are the most heroic, performing feats of strength, intelligence, bravery/courage, and integrity.

Because the monster/victim protagonist stands in for so many of our weaknesses, fears and guilts, this monstrous individual is sometimes hard to see as a protagonist at all. But it is the nature of horror fiction to sacrifice its vampires and werewolves, its mad scientists and freaks of nature, in order to cleanse the individual and collective psyche of its dark and unacknowledged content, which these figures represent. In a sense, we could see these "Shadow Protagonists" as heroes for no other reason than that "they die for our sins." Since I have explored some of the types of monster/victim protagonists, and the stories in which they appear, in the previous chapter, I will move on to an examination of Fox Mulder and Dana Scully as the central continuing figures, the series protagonists, in the *X-Files* drama. First, a brief aside about the series' choices and use of characters' names.

The Name Game

Her last name is supposed to be derived from that of a sports announcer, Vin Scully, who was known as "the voice of God." It is also the name of Frank

Scully, who wrote one of the earliest books on UFOs and alien visitation. And her first name is that of an ancient goddess, "the Great Mother of the Danes and many other peoples, such as the Danaans, the Danaids, the biblical Danites, and the Irish Tuatha Dé Danaan, people of the Goddess Dana."[4]

In his novel *From Outer Space,* the author Jose Chung gives Fox Mulder the pseudonym Reynard Muldrake. The last name suggests the "mandrake," a plant ruled by Mercury and considered in folklore and folk medicine to be poisonous as well as magical. The first name echoes Reynard the Fox, a humanized animal character in a collection of tales that originated in 12th and 13th century France but became popular in other parts of Europe. These stories satirized the church and nobility of the time and repeatedly showed that the tricky Reynard could outwit more powerful and confident opponents.

The above are only two of the examples of the Name Game that *The X-Files* plays with its viewers. Arcane and obscure allusions abound. Mostly these amount to giving peripheral characters the names of real-life persons associated with the *X-Files* production company. But the show also gives characters names with relevant Biblical associations — Jeremiah or Samuel — or ties to Greek or Roman myth — Cassandra or Diana (also mirroring Dana) — or paralleling the names of famous serial killers (1X12 and 4X08). In "Teso dos Bichos" (3X18), a Dr. Roosevelt, an archeologist adventurer, is killed at the beginning. And another character is named Dr. Lewton, after Val Lewton who produced the *Cat People* (there are cats in the episode). The nurse Rebecca Waite in "Sanguinarium" (4X06) is also a ritual magician who fights the black magic of a doctor who lives at 1953 Gardner Street. Rebecca Nurse was one of the witches prosecuted at Salem; Waite was the designer of the most popular tarot deck, the Rider-Waite. Gerald Gardner published his first book on witchcraft in 1953.[5] The name of the writer Jose Chung originated in an ongoing practical joke among the *X-Files* script writers. In addition to the outlandish combination of ethnic tags, Jose's initials are J.C., as in Jesus Christ. To me, this persistent feature of naming is a kind of "word magic" similar to the "number magic" discussed later in the section on Style. As indicated, some names appear to have a clear dramatic purpose. The fathers of both Dana and Fox, for example, are William (her father is called a more familiar "Bill"), and Fox's middle name also is William. In addition, Bill is the first name of Agent Patterson, once Fox Mulder's mentor, who is possessed by an evil demon in "Grotesque" (3X14). These associations are significant in light of the plot issue of paternal heritage, part of the series action code. The connection also has thematic dimensions: "the sins of the fathers," as well as the entry of the protagonists into the World of the Fathers, and their potential or actual status therein.

Where the names of the main characters are concerned, the suggestive fogginess of the show's *mise-en-scène* takes on a verbal form. "Fox" must certainly be linked to the Fox Network, the unusual "X" in his name to *The*

X-Files, to "X" the unknown, to "FX" as the abbreviation for special effects, to the fox as a trickster archetype of the same sort as the Native American figure of Coyote. In "Shapes" (1X18), the old Indian points out to Fox that he has an Indian name. And the family names of the three characters most consistently featured on the series are a touchstone to the genre of supernatural horror fiction. They could have been derived from an EC *Vault of Horror* comic book: skull (Scully), skin (Skinner) and mold, or more gothically, mould (Mulder — which is almost always pronounced as though the first syllable contained an O instead of a U). This subliminal tie to the horror genre is surpassed, though, by a reading of the name "Fox" in terms of numerological divination, as follows:

1	2	3	4	5	6	7	8	9
A	B	C	D	E	F	G	G	G
J	K	L	M	N	O	P	Q	R
S	T	U	V	W	X	Y	Z^6	

Essentially, each of the three letters F-O-X have the value of the number 6, or altogether, 666. Traditional numerology holds that while "odd numbers are masculine, active, and creative, even numbers are feminine and passive" and the array of sixes indicates the sensitive and androgynous aspects of Fox's character, which are examined later in this chapter. One source reports that in the Greek mysteries, "the number 666 represented the Mortal Mind" (appropriate for Mulder, who is an adept practitioner of logical reasoning), and "in the New Testament, 666 is called the number of 'the Beast.'" (We could jokingly relate this association to Mulder's religious skepticism versus Scully's conventional Catholicism; it's more likely, however, that this signification points up the paradoxical nature of Mulder's character.) But to go just a little further with popular numerology, the three sixes of Fox, added together, make a total of 18. When one and eight are added, the total is nine, and the interpretation of that number indicates a focus on "spiritual, mental achievement." Mulder, calculated numerically in the same way, results in a number one. Fox Mulder as a unit is also a one, a number that represents "unity, creation, and independence."[7]

Anyone who feels inclined to scoff at the preceding analysis as New Age nonsense is correct about the "New Age" part anyway. The one overriding assumption of this study is that *The X-Files* is a many-faceted embodiment of who and where we are at the present time. Whether someone consciously considered all the above allusions and number-meanings before choosing a name for the main character, or whether these resonant elements are simply examples of Jungian synchronicity at work (or a combination of both) doesn't really matter. Ideas, beliefs, traditions and myths of prior decades, prior centuries, are still with us. The cultural tapestry has expanded to include them all. And such subliminal strategies as what I call "name magic" spin a web of resonant correspondences between *The X-Files* series and the world that surrounds it.

The Good Guys

The high school Science Club sponsor is opening a club meeting attended by five students who appear to be stereotypical "science geeks":

TEACHER: Let's discuss the most important scientific discovery of the last few months — the possibility of life on Mars. What does that mean to you?
STUDENT: It proves that Mulder and Scully were right!
OTHER STUDENTS: (excitedly) Yeah! Yeah! Right!
TEACHER: How many times do I have to tell you? *The X-Files* is not real. Scully and Mulder are played by actors.
STUDENTS: (abashed, hanging their heads) Aww w w....[8]

FOX MULDER, ZEITGEIST ICON

"The first Internet sex symbol with hair" is how Maureen Dowd describes FBI Agent Fox Mulder.[9] For my purposes here, a more pertinent description comes from Laura Jacobs, who observes that Mulder is a "Zeitgeist Icon,"[10] an image with mythical resonance that somehow reflects "the spirit of our age." One reason the character has become larger than life is his intertextual links with past and present heroes of other familiar popular texts, especially the detective or police hero. Another, perhaps more powerful reason for his icon status is symbolic and thematic. After a brief discussion of some of the former connections, I will explore the latter mythic links more fully. To do this, I draw heavily on the archetypal theories of psychologist Carl Jung, whose belief in the paranormal, and whose ideas about individuation, synchronicity and the universal unconscious, have made him an important force in the cultural influences that have given rise to *The X-Files*. To a large extent, his ideas have eclipsed the psychoanalytic theories of Freud in the popular imagination. While not fully accepted and seldom used by literary critics, who prefer to get their mythic constituents (when they get them at all) from Northrup Frye, the constructs that Jung proposes are particularly relevant to this study, and to the character of Mulder especially.

Many seasoned television and movie viewers would recognize that Mulder follows in the footsteps of two earlier icons of individualism, the Private Investigator/Police Detective or the Western Gunfighter. Although these figures arise from different times and "zeitgeists," both, like Mulder, are marked by their own strong personal code of honor. This permits them to move outside the confines of the law and make their own rules. As their successor, Agent Mulder must show that he has the same kind of transcendent autonomy, the power to move beyond the prevailing discourse of a repressive law enforcement institution, and to defy its dictates. Thus Mulder, like his predecessors, frequently disobeys his superiors and takes action on his own. (Whether the hero follows or ignores orders, he always does the right thing.)[11]

Agent Mulder is able to act upon his intuition and instinctual choices because he follows a higher ethical code (his own) and because he recognizes, and trusts, beyond the official discourse of his agency, a higher and more honest use of language: the authentic first-hand story. Mulder repeatedly validates the personal experiences of ordinary people. In the episode "Drive" (6X02), for instance, he listens to Mr. Crump's story, believes it, and acts on it — correctly. In the cultural moment of the '90s, the era of abduction narratives, Internet chat rooms and television talk shows, the individual's own story has assumed immense importance. Social, literary and political theorists Michel Foucault, Mikhail Bakhtin and Frederick Jameson have all observed variously that the body's talk can stand against, even subvert, discourses of power and structures of social control. Jameson calls attention to the ability of the authentic to break through the cultural trance.[12] And Mulder consistently links his energy and action to the truth value of the first-person narrative. In "Terms of Endearment" (6X07), when a small-town sheriff reports a strange case involving his sister to Agent Spender, Spender assures him that he will make it a priority case. The sheriff is relieved and thankful, saying that his sister is anxious to tell her story to a person who will "really listen to her." When the sheriff leaves, Spender immediately consigns the man's report to his shredder, but in the next scene Mulder is on his way to interview the woman and investigate the case.

According to John Cawelti, vitalized stereotypes like the detective or Western hero become archetypes by combining opposed stereotypical traits with touches of human complexity and frailty.[13] Mulder's habitual smart mouth and penchant for pornographic entertainments contradict his empathy and sensitivity and fog the traditional heroic image just enough to make it believable. Compared to another recent FBI television protagonist, Agent Mulder's sly sense of humor stands in contrast to *Twin Peaks*' Agent Dale Cooper's reticence and seriousness. Cooper's sometimes ludicrous dreams and visions, and his subjective deductions, differ in content and effect from Mulder's harrowing memory flashes and his more orderly and informed logic. The significant odd trait that both agents share is that they operate on paranormal premises. Although rare as television characters, literary prototypes exist for detectives that deal in the occult. Three kinds of investigators appear in what Hazel Pierce calls "Science Fiction/Fantasy Gothic mysteries": the bumbling amateur, the private investigator using ordinary methods, and the occult or psychic detective.[14] The latter include such figures as author Randall Garrett's Lord Darcy, a forensic sorcerer who lives in an alternative world where "psi powers complement rational thought and conventional logic," and Frank Lauria's *The Seth Papers*, which features Owen Orient, a medical doctor with psychic abilities. His adventures take place in this space/time dimension and involve a worldwide conspiracy—"The Company" wants to take over and use his powers.[15]

Mulder is an even more unlikely character than these progenitors: He works for a law enforcement agency, but rather than policing boundaries and borders, he expands them to include extreme possibilities. He is personally involved in his work. It is the stage upon which he engages his destiny. And it is essential to his search for the truth, which at one level is the search for "rightful occupation," for the constructive and honorable way to live. Suspended for his thirtysomething moment between the hierarchical and coercive World of the Father and the indistinct image of the Alien Other, he makes recurring contact with monsters: with men whose powers estrange them from even the male dominated culture and women whose sensitivity and emotional openness allow him to make intimate focused contact with both his own anima and an alternative cultural consciousness. *Entertainment Weekly*'s Ken Tucker certainly understands the significance of Mulder's career when he recommends *The X-Files* as one of 1998's top ten shows largely on the strength of what he sees as its message, "that work—what you choose to do with your life as a productive human being—is at once the ultimate pleasure and the ultimate torture."[16]

As a joker, or a trickster archetype, Mulder represents a force for change, even chaos, and he exerts that kind of influence in *The X-Files* world. The third episode of the series, "Squeeze," establishes this characteristic, as Mulder throws off Tom Colton's by-the-book investigation and thwarts his drive to be a department star. As usual, Mulder operates logically and collects and interprets evidence creatively—he finds and correctly interprets Tooms' elongated fingerprints—but he works from premises that are beyond the pale, and with data and precedents that are outside of the boundaries of ordinary, respectable FBI protocols. Other, run-of-the-mill and less imaginative agents make fun of him, disparage and discredit his ideas and his work. He is treated as "an intrusion from an alien landscape."[17] And yet, Mulder is not an all-round loud-mouthed misfit and trouble-maker like the Kolchak character upon which he is supposedly modeled. He is a later version of the believer/rebel, who pleases viewers to the extent that their consciousness resembles his. Then, as long as he is out there to be more an outsider, more questioning, and perhaps more dangerous to the system than they are, they feel relatively safe. He's the one sticking his neck out, like Joe Frady in *The Parallax View*, and, also like Frady. he'll go down first—or someone like him in the real world. A paranoid vision, but the '90s is a decade awash with paranoia. And to audience members with this suspicious world view, the character Mulder functions meta-textually as well as within the text as a sacrificial being (as do protagonists of the free episodes, but differently). To be a communal sacrifice is also one of the roles of the trickster.

In the "Trickster Cycle" of world myth, this archetype develops from a more primitive and more "brutal, savage, stupid" and insensitive state into a creature who is conspicuously clever, "useful and sensible."[18] This kind of transformation can occur in the traditional characters of folklore and of genre literature. A good example is Arelecchino, a popular farcical character in Commedia dell' Arte or Italian folk drama. This changling begins his stage life as a hungry jokester, a vulgar, clumsy dimwit. But he gradually transmutes over several centuries into a sophisticated trickster, the elegant and acrobatic Harlequin, perhaps the most popular stock character of 17th and 18th century French pantomimes and "Harlequinades." Another example, of course, is the Kolchak to Mulder evolution.

Looking back toward trickster origins in Western belief systems, Carl Jung finds the alchemical figure of Mercurius to be even older than the Greek deity Hermes. Mercurius is a site of contradictions characterized by his "sly jokes and malicious pranks" along with a nature that is both animal and divine. He is regularly exposed to torture and — from that — also comes to approximate a savior figure. In this way he corresponds to a shaman or medicine man who gives expression to "the mythical truth that the wounded wounder is the agent of healing, and the sufferer takes away suffering."[19] The later deity, Hermes, is also a prankster, and he possesses other qualities of Mercurius in a shifted form. Thus Mercurius' position as a sacrificial "wounded healer" becomes Hermes' link to the practice of the medical arts. As with Mercurius, some of Hermes' features relate to the mythic dimensions of Fox Mulder's character. Hermes is the messenger of the gods and the patron of travelers. Movement and change are natural to him. He performs the function of leading the souls of the dead to the underworld, and he rules over crossroads and chance, as well as having responsibility for healing. He is a shape shifter and is also often depicted as a phallic icon. In contrast, he is androgenous, capable of taking on female form, which could configure him either as a duality or a dynamic unity. This confluence of features shows the dynamic mythic relationship between the two *X-Files* protagonists. Perhaps because of his role in healing and in communication, Hermes is the Olympian considered to have the closest ties to the human race.

But there is another well-known sacrificial figure in the Greek pantheon who has an affinity with humanity together with trickster characteristics — especially from the point of view of Zeus and some of the higher gods. Prometheus stole fire from Apollo and gave it to human beings, violating the express prohibition of the patriarch of the gods. And even before this incident he had consistently been a supporter of humanity, while Zeus was its implacable enemy. When Prometheus' crime was discovered, Zeus punished him by chaining him to a rocky mountain top where a vulture unendingly fed upon his liver. Mulder's search for the truth challenges the dark gods of the *X-Files* universe, making him a powerful contemporary archetype with roots in the mythic unconscious of the distant past. He gives expression to the qualities, described above, of gods or demi-gods who are tricksters, healers and friends of humanity. In contemporary terms, Mulder's work, like that of the cop hero of police dramas, is to suffer for society, to risk "his own sanity, life, and loved ones" in the pursuit of his duty.[20] But it is Mulder's choice to suffer for his quest, for the truth he wants to find and share. Interestingly enough, the series has established that Mulder has a morbid fear of fire; doubtless he realizes the potential danger resident in his stubborn pursuit of *enlightenment*.

In his study of traditional folk tales, Vladimir Propp found two kinds of heroes — the victim hero who is the focus of the action and suffers from villainy, and the seeker hero. With the latter, the focus is not on the protagonist, but on those helped by him or her. It seems reasonably clear that Mulder plays either one or the other of these roles, depending on the story. In the bound episodes, he is the center of the action, although Scully sometimes assumes this position, as she does in "Emily" (5X07) and "Christmas Carol" (5X05). In the small array of bound episodes, one of the protagonists tends to suffer, but not always from villainy. In the more numerous free episodes, the attention of the audience is directed to the protagonists-for-a-day, whether monsters or victims. In these episodes, Mulder, like the traditional detective character, is a "consciousness in which the meanings of other lives emerges."[21] Again, this seems to support his function as both a sacrificial hero and a victim, as well as a seeker and a trickster.

Being duplicitous, two-faced, or "not what or who one seems to be" is an aspect of Mulder's trickster identity that is featured in several episodes, especially the later more reflexive ones like "Dreamland I and II." In the fourth season's "Small Potatoes" (20) — an all-time fan favorite — actor David Duchovny plays his witty, too-cool agent role and also the role of a shapeshifter impersonating him who is anything but cool. Significantly, this character's shape-shifting powers are not supernatural nor superhuman. He is simply another of *The X-Files'* genetic anomalies, born with a layer of subcutaneous muscle all over his body that allows him to change his appearance at will — and with a tail, which identifies him with the trickster Mercurius' animal nature. His name is Eddie Blundht ("with an 'H'; the 'H' is silent"— and the "D" isn't?) and his natural appearance is that of a chubby and rather pitiful nerd, his manner vacillating between self-deprecating introversion and mild outbursts of spunk, insight and sincerity. Early on, Mulder dismisses Eddie with a classist quip when Scully asks, "Are you saying that Van Blundht is an alien?" and he responds, "Not unless they have trailer parks in space."

However, by means of the script and Duchovny's portrayal, Eddie's character attains a deeper, more sympathetic and resonant level as the story progresses.

The first time Duchovny assumes Eddie's persona occurs when the supposed agent is interviewing a woman who had been Eddie's high school girlfriend. As she tells Mulder/Eddie what a dork Eddie was then, very subtle reactions move across Mulder's face. The plot has not yet revealed that "Agent Mulder" is, in fact, Eddie at this point. The viewer can only become aware of this by noticing the lowered set of Mulder's shoulders, the faint suggestion of hurt in his eyes, the way he gestures stiffly, as if not really at home in his body, and some uncharacteristic vocal mannerisms and small random movements of his hands and fingers. If one guesses that this is not Mulder, but the impostor Eddie, the softness around the mouth and the expression in the eyes can be interpreted as pain caused by the unflattering description of him that he is hearing from a woman who had been his teenage sweetheart.

Even though many viewers may miss the facial and body cues being given at this point, they are being prepared for similar cues in a longer sequence at the end of the episode. At that time, audience members can be more certain that a switch has occurred, and can enjoy being more "in on the joke" the second time around. Eddie also takes on other identities. In typical trickster fashion, he has fooled four women into thinking that he is their husband and fathering a child with each of them. All the babies have a tail. In the third Act of the episode, Eddie has assumed the guise of his own father and disparages his son (himself) in absentia to Mulder and Scully. The critique rings so true that it is clear that Eddie, like many children, had probably heard these criticisms and insults over and over from his father as he was growing up. He finally says that he always told his son that at least he had a tail. Without that, he was just "small potatoes."

In Act Four, Eddie becomes Mulder's doppelganger image. He assumes Mulder's appearance after telling him, "You're a damned good looking man" and locking him in a maintenance room at the clinic where he (Eddie) works. When Scully arrives, he tells her that he's sorry he dragged her into the case and she asks him if he means that the case isn't an X-Files. Eddie/Mulder's expression shows that he has no idea what an X-File is. But he takes a stab at it, replying, "No, no, I think the only thing that's here is small potatoes." At that point, most alert viewers realize that Mulder is Eddie and can appreciate Duchovny's depiction of Eddie's persona, which is not physically exact but highly suggestive. Act Four begins with Scully and Mulder/Eddie in Skinner's office after they have submitted their report on the case. Skinner asks who wrote the report and, when Mulder says he did, tells him that he spelled Federal Bureau of Investigation wrong. Mulder/Eddie mumbles, "Typo," and looks sheepish after Skinner snaps that he did it twice. When Mulder and Scully leave, he — unusually and surprisingly — puts his hand on her shoulder. They part, and Mulder/Eddie, after some fumbling with keys, enters

Mulder's apartment and tries out his chair, has trouble, almost falls out of it, finally succeeds in sitting, looks around and exclaims, "Good night! This is where my tax dollars go?!"

He turns on the answering machine and hears a message from the Lone Gunmen about new/reconstructed evidence from the JFK assassination and an invitation to go out for cheese steaks as well as an admonition to erase the message. Then a woman's voice from a telephone sex line asks "Marty" to give her a call, they've lowered their rates and she's anxious to hear his sexy voice again. At this point Mulder/Eddie apparently catches his image in the mirror and—looking directly into the camera—he practices flashing his badge and saying "FBI" a couple of times in different, but Eddie-like, ways. He then plays around with the voice and facial expression of Travis Bickel from *Taxi Driver*, menacingly mouthing "You lookin' at me?" in several ways, after which he practices drawing his gun—inexpertly, clumsily—once or twice. He poses in front of the mirror and tells his Mulder reflection that he's a damned good looking man.

The impersonation continues, expanding the deception to include Agent Scully in a very personal way. Alone in her apartment that evening, she answers a knock on the door. She looks out the peephole, and we see a rounded aperture framing a ridiculously foreshortened Mulder with a silly grin on his face. She lets him in and is puzzled that he has brought a bottle of wine, but opens and serves it. In the meantime, Mulder/Eddie goes through a few hidden moves with a pillow to try to make himself comfortable on the divan. He still looks stiff and self-conscious. After Scully also seats herself on the divan, he asks her, "We don't really talk much, do we?" At this point one begins to see Eddie somewhat differently. A combination of Duchovny's portrayal of wistful sincerity and the perceptiveness of the line, which *does* comment accurately on Mulder and Scully's working partnership, shows that Eddie, the loser, has both empathy and insight. Scully is nonplussed: "You mean, *really* talk? No, we don't, Mulder."

The two finish the bottle of wine, and Scully, a little tipsy, tells a story about her high school prom night and confesses that she can't believe she's talking about this. Just as Mulder/Eddie leans over to kiss her, the real Mulder breaks in, and Eddie reverts to his own appearance. In a closing scene, Eddie is in a clinic under psychiatric observation. He tells Mulder that he's now taking a muscle relaxant that prevents him from "making faces," and he goes on to offer a commentary on Mulder's life, and a little advice: "I was born a loser, but you're one by choice. You should live a little. God knows, I would if I were you." With Eddie's removal from the scene, Mulder's trickster persona is no longer externalized and exposed, but re-integrated into his single self. The role of Eddie has been a dramatic trick to show the audience Mulder's strengths in relief, while also suggesting his weaknesses in achieving true intimacy and in the full expression of his animal or procreative energy.

Psychologist Carl Jung insists upon the interpenetration of the trickster, the shaman and the shadow archetypes, each flowing into or overlapping the other. Then he sees the anima, the hidden female dimension of a man's nature, standing behind the shadow. In order to become a wounded healer, the trickster must face this shadow, which Mulder does more than once in varied ways. In "Firewalker" (2X09), as in "Small Potatoes," the approach is secondhand, through a doppelganger image. Dr. Trepkos, the episode protagonist, is delineated as a driven man, like Mulder, and his own fervent quest a projection of Mulder's own. Trepkos destroys his lover, his colleagues and himself, an object lesson which Mulder sees and understands. In "Demons" (4X23), Mulder relives the trauma of his sister's abduction and allows himself to be drugged and physically wounded in order to know more about this event of his past. In "Quagmire," Scully compares him to the "megalomaniacal" Ahab of *Moby Dick,* who pursues the white whale to his own death.

The figure of Mulder as an empath who both feels with and offers aid to those who suffer (see "Fallen Angel" 1X09, "Oubliette" 3X08, "The Field Where I Died" 4X05 and "Minds Eye" 5X16) suggests mythic depths in his character that are not really communicated any other way. Seen in this light, he is the shaman of native cultures worldwide whose powers come because he himself has faced the deepest abyss of terror and pain — his sister's abduction, his own death and resurrection. He knows the darkness without (in corrupt institutions and powerful enemies) and within (his own fears, doubts and powerlessness). He is shown as a shaman, a sacrificial savior figure, and an avatar, or a god/human who participates fully in both spiritual and material existence.

This last aspect of his character is suggested in "Tempus Fugit" (4X17), the second of two later episodes featuring Max Fenig of "Fallen Angel." In these episodes, the first time a jet liner is intercepted in mid-air the plane crashes and Max is killed. The interception happens again, then, to another plane, and Mulder rather than Max is on board. This plane lands safely, and Mulder is the only passenger who recalls that the incident occurred, or what happened during the period of missing time. Not only does Mulder occupy a privileged position in the ongoing story, but his is also the privileged view of reality, one that is able to give the viewer a near-to-godlike perspective of the action.

In "Fallen Angel," Mulder is thrown out of the emergency room when new burn casualties are brought in. The officer who orders him to leave, Col. Henderson, grudgingly allows Scully to stay. As intuitive or mystical healer, Mulder stands in contrast to Scully, whose healing powers are connected to institutionalized medical training and supported by the research and paraphernalia of modern science. She is allowed to stay in the emergency room because she is a certified and degreed physician. She may be able to help. However, when she sees Mulder later, she is weary and dispirited and tells him that they had lost all but two of the eight casualties, and those two had been flown out to the more advanced burn unit at Johns Hopkins. In an immediately preceding sequence, Mulder has effectively diagnosed and cared for Max during an epilepsy attack. The proximity of this scene highlights Scully's relative failure in a life-or-death situation, which does not, of course, discredit the accumulated wisdom of either medicine or science, or Scully's professional skill. The crucial factor here, I think, is that scientific truths in the service of lies or corrupt purposes become ineffective, unnatural, destructive. Mulder simply represents the good man doing well.

In another episode, Mulder speculates about how Oppenheimer, the atomic scientist, must have felt when his discoveries culminated in the atomic bombs that leveled Nagasaki and Hiroshima. In one of the series' many subtle cross-references, the doctor in charge of the emergency room in "Fallen Angel" is called Oppenheim. However, *this* doctor, rather than remaining silent in the face of military opposition and bullying, tells Mulder and Scully that he hates fascism and later stands up to Col. Henderson, asserting his control over the ER and its personnel. Symbolically, the figure of Dr. Oppenheim seems to pose a question from the angle of revisionist history: What if the earlier Dr. Oppenheimer and other scientists in his position had opposed the politicians and military/industrial leaders? And then, a further question, do contemporary scientists also keep quiet about the uses that corrupt institutions make of their work? They know the history. If they act consciously and honorably, aren't they obligated not to repeat it? Won't they stand up, like Dr. Oppenheim has done? In a related subtext, Mulder, Scully and Oppenheim make up a triad of healers that complement one another: Mulder the intuitive, empathic shaman figure; Scully the intelligent, well-trained medical practitioner; and Oppenheim, the ER physician, ever under fire, who must negotiate his position as a healer with outside hostile forces, making him something of a heroic civilian warrior.

The Goddess Dana

> On *Buffy the Vampire Slayer*, Buffy's mentor Giles offers a rather long-winded scientistic "explanation" of supernatural phenomena and Buffy tells him, "I can't believe that you, of all people, are trying to Scully me...."

The character of Agent Dana Scully resembles the typical sidekick in a series of fictional partners, that is, her Dr. Watson to Fox Mulder's Sherlock Holmes, or her Miss Kitty to his Marshal Dillon (*Gunsmoke*), or even her Nora Charles to his Nick (witty, boozing husband and wife team of the 1930s–40s *Thin Man* detective movies). This comparison suggests that Scully is a secondary character perhaps not as mythically complex or important as her partner. Yet there is evidence to the contrary. The episode "In the Field Where I Died" depicts Mulder under hypnosis, recalling a past life in which Scully had been his father, and another when he was an officer in the Confederate Army and Scully had been his sergeant at arms. These transpositions of gender for Scully imply that she is an anima figure, the female element within Mulder's psyche that "sums up everything that a man can never get the better of and never finishes coping with. Therefore it remains in a perpetual state of emotionality which must not be touched." Mulder has an ongoing need to face and integrate his shadow in order to achieve individuation at ascending levels of knowledge and understanding, and Jung tells us that "the problem constellated by the shadow is answered on the plane of the anima, that is, through relatedness."[22]

The relationship of the individual to his anima (or a female to her animus) takes place entirely on the level of the psyche and is a dynamic interaction from which selfhood is constantly being negotiated. Mulder has several potent anima figures in his life: his mother, his sister Samantha and his partner Scully. Where Scully is concerned, producer Chris Carter seems to understand that the relationship with the anima is never completed; meaning, in story terms, that it should never be romantically or sexually consummated. Now it is possible that Scully and Mulder will establish a romantic coupling of some kind — the X-Philers who call themselves "Shippers" certainly hope so — but that development could diminish the psychological subtext that makes the symbolic code of the series so richly layered. From the first season on, scripts have carefully withdrawn the possibility of romantic love or a conventional relationship for either partner. In "The Jersey Devil" (1X04), Mulder pursues a beast man who turns out to be a beast woman. She is killed by another officer, but Mulder tenderly closes her eyes in death and tells Scully later that she was beautiful.

In the meantime, Scully has met and dated a man with a young son about the same age as her godson, yet when he asks her to go out again, she opts to join Mulder on a research project instead. Phoebe Green, Mulder's girlfriend from his Oxford days, turns up — an old "flame" — in the episode "Fire" (1X11) and shows herself as duplicitous and conniving. And in "Genderbender" (1X13), although Scully falls under the pheromone-induced spell of a shapeshifting alien, Mulder rescues her in the nick of time. Then, in the very next episode, "Lazarus" (1X14), an old boyfriend and FBI mentor of Scully's undergoes a soul-shift with a criminal he has been pursuing and whose impassioned Bonnie-and-Clyde relationship he has envied. In this case, however, "Bonnie" betrays "Clyde" in the end. Later, in "3" (2X07) and "Never Again" (4X13), Mulder and then Scully have disastrous one-night-stand encounters, and from time to time they engage in flirtations or experience attractions, an entertaining version of which is Scully's interplay with a handsome small-town sheriff who is also a vampire in "Bad Blood" (5X12). Young Agent Pendrell, who is smitten with Scully, is shot and killed in "Max" (4X18). But none of these associations or encounters could possibly develop into romantic love, nor, by extension, could their own partnership. Carter has said that the partners are "best friends beyond what lovers could ever be" and that "Mulder and Scully love each other. It's a wonderful romance. It's just not a sexual romance. It is a caring, tender, respectful relationship. It's an ideal."[23] I would say that their love is the kind of moral fantasy achieved by popular fiction at its best, a romantic ideal grafted upon some basic truths about how autonomous, self-defined people learn and change and grow. The X-Files externalizes, in the relationship between Mulder and Scully, a vital process that is actually interior and ongoing in every individual.

In another view of Scully's function and nature as a character, Lisa Parks proposes dimensions that are visible from the perspective of feminist theory. She points out that Scully not only investigates "monstrosities that threaten the social order," but that Scully herself evinces some of the characteristics of a monster. She is monstrous because "she visually conforms to the image of traditional heterosexual femininity but also gives voice to the historically masculized discourses" of science, medicine and the law, thus is a freak of nature from the viewpoint of the patriarchy.[24] Scully can also be considered a monster in that she has physically assimilated the monstrous, having almost certainly been impregnated with alien DNA during her abduction. In addition, she develops cancer after removing an alien monitoring implant, necessitating its re-implantation to effect her cure.

These experiences have made Scully a monster as well as a scientist and law enforcer. Thus she has evolved into an image of the woman seeker, of the feminine "ultimately in search of itself," or the possibilities inherent in her Self. Parks goes on to advance the idea that through Scully The X-Files raises the question of whether feminized monsters (as in "Eve" 1X10, "Aubrey" 2X12, "Die Hand Die Verletzt" 2X14, "Kitsunegari" 5X08, "Terms of Endearment" 6X07) and officially masculized females like Scully, co-opted into the power structure, could join forces for social change.[25] Or, the writer asks, is no reconciliation possible in a patriarchal culture? Her partnership with Mulder seems to suggest that reconciliation is a possibility, but the question Parks asks is one the series opens up and, in true X-Files fashion, does not answer.

In Scully's partnering with Fox Mulder, both are Promethean figures, emissaries or go-betweens bridging the gap between the Dark Gods and human beings, willing to experience in concrete form humanity's most terrible fears — those buried in our subconscious in the shape of monsters and apocalyptic visions. Scully, however, is less a trickster, more a goddess, an icon of female strength, beauty and virtue. That viewers recognize her strength comes through clearly in the results of a poll taken by a British cult television magazine that placed her among the top "kick-ass" female TV heroines of all time, along with Emma Peel of The Avengers and Xena, Warrior Princess.[26] Her protective role is a part of her job that she takes very seriously, particularly in cases involving children, as below. When she consults a counselor for the first time in "Irresistible" (2X13), it is because she is disturbed by the necrophiliac monster Donnie Pfaster, and she seeks help because she fears that she has lost the confidence that she can protect innocent people from predators.

Scully's beauty is enhanced by the way she is consistently lighted and photographed — iconographically, romantically, in the way of Hollywood stars of the '30s and '40s. Her virtue is imaged in her sensible hairdo, her professional clothing and demeanor. Her character also gives inter-textual resonance by echoing the recent popular *Star Trek* physician, *Next Generation*'s red-haired, compassionate and sensible Beverly Crusher. In the show's narrative, Scully struggles with issues of religious faith and assumes a focal position in episodes involving suffering or threatened children — Kevin Kryder the stigmatic, her own genetically manipulated child Emily, the damaged girls in "All Souls," and young Gibson Praise, the mind reader. In these instances, she takes on an almost saintly role, in the Christian sense, and this aspect of her persona complements Mulder's as trickster, for Jung reminds us that "the trickster has a compensatory relationship to the saint."[27] Each gives what the other needs; each has what the other lacks.

A further, albeit more tenuous, religious connection might view Mulder as a modern manifestation of a sacrificial being, the "king who must die" of early pagan fertility rites, and of Jesus Christ, the inheritor of this sacred role. In this light, Scully, in her motherly or nurturing aspect, would be Mary, the mother, and in her partnering role, Mary Magdalene. This possibility fits the cultural context of the 1990s because during the last 30 or more years, information about ancient and alternative spiritual paths has been available in this country as never before. The '60s brought an interest in Eastern religions and native shamanic traditions, and the '70s and '80s witnessed a revival of goddess worship or modern paganism in the U.S. and worldwide, as well as apocryphal ideas about Christianity and Christian history. Along with these developments, the rising ecological consciousness of the times embraced the biological and numinous concept of Gaia, the earth, as a living organism. Sightings and visions of the Virgin Mary also increased significantly, seeming to indicate a drive toward or human need for a female aspect of divinity, perhaps as a counterbalance against the male "gods" of mechanistic science and technology.[28] Barbara Walker comments that "once more it seemed that God (or man) depended on his Mother (or woman) to straighten up the mess he had made, even if it meant ceding supreme power to her...." Today, some who are spiritually inclined would agree with Wolfgang Lederer, who writes that "two rivers of common source, Mary and Maya, the Virgin and Shakti, once again run into one: and the Goddess is once more, as she ever was, the creatrix of the universe, the self-revealing energy of the unknowable God."[29] On the Internet in July 1998, a fan identified as "peregrine" asked a question about Scully's religious significance and answered it. "Could [Dana Scully] have been

sent by an even larger force to aid Mulder in exposing certain truths, not necessarily the same truths that Mulder has been searching for but truths more
divine in nature? Is this her pre-destined role on this earth? Saint Scully—
yes, for all the obvious reasons and all of those which aren't so obvious...."[30]

A Gnostic scripture of the third century C.E. "made Mary Magdalene the
questioner of Jesus in the Oriental manner of the catechism applied to the god
by his Shakti or Devi (Goddess). The female questioner then was addressed
as 'Dearly Beloved.' Jesus used the same form of address, though later editors
eliminated all traces of the identity of his questioner; but it was apparent that
his 'dearly beloved' was Mary Magdalene."[31] His partner Scully is Mulder's
inveterate questioner, continually challenging his ideas and information, and,
far from being annoyed or resentful, he has told her that she keeps him honest. Their ongoing dialectic of faith and skepticism has a psychological aspect
as well as a spiritual one. Mulder's position of "wanting to believe" expresses
an openness and comfort with uncertainty. He does not operate in the realm
of airtight facts, coercive logical structures or institutionalized dogma. His
tolerance of flexible and permeable boundaries is a condition that is usually
associated with the female psyche, women as a gender being attuned to a penetration of body limits in sexual relations, and childbirth. These are natural
penetrations whose effect is not normally a wound or death, but the generation of new life. The male psyche, on the whole, regards body boundaries and
borders in the world at large as more rigidly defined, less loose and open, than
does the female. Thus Mulder's thought processes and attitudes toward truth
and evidence have an aspect that is androgynous, in harmony with his trickster nature and standing in a compensatory relation to Scully's animus-dri-
ven faith in science and objective evidence — the position from which she continues to challenge Mulder's perception of the truth.

Who Owns the Story? Character and Narration

Point of view is often a consideration of narrative analysis: Who is
telling — and in essence controlling — the story? What's the point of view? If
Mulder and Scully constitute a dual protagonist, each having a more or less
equal status, do they, in fact, have equal control of the evolving story? As mentioned earlier, film and television do not have as many options as prose fiction
does when it comes to having a character actually narrate the story. Voiceover narration is traditionally used for this purpose, and is the trademark of
the male Private Eye in the American film noir tradition. Before the current
decade, few women in film had controlled the story in this way. As late as the
1980s film version of Margaret Atwood's *The Handmaid's Tale*, having a
woman protagonist's voice tell the story was unusual, even controversial, and
the idea was scrapped in production, although the tale was supposedly the

fictional heroine's journal and would logically be told in her voice. This decision meant that viewers could not share the woman's innermost thoughts and feelings. It also, perhaps coincidentally, blunted the movie's cultural critique.

In *The X-Files*, a kind of voiceover narration occurs when Scully or Mulder (usually Scully) prepares an official FBI report on the case at hand. Scully has a story-motivated justification for writing such reports, as she was assigned her partnership with Mulder to keep track of his activities and communicate her findings to their superiors, who worry about his renegade mindset and what he may find out — and reveal — about the X-Files materials. Typically, these report-writing sequences do not involve narration over action. They instead depict Scully in the closing scene silently typing at her computer with her voice on the soundtrack commenting on the events which have just transpired. Although more private, these summary remarks are reminiscent of the detective's revelations at the end of the classic detective story. In the same way, Scully's final words provide a sense of closure to the events that have taken place in the episode. However, she does not use this venue to present a solution to the crime or the mystery; instead, she discusses the case in a philosophic mode with rather detached and impersonal concluding remarks.

Through the end of the fifth season, only one episode, the fourth season's "Memento Mori" (15), uses voiceover narration to accompany the action and communicate the private thoughts and emotions of a character. It does not, however, describe action as it is occurring. Scully speaks indirectly to us and directly to her partner by means of a journal she is keeping as she faces treatment for cancer. Entries and parts of entries, read in Scully's voice, are heard over appropriate scenes, three altogether: the first during the first Act or "teaser"; the second during the third Act as she enters the hospital and begins treatment; and the third during the fourth Act while she is still in the hospital and Mulder is breaking into a research institute where he learns that Scully's doctor is not to be trusted, among other things.

The first segment of the journal is actually a flashback; it is composed while Scully is undergoing treatment but is read over the scene in which she looks at x-rays that reveal her condition for the first time. In the voiceover, she links the passage of time to the beating of her heart, contemplating a "truth" (and thereby crossing the line into Mulder's territory) that is no longer distant and mysterious but imminent and threatening. She acknowledges that she expects Mulder to read these words some day and feels comforted that he will. She also expresses her gratitude for his influence on her life, and hopes that he will forgive her for leaving him. With these words the viewer achieves privileged access to Scully's emotional life at the same time that the series introduces a dramatic new turn of events — her almost certain death. Thoughts then become a feature of the action code equal to dialogue in this one episode, a pivotal one in the ongoing story line of the series.

From that beginning, "Memento Mori" proceeds along two parallel lines of action. Scully learns her cancer was possibly caused by removal of the computer chip implanted in her neck during her abduction (in the second season's "Duane Barry" and "Ascension," 2X05/6). She then enters a medical center in Pennsylvania where she begins a friendship with another hospitalized abductee who is suffering from cancer — Penny Northern, who dies at the end of the episode. While Scully pursues this uncharacteristically self-determined course alone, in dreams, and in quiet scenes with other women (her mother and Penny Northern), Mulder launches a covert investigation of a federal fertility clinic and a connected research facility. As this concurrent plot line unfolds, Mulder deals primarily with men in scenes full of activity, suspense, secrecy and danger. These scenes are cross-cut with Scully's quieter and more lyrical monologues and dialogues during the third, fourth and fifth acts.

The penultimate scene is a quiet one between Mulder and Scully in a hospital corridor, an echo of the beginning. Yet even though her voiceover begins "Memento Mori" and ties the narrative sequences together, Mulder has the last word in this scene, saying that he thinks that the truth will save them both, obviously not meaning the inescapable truth of mortality. Ironically and tellingly, he has in his pocket a vial of her ova — removed during her abduction experience — which he discovered at the research institute. Although he holds her in his arms, he does not tell her about this discovery; thus he is not dealing in the complete "truth" himself. It seems that Mulder, even in his most tender moments, never completely disengages from his trickster persona.

It is significant too, I think, that "Memento Mori" does not end with the elegiac and tender hospital scene, but returns to Skinner's office and a last disquieting encounter with the Smoking Man who observes that there is always another way — if one is willing to pay the price. Although these words refer to a previous scene, their referent is uncertain enough to arouse viewers' speculation. In this way, what is immediate and personal gives way to a contested larger reality, preserving tension and suspense across episodes and into the future. At no time is Mulder given controlling narration of the sort delivered by Kolchak in the *Night Stalker* movies and television shows, because Kolchak is an investigative reporter exhibiting many of the qualities and prerogatives of the private investigator character, some of which Mulder does not share. He is not a free agent, for one thing. Generally, what little voiceover commentary there is does not privilege either Mulder or Scully, and both characters are vital to the construction of the entity that is the show's true protagonist, which is the partnership, the team.

Family Matters

A detective is meeting with a woman who wants to hire him. She is sultry and seductive in the noir manner, but instead of wanting the detective to work on an immediate and personal problem, She wants to hire him for a group who believe that the Chinese are plotting to undermine the American Spirit by dropping leaflets that would somehow "destroy the family."[32]

The ongoing family drama, though foregrounded in very few episodes, contributes strongly to the series' structure, content, and theme. It does this by —

- becoming part of an ongoing mystical, spiritual and mythic subtext;
- giving Mulder and Scully a base of "real lives lived" which carries over to episodes that are not directly concerned with their personal lives or their family history;
- constructing as well as showing the emotional and psychological complexity of the two protagonists;
- creating narrative unity and an impression of continuity by linking the free-standing plots to the plots of the mythic arc.

One significant mythic aspect of the show is that both Mulder and Scully have lost their fathers and are searching for them — actually, seeking the truth about them. Mulder's involvement in this thematic construct is much more obvious than Scully's. Her position vis à vis the father subtext is both more subtle and more complex. Since William is Fox's middle name and is also the first name of both of their fathers, these male characters are in some way interchangeable. With the death of Dana's own father, Fox becomes a father surrogate. In "Never Again" (4X13), Scully tells her male companion for the evening that she worshipped her father and still does, and that she tends to gravitate to men who are authoritative and controlling. There is a temptation to infer an Oedipal connection, and that interpretation probably does accord with one level of meaning.

Another level would be one somewhat closer to the surface of the narrative. Scully tells her mother that she wishes she could know if her father were proud of her, and the episodes that feature her religious beliefs suggest an enduring yearning toward the Father God of her Catholic upbringing. Yet, as has been previously noted, Mulder and Scully together form the two parts of a complete entity — the yin and the yang, the anima and the animus, a pair of dynamic polarities contained in one single human being. As such, this combined or dual protagonist appears to be working on the primal task of finding his/her place in the world of the father, a world which requires that Fox reject his mother in order to join a world in which Dana, no matter how fully qualified, no matter how competent, will never be totally accepted. In her several appearances before review boards and official hearings, Scully confronts this pervasively patriarchal world, but the *X-Files* text overwhelms her with its ubiquitous depictions of "official" institutions — from small town police departments to government agencies and the military, ultimately to the shadowy cabal of old white men that sums up all of the behind-the-scenes machinations and deceptions of a worldwide patriarchal system. (The international aspect is suggested by John Neville's classy British accent and aristocratic demeanor, by the Elder's vaguely Italianesque/Mafioso appearance and voice, and other cues.)

"Beyond the Sea" (1X12) is the earliest and perhaps the best example of an episode that links the family matters of the mythic arc with the partners' — and especially Scully's — daily investigative experience, their occupation in the world of the fathers. The episode also helps to construct the emotional and psychological complexity of the two protagonists. Act One takes place in Scully's apartment where she is entertaining her mother and father for dinner. As they prepare to leave, his wife prompts Bill Scully to express his feelings about his daughter, but he fails to do so. At home, later that evening, he is stricken with a fatal heart attack and appears before a half-asleep Scully, sitting in one of her living room chairs, silently mouthing an indecipherable message and not looking directly at her. A final message? A judgment? Scully longs to know if he was proud of her. The family had been disappointed when she did not use her medical degree to become a doctor, but joined the FBI instead. After her father's funeral, Scully opts to plunge back into work immediately, and the case at hand involves convicted serial killer Luther Lee Boggs.

By killing off his entire family at Thanksgiving dinner, Boggs might have believed that he released himself from their expectations. And yet they continue to judge him. When he walks down the hall toward his execution on two occasions (the first one was botched), his murdered family members line each side of the corridor — but for his eyes only. Boggs has psychic ties to Scully growing from his unsuccessful rejection of and her deep concern about family expectations. Mulder, too, has concerns about his parents, though these emerge later in the series. Have his mother and father deceived and betrayed both Fox and his missing sister Samantha?

Both of the agents, then, have potent, deeply founded family issues. Their middle-class background has made them intensely competitive and successful need-achievers with notable academic accomplishments, supposedly fulfilling the expectations instilled by bourgeois family values. Yet Scully has been shown by the attitude of her naval officer father that these goals are moving targets and cannot be accomplished in a clearcut, definitive way. And Mulder has reason to doubt the trustworthiness of his parents and the security of their world and values. They cannot be trusted if his sister can be abducted from their home in the middle of the night in an incident that has never been solved. In Mulder's world, "trust no one" also means Mom and Dad.

In a departure from his usual openness, it is the empathic "believer" Mulder, who has no sympathy for Boggs in "Beyond the Sea," and no belief in the powers of clairvoyance which Boggs claims for himself. One possible reason for Mulder's suspicion is that he is the agent who originally tracked and apprehended Boggs. But also, Mulder has been affected deeply by the failure of his parents and himself to protect Samantha, to explain what happened or to find either his sister or her abductors. The agent harbors great but unexpressed anger and resentment, complicated by his own sense of guilt. Bogg's slaughter of his own family on Thanksgiving, the exemplary and specifically U.S. family holiday, reflects what a family's "failure" might bring a man to do, to become. If family standards or values (even though socially determined) don't work in the world, if they don't take care of you and protect you, what are they good for? Even though Mulder continues to perform the role of the good, grown-up middle class boy — independent, assertive and highly competent — the breakdown of his family-instilled value system simmers beneath this exterior. Both Boggs and Scully recognize the power of family-created judgments and expectations, Scully by desiring her father's approval, Boggs by obliterating his family, hoping to kill their judgments (of him) with them. He cannot, of course, escape these judgments because he has internalized them himself, as everyone does.

Mulder is uncharacteristically dismissive of Boggs, sneering that Boggs doesn't kill because he is driven to it by rage or madness, but because he likes it. This relishing of the murderous act is never depicted in this episode, so the viewer is left with an impression of Boggs that does not entirely coincide with Mulder's description. Boggs communicates with Scully, he says, on behalf of and for her father. He also assists in locating and apprehending a murderous kidnapper in hopes of having his death sentence commuted. But the motive for his Thanksgiving Day massacre is never examined. It could be assumed that "Beyond the Sea," the first *X-Files* episode in which Scully is the believer and Mulder is the doubter, purposely sets about to flesh out the family influences which have caused the two protagonists to become the kinds of people that they are today, extrapolating into the achievement-oriented society, the kinds of people that many of us are today. Either our parents were paragons, representing impossibly high expectations, or treacherous failures, whose expectations could not be trusted. Thus, Trust No One.

By dint of socio-economic class alone, Fox Mulder is destined to enter the world of the Symbolic, of the Father, in terms that *The X-Files* has established as the metaphorical Land of the MIBs and, visually, the World of the Suits.[33] In fact, he has already entered this world, as indicated by his own impeccably tailored suits; his (Oxford) university education; his command of logic, explanation and information; and his coolly ironic manner. Add to this the fact that he works for a government agency on the cutting edge of this culture's domestic structures of control, and it is clear that his quest for the kind of truth that almost certainly would compromise both the government and that agency, is quixotic at best. Perhaps we can say that he is resisting his inclusion into the patriarchy and its ruling class prerogatives, crimes and secrets. Perhaps he wants to figure out where he is going, to lay a foundation for determining what is factually and philosophically true in a confusing world.

As he seeks the truth about his family and how power operates in the world, Mulder tests the parameters of what is known in Buddhism as the Eightfold Path. He seeks his own conception of right speech, conduct, livelihood, effort, mindfulness, concentration, views and intentions. In the episode "Ice" (1X07), the suspicious male doctor, one of three civilians brought in to assist Mulder and Scully in their investigation (and the only one of these people to survive), aptly expresses one of the essential paradoxes of the series. He tells the two agents at the end of the episode that "they" torched the research station that might have held evidence of extraterrestrial life, and Scully asks him, "Who did?" He replies, "The military, the Center for Disease Control, you ought to know. They're *your* people." The same accusation is repeated in the sixth season episode "Drive" (02), when Mr. Crump suspects that "they" are experimenting on him and states that Mulder is one of them. The paradox is that Mulder cannot be part of the solution without being part of the problem. Many episodes depict the relationship of the state to its citizens as parent to children in the stereotypical dysfunctional family of the late 20th century, showing Mulder and Scully — and by extension us — as the children of a clan who won't let their offspring grow, won't let them *know*. As I point out later in a different context, the government is the only institution that regularly lies to everyone — "for our own good."

Style: The X-Files World

The television viewing experience is quite different than that of watching a motion picture in a theater. Rather than sitting quietly in the dark, gazing up at larger-than-life iconic heroes and heroines, we sit in a familiar lighted room, looking at faces that are close to normal size and situated at just about our eye level. Thus television promotes an intimacy and a sense of accessibility that the size and distance of the movie screen doesn't allow. Also, the state of enthralled voyeuristic "dreaming in the dark" that movies induce is quite unlike the kind of loose connection viewers experience when they watch a TV show in their own homes, where the entertainment is broken up by commercial breaks, people can talk to one another, the channel can be switched instantaneously, and the sound can be turned down or the set turned off at will. The person watching a television show is in the subject position of "the fully socialized family member, making the medium especially suited to stories encouraging cooperation, understanding, empathy, and forgiveness" — familial kinds of relationships.[34] Stylistically, this quality translates to certain kinds of camerawork that are more characteristic of television than of films, such as using many close-up reaction shots or generally avoiding shots taken from the point of view of a dominant character, which encourages a detached voyeurism. Both in style and in story, the generic conventions of television drama "refuse the subject/object positioning ... [of] classic Hollywood cinematography by constructing the viewer simultaneously as voyeur and participant, possessor of knowledge and investigator."[35]

This means that when two people interact in a scene, shots of each person alone on screen, each in turn absorbing our full attention, are often cut together to create a visual dialogue. When the two are both present within the camera's frame, over-the-shoulder shots which establish relations of active/passive or strength and relative weakness are not used frequently, nor are balanced two-shots. More common are camera placements in which two (or more) individuals together are photographed off-center or from a slightly skewed angle or on differing levels or planes within the frame. In contrast to the usual TV situation comedy (there are recent exceptions), the long shot that depicts two people full-length and equidistant from the camera in an interior setting is seldom used in *The X-Files*, not even for satiric episodes. *X-Files* visual strategies have the effect of suturing the spectator into the action, thus enhancing affectionate identification with all characters — Mulder and Scully at least partly because their on-screen time is proportionately greater, but also such victim-monsters as B.J. in "Aubrey" (2X12) and such villainous figures as Alex Krychek (fondly dubbed "Rat Boy" by admiring fans).

EXPRESSIONISM AND FILM NOIR

In Chapter One, I noted that *The X-Files* uses expressionistic techniques descended from early 20th century European art and German filmmaking through the American horror and gangster movies of the 1930s and the film noir dramas of the '40s and '50s. Although the early expressionist painters used color media, they achieved their highest and most lasting influence in the area of graphics, especially woodcuts, in which they simplified composition into contrastive areas of black and white, suggested perspective by interrelating planes, and rendered both outlines and negative spaces as a positive force in the overall composition. Thinking of the difference between black-and-white and Technicolor cinematography, note Edvard Munch's painting alongside his woodcut version of this, his most famous work, *The Scream*.

Expressionists like Munch rejected the prevailing doctrines of realism in order to express a reality that was both deeply personal and political, an "artistic 'documentation' of emotional states and ideological convictions ... their sympathy for struggling humanity and their protest against ... universal oppression...."[36] The emotional power of these black-and-white graphics translated well into the emerging medium of cinema, also black-and-white, where the style was used to depict the affective content of the story and to heighten it. In the U.S., movies employed this chiaroscuro visual language in the antisocial melodramas of crime and horror throughout the '30s until it became a signature of these genres. The style was adopted by the noir films of the 1940s and 1950s, which tapped into the hidden anxieties of the culture. These crime, mystery and detective dramas continued to be photographed in black-and-white, along with most of the serious film dramas of the period (*Twelve Angry Men, Gentleman's Agreement*, even *To Kill a Mockingbird*). The noir visual language had a few central components, most of which are employed by *The X-Files*, but in such a way as to reflect a characteristically 1990s flavor, which must take the factor of color into consideration.

The conventional motion picture lighting scheme uses three sources of illumination: *key light*, which is located above and to the side of the camera; *fill light*, placed beside the camera; and *back light*, which gives characters form by separating them from the background and adds attractive highlights. Scully is usually photographed with a balanced lighting mix, which assures that her face will be "attractively modeled."[37] However, the most suspenseful, exciting, and frightening scenes in the show ordinarily take place at night or in darkness, and for these sequences *The X-Files* uses the typical "low key" lighting (that is, a relatively low level of overall illumination) traditionally associated with film noir. Also, noir films and *The X-Files* vary the three types of light (*key, fill, backlight*) away from the norm to produce unusual combinations of light and dark and striking contrasts. One technique that is used so often that it has almost become a hallmark of the series is the backlit scene with flared or diffused light coming through windows or from other sources visible behind the characters. In the paranoid thriller *The Parallax View*, this technique is featured a couple of times, as in a scene which takes place in the loading area for a children's train ride in a park; this "station" has a roof but no walls, so the characters standing beneath the cover are thrown into black silhouette, along with a tall spiked iron fence, against the background of sunlit green vegetation. Another variation of the norm in *X-Files* lighting schemes is the vignetting of areas or people by picking them up in light from within or above in a black and otherwise featureless space.

The *mise-en-scène* of film noir is designed to disorient the viewer. There are abrupt changes in camera angle and distance, and sometimes the "orienting" sequence of long to medium to close-up shot is ignored. Threat or entrapment is implied by claustrophobic framing by objects or shadows, by "choker" close-ups that frame a head to the chin. Shadows from venetian blinds crossing faces, bodies and walls is a noir trademark, as is an extreme high-angle long shot, looking down on a character in a street scene or other restrictive location that makes him/her appear to be the prisoner of fate. The *X-Files* equivalent of this shot maintains the camera distance, the darkness and the walls rising up in a dank and deserted alley, but the camera is positioned only slightly above the scene or on eye level, as one of the protagonists runs into its stygian depths. The altering of camera angle to a more human perspective hints that the television series may be somewhat less fatalistic than its noir drama predecessors.

In general, motion pictures use a montage style (cutting and editing) for action sequences and *mise-en-scène* (moving camera) techniques for scenes that are quieter, perhaps more thoughtful or psychological. Film noir tends to favor a montage style. In Season Six, *The X-Files* experimentally and reflexively reversed this tradition by depicting action scenes on shipboard ("Triangle," 6X03) and in an office building where characters were either followed by or led by a tracking camera (facing backwards) as they raced down corridors into locations like offices, elevators, ballrooms and engine rooms. *The X-Files'* special effects are effective in that they are for the most part skillfully conceived and executed, and also that they are photographed to carefully preserve believability and immediacy. What viewers may lose in mystery and suggestion by clarity and detail in representation, they more than gain in total sensory impact. Many scenes, also, do *not* show the gruesome details fully, especially when these emerge through acts of extreme violence or perversion. The show walks a fine line in such matters, stressing sensory richness to the point of "gross-out" without pushing the grotesque into the ludicrous, the clumsy or the offensive, as judged in the "home viewing" terms of the TV medium.

The *X-Files* use of chiaroscuro patterning differs somewhat from the '50s noir prototype in that backlit and other dimly lit scenes are less prone to harsh shadows and extreme contrasts of light and dark. Instead, especially in the early and middle years of the series, the set is often suffused by a misty or smoky haze that blurs boundaries and loses the clear distinction between black and white, suggesting the softening or negating of polarities, which is one of *The X-Files'* central thematic constructs. According to several experts on trends in contemporary design, this haziness is also a hallmark of the 1990s. Phil Patton reports in *The New York Times* that blurred typefaces and out-of-focus images are being used in photography, advertising and in print and other media because "we live in unfocused times, and in a society where the speed of change reduces things to a blur. Blur suggests confusion, lack of clarity, but also velocity."[38] The blurred "X" in the *X-Files* logo as well as the atmospheric fogginess of some *X-Files* locations are linked to these developments in photographic and print representations in the culture at large. Art critic Loretta Staples writes in *Eye*, a design magazine, that "the focus of today's visual landscape is the indistinction between things." And Patton forwards the idea that new blurry graphics "may mean several things: a parody of such technological and scientific concepts as fuzzy logic and chaos," a "dissolution of media boundaries — computers, television, print — and of national boundaries," and "privileging continuity and ambiguity above legibility."[39] I would say that in *The X-Files* a blurred indistinctness probably suggests all of these things.

Another effect and function of this atmospheric density is to physicalize the light which is also a primary motif in the series. Thickening the air gives a palpable material reality to what is symbolic and metaphoric — enlightenment, illumination, the light of reason, and so forth. In misty interior scenes, a strong back-lit glow will flare out, obscuring furnishings and selected characters, so that some may be selectively silhouetted or lighted. In the dark, unknown and dangerous places that Mulder and Scully must often explore, their high-powered flashlights cut through the murky gloom with the force of Han Solo's light saber. The murky environment gives palpable form to the haloed beam of light while it provides a noir contrast between the white of "clear vision" and the black that we understand means "being in the dark."

COLOR, COMPOSITION AND SOUND

One difficulty in translating the noir style to current motion picture and television productions is the color factor. All of the conspiracy-oriented films discussed earlier are in color. *Klute* adopts a straightforward noir style to the muted color palette, mostly interiors, of an urban location. *Chinatown* takes another approach more suited to its 1930s Southern California chronotope: "Shots are composed in a constricting fashion, giving the impression that important things are happening just beyond the frame.... This gives the film an airless, suffocating feeling that befits the dusty, hot climate.... Elemental colors ... enhance this desert-like aura, using earthy browns and sundrenched yellows."[40] *The Parallax View* uses noir interiors; the newspaper office where Joe works and meets with his editor is especially dark and shadowed, but the movie's primary achievement in terms of color is the way it adapts a red, white and blue color scheme throughout and manages to preserve verisimilitude in spite of the artificiality of this conceit. In almost every scene, decor and costumes are versions of these colors, and the combinations are dramatically heightened and brightened during the several political events. *The X-Files* draws color into its noir sensibility by the use of light in the complementary colors of blue and reddish orange, as Munch did in the painting of "The Scream," sometimes one in a limited area, as when the blue glow of a computer screen is reflected from Scully's glasses, and sometimes one flooding an entire scene or both used in different areas. The effect is also rather artificial, as with *The Parallax View*'s red/white/blue scheme, but in most cases the color enhances the emotional intensity of scenes in an expressionistic manner without calling attention to itself.

Composition within the television picture is often used to influence audience feelings for and understanding of *X-Files* characters. As early as the episode "Fallen Angel" (1X09), we see an instance of a visual motif that is echoed in the later "Oubliette" (3X08). This image drives home the notion of Mulder as a nurturer, comforter and healer. In it he holds, in a strong, compassionate way, someone who is suffering mental or physical distress, or is dying. He assumes the attitude ordinarily found in the figure of Mary holding the prone figure of the crucified Christ in many well-known renaissance paintings, a compositional motif called the Pieta. In the *X-Files* version of the scene, one senses not simply grief on Mulder's part, but a willingness and ability to share the other person's suffering. The concept of a redeemer "dying for our sins" has been around since the beginning of the Christian era, and is descended from earlier sacrificial figures, but a hero or a leader who can "feel our pain" has a quintessentially 1990s ring to it.

In "Fallen Angel," Mulder has also been following the official activity surrounding what appears to be a downed UFO. When he visits the trailer of an abductee, Max Fenig, he finds Max lying on the floor, shuddering and jerking. Mulder drops to the floor as well, picks the other man up and holds him tightly in his arms until the seizure passes. The composition of the scene has both men facing the camera, Mulder's head above, Max's below, with Mulder's arms clasped tightly around the other's body at shoulder level. Most of Max's body stretches out below this, out of the frame, an arrangement suggesting Pieta renderings. In order to infuse the tight scene with movement and vigor, the camera cuts back and forth between the two men's faces. When Max regains consciousness, he says that the seizure was not possible: His last attack had been seven years ago—before he began taking medication for his epilepsy. Exhausted, Max lies down to rest. Mulder then spots a scar behind the other man's ear and realizes that Max is an abductee, and that this fact could explain the resumption of his seizures. In this brief sequence, Mulder has been shown in action relieving another's suffering and performing a diagnosis in line with his Mercurial and shamanistic nature.

Some features of *The X-Files'* overall artistic design should be mentioned, even if only briefly, because they add so much to the building of an effective and unique dramatic environment. The music accentuates mood and content as both background and diegetic sound. A relevant example of the former is the consistent use through the series of the conspiracy theme from *The Parallax View*, a singularly eerie and suggestive melody behind quiet scenes of building suspense or behind scenes featuring members or meetings of the Cabal. The show's uses of diegetic music and TV shows are too numerous to recount, and often these echo content, as with the howling rock anthem "Unmarked Helicopters" blasting from the sound system in Max Fenig's trailer, which has been trashed by unknown interlopers (in "Max," 4X18). Other notable instances are parodic in the post modern manner: Among these are the use of the syrupy ballad "Twilight Time" as an auditory cover on the tape to disable the rogue Artificial Intelligence (AI) in "Kill Switch" (5X11) and the darkly humorous use of a Johnny Mathis–like version of the song "Wonderful, Wonderful" on the episode "Home" (4X03), sharpening its biting satirical critique of "family values." In homes, motel rooms and other interior locations occupied by mostly bourgeois, small-town characters, we see Rosalind Russell and Cary Grant arguing about marriage (in "Aubrey," 2X12), Claude Rains removing his concealing bandages in *The Invisible Man* (in "Detour," 5X04), the child telepath Gibson Praise watching the TV cartoon comedy "King of the Hill" and commenting that it is a great show and that he wishes they carried it where he lived (in "The End," 5X20), and Mulder and Scully exchanging Christmas presents in the early morning hours while the character of Scrooge from Charles Dickens' ghost story "A Christmas Carol" is speaking from the television set (in "How the Ghosts Stole Christmas," 6X06).

Word and Numbers and Synchronicity

A related but stranger and more numinous aspect of the overall style of the series is its dependence on an odd form of allusion that I have already mentioned at several points in this study, as well as on creative strategies that are serendipitous and synchronistic. I call the former name- word- and number- "magic" because it binds the interest and the attention of regular viewers in a seemingly "magical" subliminal way. Few people who are not fans would notice the regular use of Chris Carter's birthday and month (10/13) for content features like Fox Mulder's birthday or the number on the underground door of the missile silo where Alex Krycek is buried in an alien vehicle. The use of dates and addresses that mean nothing to anyone but the members of *The X-Files'* production company connect the ongoing sequence of episodes to each other and to both the real and the imaginal universe that the series occupies. We might recognize the allusion to romantic poet William Blake's "The Tyger" in the title of the episode "Fearful Symmetry" (2X18) and also catch the reference to the poet in the name of a construction site referred to as "Blake Towers." We might chuckle with recognition at the ties to the occult and to suspense genres foregrounded by locating "Die Hand Die Verletzt" (2X14) at "Crowley High School" (referring to notorious 20th century ritual magician Aleister Crowley) and by titling Jose Chung's previous novel, greatly admired by Dana Scully, as *The Caligarian Candidate*. (*The Cabinet of Doctor Caligari*, discussed in Chapter One, is an Ur film text in the horror tradition and don't forget *The Manchurian Candidate*.) But who of us would notice that in "Unruhe" (4X02), the brand on a camera, "Etap," is the name of the assistant prop master spelled backwards?[41] It's possible that the profusion of in-group jokes and references are merely devices created to entertain members of the production company, but I would like to suggest that they nonetheless contribute to the appeal and coherence of the show through the personal, cultural and intertextual resonances they create.

The X-Files has another type of magic in its repertory: the capacity to use seemingly random or chance events — synchronicity — to the advantage of its creative product. Perhaps the most well-known example of this capability is the integrating of Gillian Anderson's unexpected pregnancy into the plot line of the series. When the decision was made to explain her short absence during the second season by having Dana Scully abducted, possibly by aliens, and to use Anderson's pregnant body (visualized by Mulder) in scenes that suggest the conducting of genetic experiments, Scully is awarded an awesome source of numinous power:

- In Mulder's eyes, at least, she achieves "first contact" with extraterrestrial beings, and at the same time participates in an experience (childbirth) that he is perpetually denied.
- The utilization of her ova for the creation of the child Emily ("Christmas Carol" and "Emily," 5x05/7) means that, of the two partners, she is the only one who has taken part in the creative act of producing life, rather than only taking it.
- By being abducted, Scully undergoes a shamanic near-death experience, giving her official role as a healer metaphysical dimensions. In this also, she precedes Mulder, who experiences a like shamanic transformation in "Anasazi" and "The Blessing Way."

Scully's abduction also marks the beginning of the family mythos which gives the series so much of its emotional content and unity. Another fruitful synchronicity was the evolution, unanticipated at the beginning, of the Smoking Man from a silent but threatening MIB onlooker in the pilot episode to the arch-villain of the series, one with a history and a fully rounded persona that almost rivals that of the two protagonists. Also synchronistic and constructive was a visit made by an *X-Files* producer and writer to a UFO convention in Los Angeles in June 1993. They saw a trio dressed like Langly, Byers and Frohike (conspiracy theorists The Lone Gunmen), who were convincing attendees to tear up $20 bills to see for themselves the hidden metallic strip that the government could use to track monetary transactions. The characters were written into "E.B.E." (16) in Season One for comic relief, and received such positive Internet response that they were resurrected in the second season. Another crucial *X-Files* synchronicity (meaningful coincidence) is the fact that the actor David Duchovny's own witty and sardonic sense of humor has permeated the character of Fox Mulder, not only influencing his portrayal of Fox, but also underscoring the character's role as trickster in the ongoing narrative. This development has, in turn, caused the series to take on a more ironic tone over its first six years. Smaller happy accidents also abound in the show's history, as when producer Glen Morgan "was Christmas shopping at a Los Angeles mall and saw men working on the escalator, which was open and exposed. That prompted him to consider the scare factor of an urban myth stemming from some sort of monster living underneath an escalator." This idea was then put to work in "Tooms" (1X20), the second episode featuring the genetically anomalous human-liver-eater, Eugene Tooms.[42]

THE CHRONOTOPES OF THE X-FILES

In *The Dialogic Imagination*, Mikhail Bakhtin develops a concept of setting that has unique relevance to the *X-Files* world. Although Bakhtin's work pertains to literary genres, most especially the novel, his ideas regarding the chronotope in a work of fiction are appropriate to a discussion of *The X-Files'* wide-ranging settings and overall ambiance. This is true because of the close relationship the show has with its time and place — its context, its historical and political setting, its cultural moment. A chronotope works to materialize time in space, giving the work a focus for concrete representation. Through a chronotope, "the work and the world represented in it enter the real world and enrich it, and the real world enters the work and its world as part of the process of its creation."[43] Bakhtin notes that more abstract matters like ideas, social generalizations, deductions and so forth, are matters of thought that gravitate toward the chronotope and through it take on concreteness and imagaic power.

Three chronotopes explicitly discussed by Bakhtin define the immediate space-time environment of *The X-Files*: the encounter, the small town (provincial) and the threshold. The *X-Files* world is basically a place of comings and goings, a place of encounters among people of varying ages, race and social class, where temporal/spatial paths move fluidly but intersect at certain points. Working out a clever reflexive demonstration of this chronotope, the episode "Monday" (6X14) shows us strangers who are stuck in a time loop and continue to encounter one another time after time at a city bank — until they "get the day right." While other meetings may be random or accidental, fates collide and interweave. Social distance collapses as the encounters which determine human lives and fates become more complex and concrete. A literary type which utilizes the encounter chronotope is the "road," novel from *Don Quixote* to Jack Kerouac's *On the Road,* and the road (as in "the road of life") has been a perennial metaphor for the flow of time. Mulder and Scully spend most of their time "on the road" and very little "in the office." And the office environment is not regarded as desirable or challenging by either protagonist. In the encounter chronotope, individuals do not pass through alien territory, though they may come into contact with "social exotics," because their business is with "the socio-historical heterogeneity" of their own country.[44] This feature of *The X-Files* is well depicted in the U.S. maps marked for X-Philes with the many and diverse locations of Agents Mulder and Scully's adventures over the seasons.

And many of these locations are small towns, which Bakhtin describes as being the locus of everyday cyclic time, a place of quotidian and repeated events and actions, "a viscous and sticky time that drags itself slowly through space." Because small town time repeats itself in cycles in the daily, weekly, monthly, yearly round of work, holiday, school, church, home, meeting rooms, cafes and bars, it cannot be the primary chronotope, but only supportive, "interwoven with other non-cyclic temporal sequences"[45] When the two agents enter a small town locale, there has been a break in the normal cycle, and more crises follow after they arrive. This sort of break or crisis marks the chronotope of the threshold. It is associated with locales of passage, like corridors, stairways, front halls — oft-repeated settings for the agents' actions — and spaces that open out from these: parking lots, streets, docks, train stations and airports, loading docks, sidewalks, parks and squares. In these areas, characters are purposeful; they fall and recover; they experience renewals and epiphanies; they make decisions and act on them. In these locations, Bakhtin points out, time is essentially instantaneous.

The ongoing combining of the chronotopes of the encounter, small town and threshold provide the space-time matrix within which the action of *The X-Files* takes place, but two additional chronotopes must be added to achieve a complete picture of the *X-Files* world: The first is biographical time, which, unlike the threshold, is continuous, has duration. In it, time is stretched out and decisions and events are not instantaneous. Mulder and Scully's office, the FBI building and personal and family dwellings create this ambiance. In addition, the locales of board roams, hearing rooms, hospitals, laboratories, prisons, army camps and similar official environments represent that pervasive set of interlocking systemic restraints that are resident in the chronotope of the disciplinary society and its discourses.

Symbolism and Theme

> Back in the late 18th and early 19th centuries, supernatural fiction
> dealt very largely with beings that were in some sense superior to mortals or to living men. Today, it is much less concerned with such
> beings than with a world view that is in direct opposition to that of
> materialism.... Modern [supernatural] fiction has erected a mirror
> world based on direct contradiction to what most of us believe, related
> through the strong principle of positive negation.[46]

The following paired thematic statements show how the tenets of a mechanistic, materialistic world view are challenged by the supernatural in literature. E. F. Bleiler, who devised this list, comments that it could even be extended, yet in its current form the second or answering statements in each case summarize well the belief system represented in *The X-Files*:

Man is alone in the universe — There are supernatural beings.
Man is the most powerful force — There are gods.
The universe is amoral — There are forces concerned with morality, gods, demons, rewards, punishments.

The universe is an uncaring place—There are temptations, prayer, faith.
Death is final—There are ghosts, heavens, hells, reincarnation.
Change can be effected only by rational means—There is magic.
Existence is material—There are fairies, vampires, little people of various sorts.

Essence is inalienable—There are transformations of various sorts, personality interchanges, possession, breaking the rule of one-man-one-personality.

Reality is closed and separate from things imagined—There are solipsistic universes, entry into literary worlds, characters coming to life.

The animate and the inanimate are rigidly separated—Life may be created; inanimate things may be brought to life.

Man's senses have limitations—There are paranormal abilities, dream worlds, foreknowledge.[47]

By violating ordinary human concepts of limits, *X-Files* characters and situations transform polarities into physical reality, and in doing so, problematize them. Individuals tend to interpret the world in pairs of polar concepts: *either* good or bad, *either* true or false, *either* personal or impersonal. The meaning of a word is established by what it is *not*, by referencing the contrasting term. *The X-Files* interrogates polarities by examining what it means to fall into the gray area between such contrastive pairs—the thematic correlative to *The X-Files*' often blurred and indistinct environment. The correlative in story or content is a high level of irony, reflexivity and paradox, as when Mulder tells Scully that he's trying to figure out what lie to believe or when Scully engages in a personal conversation more easily with a geek who is impersonating Mulder than she is able to do with Mulder himself ("Small Potatoes," 4X20). What's the difference in believing a lie or believing the truth? How does one distinguish between a personal conversation and a conversation that only seems personal? Questioned or blurred boundaries are deliberately foregrounded whenever some character in command, usually Skinner, tells Mulder or Scully (or both), "You've gone beyond your limit ... crossed the boundary ... stepped over the line."

In *The X-Files*, the question of knowing the truth goes beyond the possible existence of extraterrestrials and paranormal phenomena, although these provide an evocative metaphor for other areas of life that puzzle and disturb us. Perhaps the basic thematic question of the series concerns the truth about power in the world—who has it and how and for what purposes is it being used? Almost every episode provides a bit of the answer: The paternalism and condescension of wealthy British aristocrats, not to mention the economic differential, provokes fiery resentment ("Fire" 1X11) that is not easily extinguished; prison and internment camp wardens brutalize those who are utterly dependent on them ("The List" 3X05 and "Fresh Bones" 2X15); and military officers provoke the rage and vengeance of their men ("The Walk" 3X07,

"Unrequited" 4X16 and others). The power of institutions and expert discourses is shown again and again. The episodes of the mythic arc apply the question of power to the microcosm of the family and, through the emblematic Global Syndicate, to the macrocosm of the world, the present cultural and international context; and finally, through paranormal and alien elements, to the dimensional and interstellar universe.

When viewers of the show leave the practical, observable environment that they recognize as the series' reality (even though populated by monsters), they enter Fox Mulder's memories of family deceptions and secrets, and sometimes a bit of the fragmented and hazy world of Scully's abduction — the metaphysical zone — an area also accessed through Mulder by means of his near-death experience, dreams and visions. Connections to the universe, perhaps to a higher reality, are, in *The X-Files,* intensely personal, experiential, and idiosyncratic. Her abduction by forces unknown gives Scully a terminal disease. Mulder's unexplained and traumatic loss of his sister is linked to alien assassinations and large scale experiments on unaware human subjects. The language of the body can speak truth to the discourses of power and thereby resist them. The personal, physical stories of *The X-Files* interrogate official claims to truth by implicitly and explicitly comparing them to the truths of lived narratives, Mulder's and others'. Spectators are sutured into the text by the domestic television viewing environment and by the fact that *X-Files* episodes are intimate in style and content, focusing on individuals, personal matters and the senses. And yet the entire series evolves on an epic scale, connecting the body, the individual unique human being, to the larger sociopolitical environment, and to the illimitable reaches of the interior and exterior universe.

The history of the horror genre tells us that Mulder may be an echo of the heroes of early gothic novels, seeking his birthright, avenging and vindicating his father (or choosing not to), plotting to expose those who have stolen his title (his true self) and his rightful position in life, solving the family mystery. The patrimony issue can certainly reach a narrative resolution within the life of the series, but such a move is not likely, because Mulder's quest for selfhood is a thematic linchpin of the series, and there are motion pictures to be made. Another plot line, the Scully and Mulder relationship, can be deepened and strengthened, broken off and reinitiated, tested in many ways — but never clearly sexualized without serious changes to the thematic direction the show has established.

It seems likely that the structures of conspiracy in *The X-Files* will continue to blossom and expand. Cut one off one head of the hydra and a dozen will arise in its place. This is a conception that is not only mythically but also rationally satisfying. Of course, that means that the central questions of What conspiracy? and To what end? will never be solved. The UFO and cloning plot components also do not lend themselves to resolution. And even the monsters of the week, in their individual 45-minute picture frames, will, I'm sure, continue to be — for the most part — unexplained, and their outcomes (even when the case is closed) open-ended. One of the achievements of the series is how it makes this resistance of closure, in both macro- and micro-plots, aesthetically and psychologically satisfying. The other remarkable feature is how coherent the entire series continues to be, even though largely composed of freely combinable units. This may be attributed, in large part, to its rich and solid thematic substructure.

The X-Files has inherited the traditions of several centuries of British-American horror literature and the following areas of thought and technique are connected to historical developments in the genre. The next chapter will show how these concepts took shape through the social, political, and artistic developments of the distant and immediate past:

- The concept of the Alien Other, evil that is amorphous, uncentered and other-worldly (the shadow).
- The humanized monster/victim.
- Basic conventions like pursuit, entrapment, madness, the "double," liminality, "wrongness," and loss of control.
- Pursuit of the truth — about the past, the future, and one's place in the world.
- Acceptance of the supernatural as reality.
- Irony and parody (the trickster) played out against everyday reality, gothic iconography and atmosphere.
- Fear of the future — the threat of experts and their discourses of control, of science and technology, of a mechanistic view of the universe.
- The overriding significance of the authentic personal experience as Truth.
- The exposure of that which is hidden, secret, forbidden.
- The importance of an expanded spiritual or mystical view of the universe.

III.
THE CULTURAL CONTEXT

Chapter Five

The X-Files and the Gothic Horror Tradition

> The chief element of the Gothic romance is not so much terror as, more broadly, dread — whether physical, psychological, or metaphysical, whether of body, mind, or spirit. The Gothic romance seeks to create an atmosphere of dread by combining terror with horror and mystery. *Terror* suggests the frenzy of physical and mental fear of pain, dismemberment, and death. *Horror* suggests the perception of something incredibly evil or morally repellent. *Mystery* suggests something beyond this, the perception of a world that stretches away beyond the range of human intelligence — often morally incomprehensible — and thereby productive of a nameless apprehension that may be called religious dread in the face of the wholly *other*.[1]

The horror story in English has come a long way from the novels of the Gothic period with their haunted castles and mad Arabian princes, evolving into the many television and film versions of the horrible that surround us at the beginning of the 21st century. This chapter starts at the inception of the form and traces the literature and its motifs, along with some significant cultural influences, into the 20th century, when the gothic gives way to the modern horror story. Chapter Six, then, delineates cultural factors which have permitted a television series like *The X-Files*, borrowing from and building upon the gothic fictional tradition, to become a popular phenomenon and a major source of imaginative experience, not just to the English speakers within the tradition, but to a worldwide audience.

The horror genre developed from the oral story-telling practices of pre-literate societies — communicating dreams, myths, legends, folk tales — and, in the British-American context, at least, it has gone beyond these origins primarily due to the artistic skill and creative imaginings of a number of talented writers over the past 200-plus years. Mikhail Bakhtin observes that although a genre "lives in the present, it always remembers its past, being always old and new simultaneously."[2] Arising from the concerns of their times, many earlier texts feature themes or ideas that are nonetheless quite relevant to the present era and to *The X-Files* in particular. "The relationship between genre and social perceptions of reality is reciprocal," and an accumulated genre sets an audience's "horizon of expectations." New generic texts engage audiences in terms of previous reading and viewing experiences, and then, "by breaking new ground and manipulating generic conventions, force the horizon of expectations to reconstruct itself around new visions of reality."[3]

To illustrate briefly, the idea of the abuse of power — so often instantiated in one aristocratic villain — has been part of the horror story tradition since the earliest gothic novels until almost the end of the gothic period, roughly, the beginning of the 20th century. And the open, interconnected concepts of dark unknowable gods (in *The X-Files*, the shadowy Cabal or Syndicate); a disinterested or hostile natural world; and an actively malevolent universe began to appear in popular British and American horror fiction around the period of World War I. There can be little doubt that these fictional premises grew partly from the bloody, vicious nature of that war, the first large-scale modern conflict, which employed not only a full range of firepower in the form of bombs and bullets, but also featured the widespread use of armored vehicles, air strikes, poison gas and trench warfare. The horrors being experienced on the European continent, and especially by the generation of young men who fought and died there, were projected outward into nature and the cosmos by such British writers as Arthur Machen and Algernon Blackwood. The American H.P. Lovecraft was writing in an equally dark metaphysical vein during the same period. The ancient, lurking evil of his monstrous gods metaphorically extends man's destructive capability to potential world annihilation. The "how" is only intimated, but Edmund Wilson comments that in "The Color from Out of Space," a story written in 1927, Lovecraft "more or less predicts the effects of the atomic bomb," as if the devastation of the previous war had shown him visions of what might take place in humanity's future.[4]

Types of the Gothic Genre

The mysterious, long-ago-and-far-away atmosphere of a more barbarous time was an essential feature of early gothic texts. Horace Walpole's *The Castle of Otranto,* the first gothic novel, was first published on Christmas Eve 1764. Although written in England during the "Age of Reason," its setting was medieval Italy, and the author explains why in his preface to the first edition: "Miracles, visions, necromancy, dreams, and other preternatural events, are exploded now even from romances," but "that was not the case when ... the story ... is supposed to have happened. Belief in every kind of prodigy was so established in those dark ages, that an author would not be faithful to the manners of the times, who should omit all mention of them."[5] This first gothic text was an example of both "historical" and "supernaturalist" gothic: a story set in the (sensationalized) past and containing supernatural elements.

New literary forms do not replace old ones, but supplement them, expanding the province of available types. Three such types developed during the late 18th and mid–19th centuries, and the terms that refer to them — supernaturalist, historical and explained — are sometimes used to describe more recent horror texts. The fourth type — called ambiguous, psychological or philosophical — appeared at the end of the gothic period, at the beginning of the 20th century. Although these categories are not mutually exclusive, each does refer to certain salient and distinct characteristics found in a number of stories. As descriptors they correspond roughly to the divisions proposed by the structuralist Tzvetan Todorov.[6] He called the "supernaturalist" the "marvelous," and described it as the supernatural intruding into the normal world and being accepted there. The "explained" form, which gives natural explanations for supernatural events, Todorov called the "uncanny." And the "ambiguous" type is similar to his "fantastic," in which the story does not indicate whether the supernatural occurrences are really happening or not. He believed that the artistry of depicting the impossible in literature lay in prolonging the fantastic hesitation, as Henry James does in *The Turn of the Screw*; that is, in withholding the commitment of a story to being either marvelous or uncanny (supernaturalist or explained) for as long as possible.

Todorov's schema dealt with the larger landscape of imaginative fiction and not gothic literature only. Therefore, the category of "historical" would not be relevant to his theoretical analysis. But the historical medievalist aspect was a defining characteristic at the beginning of the gothic genre, and gradually lost its importance as the gothic evolved into the modern horror story. At the end of the gothic period, stories became less likely to justify the inclusion of the supernatural by setting the story in an antique past and a distant location thought to be more primitive and irrational. During the early part of the 19th century, the historical gothic became a popular genre in its own right, keeping, to a greater or lesser extent, the dark, threatening atmosphere that marks "the gothic" as a genre, but disposing with preternatural elements altogether. Sir Walter Scott's novels — *The Bride of Lammermoor, Ivanhoe* and others — moved the historical gothic toward adventure tales set in early England and Scotland.

A flood of highly sensational gothics continued the development of the supernaturalist subgenre from the late 17th up to the mid–19th century. Such novels as Matthew Gregory Lewis's energetic, salacious and horrific *The Monk* had many imitators. And new forms branched off, too. Beckford's idiosyncratic *Vathek* was published in 1786, and, with its heavily baroque and decadent *Arabian Nights* atmosphere, became a prime example of a sub-category of the supernaturalist type known as "Orientalist." Soon after the first gothic novel (Walpole's *Castle of Otranto*) appeared, the genre was augmented by gothic versions of an earlier non-gothic form, the sentimental novel. The most popular of these sentimental explained gothics were written by the immensely popular Ann Radcliffe and her successors. In these works, the conventions of gothic menace were preserved in setting, plot formulas and character — especially the gothic villain and his innocent, virtuous female victim — but in the end, the supernatural mysteries they promised almost always turned out to have natural explanations. This marks the difference between what is called "explained" gothic and the supernaturalist form, which takes the supernatural for granted. Those early gothic romances evolved gradually into such modern dark romances as Daphne du Maurier's *Rebecca*, as well as into the more lurid and torrid, less literary type of romance fiction that is still so popular today. Both the supernaturalist and explained gothics eventually outgrew their dependence on historical settings, most typically an exotic location during the Middle Ages. Certain attributes of the early gothic — supernaturalist, historical and explained — are still found in today's literature of supernatural horror, and the more of these attributes that show up in a contemporary text, the more purely gothic that text is. *The X-Files,* to cite only one instance, shows its relationship to this heritage by a strong continuing emphasis on claustrophobic situation, as described in Chapter Three.

Characteristics of the Gothic Genre

The condition of being trapped or imprisoned was a regular feature of all forms of early gothic literature, and such entrapment was connected tellingly to the chronotope of medieval architecture. Characters found themselves in dungeons or crypts or being chased through clammy, decaying underground passages. A turn-of-the-century version of this trope, Jonathan Harker's experiences as a prisoner in Dracula's castle, is arguably the most frightening section of Stoker's novel, and illustrates how effectively such situations can conjure up numinous dread. Edgar Allan Poe, writing in the first half of the 18th century, added being buried alive to the lexicon of claustrophobia: "The Fall of the House of Usher" and "The Cask of Amontillado" are probably the most familiar examples. Although the motif of enclosure was central to the gothic aesthetic, other features also figured prominently. Among these were extreme sensations and emotional states, madness, ghosts and terrifying objects, forbidden knowledge, the possible superiority of evil, and genealogical "complications, jeopardy and mysteries."[7]

Poe also continued the early gothic tradition of putting characters in anxiety-ridden and deadly situations, and he heightened the emotional content of these situations by adding a psychological dimension. Adopting a frequent gothic setting — the Spanish Inquisition — for his story "The Pit and the Pendulum," Poe placed his hero-victim in a limited space which became progressively more constricted and dangerous. In this story, the reader must identify with the single, suffering protagonist because there are no other characters, no distractions, no explanations or solutions. Claustrophobia then transcends the situation or action and becomes part of the character's psychological state, becomes the person trapped alone inside his (her) own head, a condition later identified with 20th century existential thought. This tortured subjectivity found expression at that later time in the modernist works of Dostoyevsky, Kafka and others. Gothic stories explored mental torture early on and even in its formative stages the genre concentrated on extremes of sensory and emotional experience, exacerbated by premonitions of impending but unknown catastrophe. Madness and inflamed passions that might result in murder or suicide contribute to a potent eroticism, as do hints of incest and other taboo acts. These psychological elements heighten the emotional effect of such dreadful predicaments as death by lightning, spontaneous combustion, being hurled from a cliff or other high place, or being crushed by falling objects.

In early gothic stories, too, the supernatural is usually a constant and accepted presence, intruding into natural space in the form of both specters and maleficent objects. The apparitions of wronged, murdered ancestors or walking skeletons and bleeding nuns were presented in these stories as being undeniably real, calling natural law into question. Both ghosts and possessed objects were sometimes inserted in contrived, inartistic ways, in order both to terrify the prisoners of the haunted or oppressive building, and, hopefully, to shock the reader. Common objects like doors, candles, books, statues, portraits, mirrors and tapestries took on special powers and a life of their own. Most readers of gothic fiction have encountered examples of these: The door opens slowly on its hinges all by itself, or the pages of the book turn themselves, as though lifted by an unfelt breeze. A number of *X-Files* episodes, noted in Chapter Three, make use of the gothic convention of animated objects, as do many transitional and modern horror and ghost stories. In H.G. Wells' "The Red Room," the candles lit by a self-appointed ghost hunter extinguish themselves one by one. And in H. P. Lovecraft's "Rats in the Walls," a tapestry wall-hanging undulates and shudders in response to the movement of unseen creatures behind it.

The motif of the forbidden book or the book of forbidden knowledge is repeated in works of the later gothic and right through the period of modern horror. In Lovecraft's mythos, the book *The Necronomicon* is supposed to contain esoteric knowledge about ancient evil as well as the rituals to call it up from the depths of the universe. In Shirley Jackson's *The Haunting of Hill House*, the ghastly book is one intended for a child but filled with hideous, terrifying drawings of the tortures of hell. In *The Shining*, the scrapbook and the boxes in the Overlook Hotel's basement contain a record of corrupt history that seduces Jack Torrance. And in *The X-Files*, the forbidden knowledge is held in FBI filing cabinets, in storage boxes in an underground Pentagon vault, behind decaying rural structures that conceal a labyrinth of cave-like corridors filled with even more records. In this way *The X-Files* connects the icon of the vault to the motif of forbidden knowledge, tying its artistic vision to the gothic and also finding a contemporary expression for terrors both of the body and the mind. The files and storage containers hold "X"— the unexplained and unknown evidence of paranormal activity — and they also hold information about citizens that may someday be used to control or exterminate them.

Many high gothic tales like *The Monk* or *Melmoth the Wanderer* end with dark powers, say, for instance, the devil or a demon in control. This suggests that wickedness might finally win out over good, enhancing the apprehension and fear that such texts aim to arouse. In order to arouse a similar apprehension *The X-Files* prolongs the question of whether evil or good will triumph. The show even refuses to commit itself fully as to what or who *is* evil or good. The serial form allows much flexibility in this regard because its conventions include plot devices like disappearances and reappearances, drastic changes of personality, recovered memories, new characters (including new relatives, new monsters and new aliens) and shifts in narrative focus. Having an open structure in which elements are constantly in flux can be unsettling in itself, but *The X-Files* also deliberately creates uncertainty about the nature of the larger threat. What is going on behind the scenes at the highest levels of the government, military and corporate establishment? Is there an alien threat or not? If so, what is its nature? And what is the potential outcome of Fox Mulder's quest for the truth? Enlightenment? Or a darker and more perilous universe than we ever suspected?

The fourth sub-category of the gothic marks the move to the modern horror genre. The ambiguous gothic form reflected 20th century skepticism, new psychological ideas about the unconscious, and associated, more subjective literary techniques. Altogether there was a rising interest in introspection. Modern horror stories like *The Turn of the Screw* and "The Yellow Wallpaper" take the gothic convention of a first-hand experience (narrated by a participant or written down in a manuscript or in the pages of a diary) to create a text capable of being interpreted in several ways. Is the Governess who tells the story in *The Turn of the Screw* psychotic? Are she or the children actually being haunted by evil apparitions? Or is her tale a fiction, a story she wrote to wreak revenge upon the representative of a system that had deluded and degraded her? This form of gothic/horror is ambiguous by virtue of permitting several layers of meaning. If the supernatural elements could be symptoms produced by guilt or other mental disturbances, the type might be called "psychological." The philosophic label would apply if the work seems to be symbolic or allegorical and therefore best understood from the standpoint of history, theory, or ideology. The questions above indicate that James' story could be called an ambiguous, a psychological or a philosophical horror text.

In Frank's description of the "genealogical complications, jeopardies, and mysteries" feature of early gothic literature, he cites the regular recurrence of villains from the hero or heroine's own family: evil twins or siblings, wicked mothers and fathers, uncles set on usurping the hero or heroine's birthright or legacy. The basic plot of many gothics is a variation on the search for a missing parent or the correcting of a misconception surrounding the protagonist's birth or parentage. The plot of *The Castle of Otranto* hinges on the withholding of the castle and its site of feudal hegemony from the rightful heir of Alfonso the Good. "The heroic unraveling of a complex genealogical problem climaxed by the moment of discovery or reunion" is a major narrative construct of the early gothic form. This resolution constitutes what Frank calls "a relocation of the self" for the hero or heroine, toward fuller individuation and integration of consciousness.[8]

Fox Mulder's search for the truth is, in fact, a quest for such a relocation of the self, and it finds narrative focus in his quest for the truth about his paternity: Whose son is he? What kind of man is or was his father? *The X-Files*, following the gothic genealogical convention, has built a structure of suspense into its action and interpretation codes regarding Mulder's father, his identity and his legacy. Viewers are led to believe that, in order to assure his loyalty to "the program," William Mulder had to decide which of his children he would give up as a hostage on a long-term basis — and he chose Fox's sister Samantha, leading to her abduction. A suspicion has also been planted that Mulder, Sr., as part of his duties at the U.S. State Department, worked with transplanted German Nazi and Japanese scientists who were performing experiments on U.S. citizens after World War II. In the episode "Anasazi" (2X25), William Mulder is shot and killed just as he is about to reveal "the truth" to Fox, so that we still do not know his actual connection to the conspiratorial government or syndicate agenda. Also some doubt exists as to whether or not he really is Fox's father. Several episodes have shown that the Smoking Man and Mr. Mulder served in the army and as FBI agents together. They may also have been personal friends, and, when CSM has a private conversation with Mulder's mother in "Talitha Cumi" (3X24), he reminds her that he was a better water-skier than her husband, but that "was true of so many things, wasn't it?" She replies unconvincingly that she has repressed it all. Whereas her son actively seeks the truths of memory, she chooses not to remember, in much the same way that Scully, and Mulder's sister Samantha, cannot or choose not to recall their abduction experiences.

If it is the question of paternity that focuses Mulder's otherwise rather amorphous quest, it is also the element that extends this quest out into the ongoing symbolic code of the series and into the world at large — the world of the fathers, our world and our anxieties about it. What kinds of men are the fathers, and what kind of world will we all inherit from them? Horace Walpole tells us in his first preface to *The Castle of Otranto* that the moral of the tale is that "the sins of fathers are visited on their children to the third and fourth generation." Walpole himself confesses that he doubts "whether in [medieval times]... any more than at the present, ambition curbed its appetite of dominion from the dread of so remote a punishment." Yet the theme has certainly not been abandoned. Stephen King's landmark 1970s horror novel *The Shining* turns on the same premise. Since the book is still widely read and enjoyed, the idea of "the sins of the fathers" obviously continues to be relevant to readers of the 20th century. It should not be forgotten that during the decade of the '80s we became aware of family child abuse as a serious social problem for the first time, and this problem has not abated as a public issue in the 1990s. *The Shining*, even though it concentrates on an intimate familial history of alcohol and child abuse, projects these onto the monstrous "American Hotel" and its entrepreneurial, undead, evil genius of an owner. He represents those whose power knows no limits, no boundaries, not even the final one of death. In this era of corporate greed and ecological and other types of anxiety, we see the shadow of the "Bad Daddy" in political, business and military leaders who do not seem to have our best interests at heart. This is true, notwithstanding the cynical view, loosely paraphrased, of a young white man commenting in a popular magazine: The world is run by old white men and it always has been, so what's all this new paranoia about?

The Cigarette Smoking Man and his colleagues of the shadowy international Cabal are currently only the most recent evocation of an entity that has been with the gothic/horror genre from its inception: the Dark Man or the shadow. The fact that it has now, with *The X-Files*, become "the Dark Men," or collective shadow, is a significant shift, resulting, I believe, from the cultural myths and conditions of life in the '90s. The developments in this numinous figure from the 18th century to the present show where these antagonists, these dark gods of *The X-Files* originated — their antecedents, their "fathers." The persistence of the shadow image and its power to frighten us — in our private nightmares as well as the public nightmares of popular fiction — suggest that it touches deep-seated unconscious fears. Carl Jung's archetypal theory regards the shadow as an ancient and universal image, or archetype, that points to a place in the cultural fabric where a knot of emotionally-charged material disturbs the collective unconscious, a correlative of the complexes that entered popular awareness with Freud's so-called Oedipus complex. When writers of horror fiction destroy the shadow, render it impotent, or defeat its purposes and hold it at bay, they perform what Carl Jung has called the function of artist as collective man: They come to the spiritual assistance of their society by conjuring up its shadow, its evil side, and exorcising it. To Jung, the shadow represents "the dangerous aspect of the unrecognized dark half of the personality"[9] He cautions that unless we admit this shadow in ourselves, collectively and individually, neither the society nor its members can experience psychic health. In its journey through the past 200-plus years of horror literature, the shadow has gone through a number of changes. Yet perhaps the most significant one of all is its gradual shift from being a single archetypal individual to becoming a group, a collective icon of external and internalized evil.

The Shadow as Gothic Villain

Manfred, Prince of Otranto, the main character in Horace Walpole's *The Castle of Otranto,* is perhaps the earliest popular villain. *Otranto* is a short novel first published in 1764, and was such a success that a second edition followed closely in 1765. The second one added a subtitle, "A Gothic Story," which initiated the gothic school of English literature. *Otranto* was so influential that it stimulated innumerable imitations during the next half century, and some authorities claim that this body of literature probably began the concept of "mass culture," because it was the first literary form to win great popularity in spite of critical disfavor. In some ways *The Castle of Otranto* is an imitation Elizabethan or Jacobean tragic drama in five acts, disguised as a novel and rather artificially punctuated with ghostly warnings, portents, revelations and a final apotheosis. The plot turns on the fact, previously mentioned, that Manfred is a usurper in the castle he occupies, and the story is a working out of a curse whereby he is forced to relinquish his identification with the castle and the power over others which it symbolizes. During the course of the action we are shown not only that Manfred occupies his position illegitimately, but also that he wields authority in a selfishly capricious way, often slipping into thoughtless cruelty, even perversity. He pursues his dead son's fiancée, callously discards his loyal wife, and trades off his daughter to get the woman and the political legitimacy he covets.

The author provides his protagonist with a fatal flaw in the manner of classical Greek tragedy: "Manfred," he assures us, "was not one of those savage tyrants, who wanton in cruelty unprovoked. The circumstances of his fortune had given an asperity to his temper, which was naturally humane and his virtues were always ready to operate, *when his passions did not obscure his reason* [emphasis mine]." Walpole, in spite of minor eccentricities and a penchant for "truant fantasy,"[10] was a man of his age, and his age was the Age of

Reason. It is not surprising, then, that his villainous hero's fatal flaw was unreason; that is, irrationality.

In the final pages of the novel, Manfred at last becomes aware of his fatal weakness. In yet another fit of anger, he has killed his own daughter by mistake. As she dies, he cries out to her, "Canst thou forgive the blindness of my rage?" Manfred, in his anguish, is finally able to "see" and reflect upon the irrationality of his own behavior. He later confirms this by avowing that his heart at last is open to moral admonitions. He has passed from distracted part-savage to sadder-but-wiser civilized man. Jung points out that the oldest stories of many religions and mythologies record similarly painful awakenings, and he holds that these tales mark the coming-to-conscious of the human race.[11]

Each such story, however, also embodies the situation of a particular culture at a particular point in its history. Immediately after Manfred attains the eighteenth century ideal of rationality (in Jungian terms, achieving a more fully integrated psyche), he is replaced as ruler by the rightful heir to the principality of Otranto, who reestablishes the legitimate feudal hierarchy. Manfred, stripped of rank and position, is now outside that world. And he cites his actions and their results as a lesson: "May this bloody record be a warning to future tyrants." Could the potential tyrants he addresses be us? Or, more especially, the readers of eighteenth century England who embraced his story with such enthusiasm? There is some reason to think so, because when feudal society crumbled, followed by the rise of the middle class, many more people became as "free" and "autonomous," if not as powerful, in fact, as the feudal overlord.[12] The capacity of the human race for evil as well as good was thus greatly extended. The protagonist of *The Castle of Otranto*, the first gothic villain, reminded the more rational, more completely individuated persons of his day of their largely unadmitted capacity for cruelty, lust, raw ambition, lies, and treachery, and warned them of their potential for reversion to a more primitive state. Manfred demonstrates the possibility of atavistic behavior through his mad rages, his contradictory actions and reactions, and his use and abuse of others. In the end, Walpole restores order — a good, sane, limited, established and organized feudal universe, comforting to the neoclassical mind. After showing civilized men what they have to fear, he exorcises that fear and erects institutional barriers against its recurrence.

If Manfred is to be seen as a shadow figure with some kind of direct connection to *The X-Files*, a few questions should be raised at this point. Due to the serial format of the mythic arc and to the god-like position of the syndicate in the ongoing narrative, that group is not likely to "come to consciousness" and reform itself. We know that greed, exploitation, and domination are devilishly persistent if not deathless — although they are sometimes punished — and the serial form requires that antagonistic forces either persist or continually be renewed. Manfred's trait most clearly instantiated in the members of *The X-Files'* syndicate is a self-serving ruthlessness that does not brook questions or opposition. Like these dark gods, Manfred is villainous insofar as his oligarchic political system gives him the opportunity to be, and he can reform himself only through the channels which that system provides — the church, or a strictly enforced hierarchy of privilege and hereditary rewards. For the syndicate to be similarly reformed, the political and economic system which gave rise to it would also have to be drastically changed. And we participate in that system. It is no accident that Fox Mulder is a government worker and not a free agent. The world has become more complicated, and when we battle evil, as CSM reminds us, we only destroy our fathers. For the modern, consciously individuating person, taking on the shadow is both a dangerous and a delicate business that requires intelligence, sensitivity, compassion, courage, a sense of humor and the recognition of the shadow within oneself.

One way the show refreshes the image of evil which weekly confronts the two protagonists is to place cabal-like characters in the free episodes and let them work out their villainy in self-contained narratives where they *can* be neutralized in the end. This happens in the episode "Revelations" (3X11) when the wealthy Southern industrialist who is plotting to kill the stigmatic boy Kevin Kryder is chopped up by the shredding machine in his own factory. FBI Section Chief Blevins, in "Redux II" (5X03), turns out to be a corporate double-agent, simultaneously employed by Rausch, a biotech company, and the government. When Mulder blows his cover, Blevins is shot by one of his own government cronies, who camouflages the murder to look like suicide. Some military officers and one prison warden are punished in their episodes, but the monstrous bosses in "Folie a Deux" (5X19) and the monstrously self-serving surgeon in "Sanguinarium" (4X06) are neither recuperated nor eliminated. These are shadow figures who act out the evil that the Cabal or syndicate represents on an "up close and personal" level, reminding us that power combined with venality is not only frightening in a general way, but can also be positively lethal.

In *Otranto*, Walpole indicates that once Manfred becomes a more rational human being, he will be able to act accordingly. *The X-Files* is much less sanguine about the transformative powers of human intellect and logic. Scientists are frequently portrayed as icons of evil — especially foreign scientists. And one U.S. scientist who supports Mulder's quest in "Gethsemane" (4X24) is duped by unknown forces that have constructed a fake alien body just to deceive him and Mulder. Although science and technological thought are often shown to be suspect, Agent Mulder uses his reasoning powers often and to great effect, despite the weird data and odd facts that make up his evidentiary base.

The figure of Manfred before his transformation exhibits traits that continually emerge in the human psyche, no matter what level of knowledge and competence the individual attains. Since Manfred represents the shadow as the feudal tyrant, he does not demonstrate the more sophisticated attributes of the archetype. These begin to surface in the villains of the gothic romances. Even so, uncontrollable anger still haunts homes, schools, businesses and public buildings in this more conscious age, giving rise to real-life stalkings, shootings, beatings and murders (an issue that Stephen King treats metaphorically in *The Shining*). Manfred's bestial impulses, insofar as they represent destructive forces from the human Id, are depicted again during the Victorian period in Robert Lewis Stevenson's *Dr. Jekyll and Mr. Hyde,* in which a human beast "hydes" behind the good doctor's civilized and moral façade. Oscar Wilde's *The Picture of Dorian Gray* is also a variation on this theme: The protagonist remains youthful and vigorous while his portrait ages hideously, showing all the effects of Dorian's life as a depraved libertine. The motif of "the beast within" finds expression again in the many 20th century film versions of the werewolf legend. It is interesting that so many of these stories evoke sympathy for the werewolf protagonist — a man who turns into a beast whether he wants to or not, making him a victim as well as an object of terror. This is also a strategy employed for the victim/monsters of *The X-Files.*

The works of Ann Radcliffe give us another vision of the shadow. Her lengthy novels, now called sentimental gothics, were the first gothic romances. All were published during the final quarter of the eighteenth century, a little later than *Otranto,* and in them, the gothic villain loses much of his crude willfulness. He no longer parades his uncontrollable passions, his selfishness, his arrogance in broad daylight and in torchlight, openly committing atrocities and pursuing nefarious schemes. Instead, he becomes an imposing shadow, more to be feared for the evil powers he conceals and suggests than for the actual power he wields in the everyday world. This kind of gothic villain echoes Milton's Satan of *Paradise Lost* from a century before. He possesses a dark and mythic grandeur as well as flawed nobility, and he is mysteriously alienated. His emotions are stronger and his powers greater than those of ordinary mortals. Unlike Manfred, this new villain is almost hypnotically attractive to both men and women. Also, in line with his larger-than-life stature, he does not respect or even recognize the limits of mundane human existence. This makes him both an appealing and a frightful figure, because it tempts us to a similar disregard of natural laws and moral restraints, enlarging the scope of the shadow within.

Father Schedoni in Ann Radcliffe's *The Italian* typifies the shadow in this next stage of his development. Schedoni is an alienated figure: "no one loved him, many disliked him, and more feared him." His presence is "terrible ... almost superhuman." Tall, but not graceful, he stalks along wrapped in a hooded robe which shadows his pale, livid face, a face that Radcliffe tells us "approached to horror." It is stamped with the deep lines of past passions, now dead, and "habitual gloom and severity." Schedoni's most extraordinary feature(s) are his melancholy eyes, which reflect, not a "sensible [sensitive] and wounded heart," but a "ferocious disposition," and are so piercing that they seem "to penetrate at a single glance, into the hearts of men, and to read their most secret thoughts; few persons could support their scrutiny, or even endure to meet them twice." Schedoni's unendurably penetrating gaze knows our "most secret thoughts," is privy to the dark side of our psyche. In fact, he *is* that dark side; at least he represents it, just as Manfred did. Villains of Schedoni's type were the fathers of the poet Lord Byron's so-called "Byronic" hero and also of the early fictional vampire. It might be said that the flawed, passionate Romantic/Byronic hero, openly embracing the perils of self-determination, represents the daylight face of individualism. The vampire, on the other hand, is the nocturnal, unacknowledged face — the face of a creature who is dangerous, not as much to himself as to humanity at large.

The Shadow as Vampire

At least three influential vampire tales preceded the publication of Bram Stoker's *Dracula* in 1897. The first of these, *The Vampyre* (1819), was written by John Polidori, personal secretary to Lord Byron. It is significant that Polidori's vampire Lord Ruthwen was modeled on Byron[13] just as Dracula was a portrait of the actor Henry Irving, who for many years employed Stoker as his business manager. Significantly, then, both novels grew out of the ambivalent fascination, fear and repugnance felt by one man toward the power exercised by another. Moreover, with the appearance of James Malcolm Rhymer's *Varney the Vampire* (1847), the tradition of the aristocratic vampire was firmly established; vampires came to represent an abuse of power, as Prince Manfred had. Before Lord Ruthwen and Sir Francis Varney, the vampire of folklore had for centuries been a mere peasant or gypsy. Ornella Volta observes that only as a nobleman did he become "a fully rounded personage, acquiring the prestige of an archetype."[14]

The fictional Count Dracula, of course, is himself the undead remains of a feudal tyrant, Vlad Tepeç, Prince of Wallachia from 1456 to 1462. Dracule, meaning dragon or devil, was the family name. Even though Vlad Dracula was not reputed to be a vampire, he exhibited many of the traits of a cruel and barbaric ruler. We still use the suggestive metaphor "bloodthirsty" to describe such qualities in leaders today, as we sometimes use the term "bloodsucker" to refer to those in power who steal from and otherwise exploit their subjects. (It is interesting to note that this term preceded the appearance of the vampire in literature, most commonly referring to the "bloodsucking" institutions of church and state or their representatives.) The primary demonstration of Vlad's power, as Bram Stoker found in his painstaking research for the novel, was apparently to murder his enemies in slow and gruesome ways, including, especially, various forms of impalement. The name that activity earned him — Vlad the Impaler — conjures up the erotic penetration of Count Dracula's bite, as well as the ritual penetration of the stake used to extinguish his power.

It would be difficult to conceive of a figure who more clearly personifies humanity's shadow, as it manifested during the Victorian Age, than does Dracula. The Count is a parasite, subsisting on the lifeblood of others. He leaves the base of his power, his castle, to seek fresh blood and new victims in England — a neat symbolic reversal which allowed British readers to see themselves in the sympathetic position of potential victims rather than as imperialists who were actually victimizers. Another symbolic reversal inheres in the fact that Dracula, like the Italian Prince Manfred, is not English, which safely identifies evil with foreigners, just as the Italian Manfred did. Yet Dracula both feeds on his own countrymen and travels from his homeland to satisfy his hunger in another country, and this cannibalistic metaphor serves both for England's economic exploitation of her industrial workers at home and her colonial empire abroad. Thus, with the vampire, the shadow in gothic literature moves into a broader, more public sphere than before. This move links self-aggrandizement on the individual level to national aggrandizement on a political level. When Dracula's throat is cut at the end of the novel, then, the reader participates in a ritual expunging of not only individual but also collective selfishness and economic guilt.

Scholars have pointed out a number of ways that the characteristics and powers of the fictional Dracula are coded representations of how the shadow archetype manifests in human life. Since he expresses our hidden capacity for inflicting evil on others, Dracula is, appropriately, a changeling who can take the shape of a wild beast or pass through barriers in the form of mist or elemental dust to appear where and when we least expect him. Although he cannot enter our dwelling unless he has first been invited in, he can control our minds hypnotically, so the invitation is almost assured. He throws no shadow (he *is* the shadow) and he casts no reflection in mirrors because we refuse to see those characteristics of ourselves that are most like those of the vampire. He is a creature of the night and can see in the dark: "No small power this," Prof. Van Helsing reminds us, "in a world which is one-half shut from the light"— just as the world of the unconscious is shut away from the light of human reason. And even though he sometimes appears to be elegant and refined, Dracula is an atavistic remnant. Van Helsing points out that the Count has a child's or criminal's brain, one that has lain in the tomb for centuries and has not grown to normal stature; nor will it in the future. Since it serves only selfish motives, it will always remain small.

While it is true that religious artifacts can control Dracula's evil, it is also true that religion plays an ill-defined role in Stoker's epic novel. Dracula's powers can be drained by a crucifix or the communion host. A forehead scar, a Mark of Cain, identifies the Count as an unholy creature; and he similarly marks Mina after establishing his power over her. But the feudal tyrant's and Dracula's gothic castle and the gothic cathedral are related images, their soaring towers and subterranean chambers calling to mind the heights and also the depths the human soul can reach. Moreover, the fact that Dracula must rest in sanctified earth suggests not only that good and evil are inextricably bound, but that religion can no more escape the shadow of man's dark side (his pride, his hypocrisy, his selfishness) than can any other human endeavor or institution.

Other Nineteenth Century Developments

> The true project of horror fiction is to discover evil, to bring it out of hiding and to make it show its face; the horror fiction of the nineteenth century shows us the progress of contemporary anxieties about the evil which others did, whose consequences could not be "interred with their bones," and about the evil which we do, whose legacy will haunt us even while we live.[15]

The so-called Romantic period in England lasted from the late 18th to the mid–19th century, also crossing the Atlantic to influence such authors as Edgar Allan Poe and Nathaniel Hawthorne in the United States. The British Romantic poets especially were influenced by the rediscovery and study of folk literature, such as popular ballads and fairy tales. This led to an increased appreciation of lyricism, spontaneity and fantasy, leading away from classical rules and proprieties which had dominated artistic production in the immediately preceding Age of Reason. Romanticism also valorized the feelings, beliefs and life situations of middle and lower-class individuals, and this new attitude — a step toward equality and away from class-bound systems — took on crucial significance as a number of popular uprisings occurred on the European continent, including the French Revolution. Accompanying and expressing the rebellious spirit of the age, Jean Jacques Rousseau and other philosophers began considering the question of individual rights and freedoms for all people.

At the same time, on the continent and in England, a new attention was being paid to death, funerals and the final resting place of the deceased. The British Victorians in particular seemed to be obsessed with death. Cemeteries expanded; monuments grew larger and more elaborate. Sentimental novels featured emotional deathbed scenes and virtuous children dying, and the art of the period produced many representations of pale and languid invalids or "the beautiful death" — usually of idealized female subjects. Correspondingly, there was a steady growth of interest in contacting the dead and in somehow obtaining evidence, not only for life after death, but also for paranormal abilities.

Mediumship, spiritualism and seances grew in popularity, leading to the establishment of first the British and then the American Psychical Societies. These groups approached the subject scientifically, accumulating careful documentation on the activities of mediums, mesmerists and spiritualists, as well as investigating alleged sightings of ghosts and other supernatural occurrences, like poltergeist activities. The preoccupation with death also showed up, as could be expected, in the gothic tales of the middle to late 19th century. The main topic of these stories was ghostly visitations — either for purposes of aiding the living or taking revenge upon them.

Brian Stapleford sees "the extravagances of Victorian mourning" as arising from guilt over the death of family members, an attempt to soothe the conscience of those left behind. But that seems to oversimplify the phenomenon and not to explain why, at this point in time, guilt for the death of relatives would suddenly become so unbearable. Also, why would it generalize out into all of the cultural areas mentioned above? Stapleford asks an appropriate question: Why would "guilty consciences [run] ... riot in the late nineteenth century in a way they never had before?"[16]

One explanation might be that people of the 19th century were attaining new levels of individuation, new powers of introspection and self-consciousness, and consequently achieving more sensitivity to racial memories stored in the collective unconscious. Carl Jung compares this repository to the current evolved state of our bodies or internal organs, all of which have gone through an historical process of change. The intermediate steps, and not just the latest stage, are part of their present form. So, too, according to Jung, the subconscious has participated in and responded to human evolution. The psyche contains a record in archetypal form of human experience through the ages, and anyone would have to admit that the history of the race has not been a tranquil one. Indeed, "Man's inhumanity to man" has made "countless thousands mourn": wars, persecution, torture, slavery, brutal punishments like drawing and quartering or burning at the stake, public hangings, beheadings and so forth. These are not "natural" disasters like fires, storms or disease, but horrors created by our ancestors. Access to the traumatic echoes of past acts, participated in or witnessed, might easily be felt as a generalized guilt which could attach to more intimate and immediate deaths in the present. Although this idea might strain credulity, I am forwarding it as an interpretation which would accord well with the Jungian leanings of popular thought in the 1990s. A Jungian conceptual field runs throughout this study and informs the archetypal analysis being applied to both the text and the context of The X-Files, past and present.

The works of American author Edgar Allan Poe (1809-1849) reflected fears that seemed to be prevalent on both sides of the Atlantic: fear of entrapment and of madness. Two of his story types, the tales of sensation and tales of ratiocination, evolved into the modern horror story and the detective story, respectively. The latter form is the progenitor of Sherlock Holmes and all subsequent classic detective fictions, and doubtless had an influence on the psychic detective stories of Sheridan LeFanu, Algernon Blackwood and others. Premature burial and madness are sites of fear often invoked in Poe's tales of sensation, which, as stated earlier, involve a central character who gets himself into a terrible predicament and then has to suffer through it — along with the reader. Stories of sensation often feature confinement, and the most dreadful sort, presumably, would be premature burial in a tomb or crypt. This common gothic motif is still part of horror literature today, as anyone who watches *The X-Files*, or has vicariously crawled through the underground drainage system of Stephen King's *It*, can testify. I would argue that this motif is so powerful and persistent because it violates ideological presumptions about individual liberty that are deeply felt in Anglo-American culture, especially in the U.S. This particular cultural ideal was just achieving force in the period during which Poe was writing, and it continues to have force now because it is, if anything, even less contested and more fervently believed than ever. In a popular text like *The X-Files*, which foregrounds Foucault's institutional structures of power and control, scenes that involve actual physical entrapment take on the resonance of a larger ideological dimension. This is one way that horror techniques serve artistic purposes, as Stephen King insists they should.

The fear of madness, one's own or someone else's, has also carried over from Poe's stories to the present. And this fear can take several different directions. In "The Tell-Tale Heart," Poe's narrator begins, "True!— nervous — very, very dreadfully nervous I had been and am; but why *will* you say that I am mad?" The speaker of "The Black Cat" confesses, "Evil thoughts became my sole intimates — the darkest and most evil of thoughts. The moodiness of my usual temper increased to hatred of all things and of all mankind; ... [leading to] sudden, frequent and ungovernable outbursts of fury to which I blindly now abandoned myself." The first excerpt illustrates a new concept of madness that was developing in the 19th century — the idea of "mental illness." This concept accompanied the belief that madness was a malady arising from guilt or moral weakness. Thus hauntings could be regarded as visions or hallucinations brought on by psychological disturbances, rather than true experiences of the paranormal. While this development opened the possibility of ambiguous or psychological readings of gothic stories, the fearsome prospect of having a diseased psyche, for the people of the times, was heightened by the fact that asylums and professionals to staff them proliferated during the 18th and 19th centuries. A person who demonstrated symptoms of mental disturbance could be institutionalized indefinitely, rigorously controlled and submitted to bizarre and terrifying procedures — a gothic nightmare. A depiction of institutionalized delusional madness is seen in the figure of Renfield and his situation in *Dracula*. Renfield is a patient in an asylum run by Dr. John Seward, one of the novel's team of protagonists. Renfield's moral flaws are obvious in his disgusting consumption of flies and progressively larger insects and animals, approximating the taboo of cannibalism as he tries to work up to consuming something bigger in hopes of becoming more like his master Dracula.

To return to the second excerpt from Poe above, "The Black Cat" shows that demoniacal rage, a bursting forth of destructive forces from the Id, was still as frightening for readers in Poe's time as it was for those who first encountered the blind fury of Manfred, Prince of Otranto. This is the kind of madness that we would fear in others and also in ourselves: being out of control and giving way to a more savage and brutal nature, the plight of the werewolf. Current horror fiction has inherited the clinical view of madness as an illness as well as the belief that madness arises from irresistible urges — the compulsions and obsessions of modern man. In the television police drama, the antagonist is almost always the crime lord or a crazy killer. These conventional villains provide the narrative advantage of a single, confrontable antagonist, even though they certainly do not represent the true nature of most police work, which involves mostly domestic disturbances or petty crime. *The X-Files* features some villains whose actions cannot be explained in any way but as resulting from the first kind of madness described above, a mental pathology, including an unnatural propensity to evil — from Eve and Donny Pfaster to John Lee Roche and Kurtwood Smith. Many other cases revolve around an individual who is in some way "not normal," villains driven by irresistible physical drives (the equivalent of madness) — like Leonard Betts, Virgil Encanto and Eugene Tooms. Both types arouse fear in us as potential victims, and they show us a face of evil that is also our face. They show us our shadow, the evil Other that is the worst in ourselves.

The Close of the Gothic Period

One direction the gothic took at the close of the nineteenth century was that, in the horror stories of the new era, the shadow archetype became a more amorphous character. As we see in Poe's main characters, the social status of the gothic villain diminished. He then faded into the background much more than he had as a vampire. At this time, his victims or accomplices begin to occupy the foreground, as in Henry James' *The Turn of the Screw* (which, although a literary work, is easily James' most popular, in both senses of the word). In this ambiguous, psychological or philosophical "ghost story," two spirits presumably haunt the children — a boy and a girl — cared for by the protagonist, a young governess. One apparition takes the form of Miss Jessel, the former governess, and the other is Peter Quint, the ex-valet of the children's absent uncle, a figure red-haired and leering like a medieval devil, dressed above his station in his master's cast-off clothes. Descriptions of a female specter resembling Miss Jessel abound in nineteenth century records of the British Psychical Society. But no figure similar to Quint is reported. Jessel is the apparition of "the woman in black," whereas Quint seems to be a creature of the author's creative mind, possibly unconsciously based on medieval devil imagery — thus an archetype. By dressing Quint in his master's clothing, James shows his assumed identification with a higher social class, which makes sense because now, commoners like Quint, ordinary human beings newly individuated, are taking on the full potential for evil once restricted to rulers and members of the aristocracy. At this point, the shadow is still typically an individual and is still identified with its house or dwelling.

More elusive versions of the shadow appear in the psychological ghost story, of which *The Turn of the Screw* is a respected early example. Another of about the same period is Charlotte Perkins Gilman's tale "The Yellow Wallpaper" (1892), in which the protagonist's physician-husband functions as menacing shadow figure. In this story, the narrator is suffering from what her husband calls "a temporary nervous depression — a slight hysterical tendency." Perhaps to achieve the "rest cure" often prescribed for women's nervous disorders in the late 19th century, the couple has moved to a country house for the summer with their new baby. The wife describes the house, in the gothic fashion, as "a colonial mansion, a hereditary estate, I would say a haunted house, and reach the height of romantic felicity." She does "declare that there is something queer about it," or, she wonders, "why should it be let so cheaply? And why have stood so long untenanted?" She and her husband take as their bedroom what she calls "the nursery at the top of the house. It is a big, airy room, the whole floor nearly, with windows that look all ways. ... It was nursery first and then playroom and gymnasium, I should judge; for the windows are barred for little children, and there are rings and things in the walls." At this point, the motif of madness begins to creep in and is reinforced when she says she has asked her husband if they could replace the hideous yellow wallpaper in that room and he tells her "that after the wallpaper was changed it would be the heavy bedstead [which is bolted to the floor], and then the barred windows, and then that gate at the head of the stairs." He also refuses to change their room for one downstairs, forbids her to work or write (although she writes in her diary on the sly, no one "hears" her story), gives her phosphates and tonics, goes in to town for long periods of time and refuses to let her have visits from relatives or friends. Gradually she becomes fixated on the repellent wallpaper in their bedroom, seeing a caged woman behind the pattern whom she tries to set free by peeling the paper from the wall, her rest cure descending into total madness.

Gilman uses the field of medicine as a paradigm of professional authority, and the story is told as an authentic narrative recorded in the protagonist's journal. Like the unnamed governess in "Turn of the Screw," the narrator of Gilman's story filters our perception of the other characters through her own consciousness, which may possibly be psychologically disturbed. Unlike James' story, though, "The Yellow Wallpaper" does not present the reader with a shifting domain of possible interpretations, but offers three clear levels of meaning within the interpretive code. One self-contained reading is the supernaturalist gothic one, which would see the room occupied by the protagonist as haunted by a madwoman who was confined there during a previous tenancy. A psychological reading, which also fits all the details and clues of the story, would interpret the narrative as the history of a mental breakdown being aided and abetted by the protagonist's husband (a common romantic gothic formula). This reading also accords with popular prejudices of the time regarding women as especially prone to neuroses (Poe to the contrary). The third interpretation, also capable of standing alone, and functioning almost allegorically, is that the protagonist is a metaphorical representation of the plight of the Victorian woman. Her husband is the personification of the shadow, the frightening archetypal image of new power relations that resulted from a period of extreme political and socio-economic change. The story arises from the following historical context.

During the 19th century, two influences brought about a drastic shift in patriarchal authority: the industrial revolution, which had destroyed the productive self-sufficient family and driven individuals from farms into cities, and the new concern for human liberties previously mentioned in conjunction with the Romantic era. Before the industrial revolution, the social order was one of fixed relations in which the cycles and forces of nature dictated the activities of most people. In that pre-industrial period, society was patriarchal yet gynocentric because women held a vital role in producing goods and caring for the household. But with the development of modern capitalism, the Market replaced nature in determining how ordinary people lived. Private and public life split apart; the former becoming the domain of affection, personal attachments and morality, while the latter became a competitive arena where only profit mattered. Women's previous realm vanished; their traditional contributions became commodities, objects of industrial production. Moreover, since the home was not any more a viable economic unit with the father as the head, he was displaced by the corporation, which took over from him the job of employing and sustaining family members.

"If the history of the West from sixteen hundred to the eighteen hundreds was condensed down to a single simple allegory, it would be the drama of the once all-powerful father."[17] Indeed, Freud's concept of the Oedipus complex reflects historical reality, in that the sons of his generation were engaged in a struggle with their father's traditional system of authority, and were thus suffering the psychological effects of envy, resentment and guilt. In this period, the sons, the new bourgeoisie, were the rebels: The French Revolution committed patricide by murdering the king and closing the churches. But even though the structures of the old patriarchy were being overthrown or dissolving, the new market economy was establishing another form of male dominance, with females as outsiders, anomalous, and a social problem to be solved.

The romantic reaction to industrial capitalism was one of horror at its destruction of nature and degradation of humanity. The new way was a brutal one, not even softened by benevolent feudal paternalism. The "freedom" that had been achieved seemed only to bring an endless struggle to survive in a cutthroat and unforgiving world. So the home became a refuge. Romantic idealists reinvented it as an escape from competitive strife, and placed an Angel in the House — the wife — to provide love, comfort and affection. The successful Angel was the antithesis of the successful Economic Man who endlessly transformed "life — human labor and effort — into lifeless capital." Where he was logical, she should be intuitive and illogical. Where he was stoic and practical, she should be emotional and tender. Where he was aggressive, she should be passive and unassuming. In this way, the middle- to upper-class woman of the late 19th century attained an idealized, elevated image which, paradoxically, placed her in a position of economic dependency and non-productivity. Her husband's wealth, largely gained by the exploitation of cheap labor, allowed the Victorian wife to be idle; domestic servants took care of household chores. The only life-function of such a woman was sex and procreation. She became a trophy, living proof that the husband could afford to keep a wife who did absolutely nothing. This kind of life often brought on an array of non-specific illnesses and neuroses, leading women to seek out the services of doctors, members of a newly established male medical profession who specialized in the diseases of women and promulgated a discourse of control with a "variety of diagnostic labels": "neurasthenia, nervous prostration, hyperesthesia, cardiac inadequacy, dyspepsia, rheumatism and hysteria." Since women were thought to be naturally disposed to sickness (especially rich women), they were especially in need of constant treatment.

The fear of madness is the obvious emotional ground of "The Yellow Wallpaper," and the largely absent but oppressive husband is the villain, representing the male power of scientific expertise and professionalism. Medicine is but one of the controlling discourses of the modern age, but it is one that has had a substantial impact on the lives of women. In author Charlotte Gilman's own life, she had consulted a famous and respected "nerve doctor" during the 1880s, and his prescription — to be completely domestic, limit mental activity and give up writing altogether — brought her, as she later said "perilously close to losing my mind." The historical foundation for this story and the story itself provide background for two thematic elements of *The X-Files*: In the transition from agrarian to industrial society, the sons overturned their father's traditional hierarchical male system (God → pope → king [bishop] → landed aristocrat [priest] → father). The early gothic preoccupation with paternity and heredity betrays a cultural nervousness about this upcoming change. And in "The Yellow Wallpaper," the shadow archetype is being connected to the powerful controlling discourse of science. Chapter Four discussed the fact that concerns about structures of control and the protagonists' relation to the world of the father are ongoing *X-Files* thematic concerns. A third relevant component of this story is macrotextual — the truth value of the authentic personal experience document. "The Yellow Wallpaper" is a combination of the real and the imaginal. Such stories have the multivalent potency of folklore, myth and personal testimony. Similar narratives are now perhaps the dominant, most interesting and certainly most accessible form of truth in the end-times of the 20th century.

Horror Fiction Enters the 20th Century

> Supernatural fiction is not, as is often believed, simply an inferior sort of mainstream fiction with a few ghosts thrown in, but is a range of literature with an extensive collection of motifs of its own, and it uses them in ultimate story abstractions that are its own. It also differs from mainstream fiction in its point of interest. Whereas mainstream fiction ... is primarily societal and to a lesser extent psychological, modern supernatural fiction is ultimately concerned with the impersonal individual and with universals of existence.[18]

At the beginning of the gothic period, neither realism nor the novel were considered to be completely respectable literary forms. Writers used the data of real life mainly to lend verisimilitude to an otherwise fantastic story and to provide the narrative with an effective chronological order that unified it and made it more coherent. However, as the 19th century progressed, the realistic novel gained in ascendancy. By the turn of the century, realism had become the dominant literary style. Spanning the middle of the century, the novels of Charles Dickens, with their recognizable characters of all social classes and their glimpses of the often miserable living and working conditions of industrialized Britain, captivated readers and engaged them as no reading matter but the gothic had done before. Dickens, though, championed the tale of the imagination just as much as he forwarded the cause of realistic fiction. He promoted the tradition of telling ghost stories on Christmas Eve and, of course, wrote the most famous Christmas ghost story of all time: "A Christmas Carol." His influence as a popular author and an editor kept the ghost story and other tales of supernatural horror alive and acceptable, though marginal as literature, in the U.K. after they had fallen out of both critical and popular favor in the U.S. when the contributions of Poe and Hawthorne ceased.

As the 20th century began, two forms of the horror story were most popular in Great Britain: the psychic detective story and the antiquarian/academic ghost story. Even though the first type is scarcely known by any but the most avid horror aficionado today, the protagonist of the psychic detective story has much in common with the character of *The X-Files'* Fox Mulder. Such early psychic detectives as Algernon Blackwood's John Silence also somewhat resemble Dr. Van Helsing, the scientist and sage who helped to rid the world of Dracula, but their purpose is "to explore rather than explain," in Brian Shackleford's words. He observes that the processes of psychic detection are scientific but not in a way that works toward clarity and normality. Instead, deduction applied to psychic events dissolves "the apparent safe solidity of the world we inhabit in a kind of metaphysical acid bath, which opens it up to the incursions of doubt, uncertainty, and the horrific reflections of our inner fears."[19] This, in fact, is a good description of Agent Fox Mulder's role and dramatic function. In the episode "Tithonus" (6X10), when Scully is sent on a case without her partner, she denies that it is an X-Files matter, and Mulder, who's been doing a little computer-based investigating of his own, immediately comes up with three explanations of what seems to be going on: murder by telekinesis, shamanistic death touch or a working-out of the Muslim belief that taking a photograph of someone will steal that person's soul. With Mulder, as with his earlier prototype, possibilities multiply; the world is various, rich and strange. This is the opposite of the conventional detective, who validates existing social mores and narrow rationality by getting the "right answer," at the same time implicitly denying the possibility of a larger morality or a more mysterious universe. The psychic detective story and the antiquarian/academic ghost story, though implicitly affirming the imagination, were transitional forms and smaller in scope than those literary types which developed later in the 20th century.

The primary exponent of the antiquarian/academic ghost story was M.R. James, a British schoolmaster whose published ghost stories were ones he told his students on Christmas Eve. *The Castle of Otranto* had been published on Christmas Eve 1767, and 100 years later Charles Dickens was championing and popularizing the idea of telling ghost stories on that evening. Although readers of the last half of the 19th century were becoming more skeptical, the Christmas ghost story tradition persisted, justified by the fact that the holiday itself was supernatural and miraculous, so it lent itself to tales that could be approached with childlike wonder. James' ghost stories are close in intent and effect to the tales of psychic deduction. Instead of showing how science and history can solve paranormal mysteries, they "celebrate the *limits* of academic expertise and scientific analysis, ... [focusing] upon the terror of moments when the rational world-view fails and collapses."[20]

One delightful facet of James' stories is the style, the way the calm, fastidious and precise language of an English don contrasts with the gruesome subject matter he is relating, as in this passage from "Casting the Runes": "... the electric light was off. The obvious course was to find a match, and also to consult his watch: He might as well know how many hours of discomfort awaited him. So he put his hand into the well-known nook under the pillow: only, it did not get so far. What he touched was, according to his account, a mouth, with teeth, and with hair about it, and, he declares, not the mouth of a human being." In the drily ironic tone of this passage we see, in its beginning stages, the kind of trickster irony that is resident in *X-Files* episodes. Several types of comic variation — parody is the most usual — are a common feature of horror texts, and are even, as Keith Neilson has noted, one of the major characteristics of the genre in its modern form. *The X-Files* has aired many humorously reflexive stories, with a large number of what an X-Phile calls "X-Files Lite" episodes coming up at the beginning of Season Six.

Among these was a show aired during the 1998 Christmas season that indicated full knowledge of the venerable Christmas ghost story tradition (as well as Dr. Seuss titles). "How the Ghosts Stole Christmas" (6X06) begins with Mulder and Scully arriving in the deep darkness of a stormy night at an iconic "haunted house." He proceeds to tell her, in excruciatingly purple prose, the story of the phantoms who are reputed to appear here every Christmas Eve; a young couple who committed suicide so that they could spend eternity together. In the course of the episode, *The X-Files'* postmodern irony develops as the ghosts enter the story. The pair of revenants are not young, but middle-aged, and they attempt to spook the agents into suicide or murder by ghastly visions and visitations, entrapment and a barrage of insulting diagnostic terminology borrowed from pop psychology.

But in this case, the "expert" discourse does not control. At one point during his psychologistic ramble, the male ghost, played by actor Ed Asner, echoes the crazy killer in "Clyde Bruckman's Final Repose" by asking Mulder if he knows why he thinks he's seen the things he has. And when Scully points a gun at the two ghosts and tells them to put up their hands, Asner, a well-known Hollywood liberal and activist, protests that he has friends at the ACLU. A little later, appearing and disappearing corpses under the floorboards, which look a lot like Mulder and Scully, are referred to as possible "Jungian symbolism," a nod to the cultural context. At the end, the agents shoot each other as they exchange greetings of "Merry Christmas," and the strains of "Have Yourself a Merry Little Christmas" play as background music. At the end of the episode, a revived Mulder and Scully exchange Christmas gifts as a filmed version of Dickens' "Christmas Carol" plays on a TV set in the background.

As the literary works of the late 19th and early 20th centuries evolved, popular horror fiction, too, expanded and progressed, moving away from its gothic foundations. It followed the lead of literary art by portraying characters with more freshness and immediacy, giving them more believable motives, and updating the way they talked and behaved. Along with more realism in characterization, the story-telling also became more realistic, even naturalistic, and at other times more self-consciously poetic or expressionistic, as writers made freer and more sophisticated use of symbolism and metaphor. In developments that have found their way into *X-Files* scripts, the turn of the century saw authors beginning to explore, in more imaginative and widely various ways, how the terror caused by the supernatural reflects our anxieties. And a social or cultural dimension of the genre began to be recognized.

The modern horror story started to reflect the same modernist sensibilities that were evidenced in the more respectable literary forms of the time. Modernism gave expression to the pervasive anxieties of the 20th century: an awareness of economic vulnerability; a reaction against the gray, dead-end urban lives that many people were living; and the seeming inevitability of human conflict and destruction. This world view gave rise to new kinds of imagery like this not traditionally "poetic" comparison from T. S. Eliot's critically acclaimed "The Love Song of J. Alfred Prufrock":

Let us go then, you and I
When the evening is spread out against the sky
Like a patient etherized upon a table.

And from poet and dramatist William Butler Yeats, both a writer of fantasy and practitioner of the occult, comes a modernist attitude with a definite atmosphere of supernatural horror:

... The Second Coming! Hardly are those words out
When a vast image out of *Spiritus Mundi*
Troubles my sight: somewhere in sands of the desert
A shape with lion body and the head of a man,
A gaze blank and pitiless as the sun,
Is moving its slow thighs, while all about it
Reel shadows of the indignant desert birds...
And what rough beast, its hour come round at last,
Slouches toward Bethlehem to be born?

The idea of "spiritus mundi" was Yeats' version of the Jungian universal unconscious, a store of archetypal materials from which he and all poets draw symbols and images. In his "The Second Coming," the rough beast is the monster of the twentieth century which will produce world wars, genocide, state and independent terrorism and nuclear annihilation and pollution, as well as an unprecedented attack on the natural world. As the horror fiction of this century develops, its universe becomes animistic and hostile. Characters experience random and capricious supernatural manifestations; they are not haunted because they have violated traditional religious or moral sanctions, and are much less likely to cause or deserve their gruesome encounters. As events appear less and less explainable by the resources of ordinary language and logic, "the unexplained," becomes an important means of intensifying anxiety and horror, leading to the narrative gaps and open-ended plots that are now a common feature of late modern and postmodern horror and are also regularly found in *X-Files* episodes.

Modern Supernatural Horror Fiction

M. R. James' work and that of other writers of the antiquarian school kept horror fiction respectable in England, and many literary authors experimented in the genre, although some pulp fiction was produced, too. But in America during the first half of the 20th century, horror was relegated entirely to the pulp magazines. Although this segregation was unfortunate, in several ways it was beneficial: It tended to liberate writers from the expectations of realistic literary fiction. They could explore new styles, write in unusual ways, affect their readers differently than could the authors of conventional literature. Pulp writers were allowed to be less inhibited in dealing with horrific imagery. Their work could be bizarre and indulge in extremes of disgusting ugliness and violence. Horror began to draw on ideas which invoked the vastness of space and the distances of time, leading to the Cosmic horror story. Concepts of unfathomable and trans-dimensional mysteries had been pioneered by Arthur Machen and Algernon Blackwood in Great Britain but reached their apotheosis in the work of H. P. Lovecraft in the United States from 1910 to the 1930s. Most of Lovecraft's work was published originally in pulp magazines.

The best works of horror by both Machen and Blackwood appeared before Lovecraft's best tales were published in the late '20s and early '30s, but the American author was very much in tune with the sensibility of both British writers. Machen was the most metaphysical of the two. One of his early stories, the atmospheric and chilling "The White People" communicates the terror of a world in which normal reality and natural law have been negated. The tale posits that real evil is not the violation of man's laws but nature's laws, the violation of patterns, principles and structures of the natural universe. Imaginative concepts such as this one show a kind of paranoia creeping into supernatural fiction before and after the first world war. Machen's contemporary, Blackwood, wrote stories that depicted nature itself — the same nature that had been idealized with nostalgia by the romantic poets — as an unknowable and dangerous sphere, whose forces were either oblivious or actively hostile to human beings. One of these forces, Blackwood's fictional figure of "the wendigo" was used by Stephen King in *Pet Sematary,* and the British author is widely considered to be one of the great horror story writers of all time. This may be the reason his last name was chosen as the working title for *Fear the Future,* the first *X-Files* film. (although "Blackwood" supposedly referred to an imaginary Texas town).

The story "The Willows" is among Blackwood's best work. It describes the experiences of a pair of sportsmen who set off to journey by canoe down the Danube from its point of origin in Austria, through Hungary, to its outlet in the Black Sea. The story begins, "After leaving Vienna, and long before you come to Budapesth the Danube enters a region of singular loneliness and

desolation, where its waters spread away on all sides regardless of a main channel, and the country becomes a swamp for miles upon miles, covered by a vast
sea of willow bushes." When the narrator and his companion reach this area,
they are out of their element. Something is "wrong." Outdoorsmen accus-
tomed to dealing with extreme physical challenges, they are not prepared for
the imaginal territory of the willows, where there are weird and ominous portents, where a terrible wind blows ceaselessly accompanied by an inexplicable booming, humming noise, where their equipment unaccountably becomes
damaged or disappears, and where the willows close in on them and the sand
banks fall away precipitously as they sleep. One night the narrator leaves their
tent and encounters an agglomeration of non-human creatures, enormous
and bronze-colored...

> [rising] upwards in a continuous stream from earth to sky, vanishing
> utterly as soon as they reached the dark of the sky. They were inter-
> laced one with another, making a great column, and I saw their limbs
> and huge bodies melting in and out of each other, forming this ser-
> pentine line that bent and swayed and twisted spirally with the contor-
> tions of the wind-tossed trees. ... I seemed to be gazing at the per-
> sonified elemental forces of this haunted and primeval region. Our
> intrusion had stirred the powers of the place into activity.

But his partner's interpretation of their predicament is much darker. He
believes that they have "crossed over the line" at a point where the space of
incomprehensible entities intersects with the space of men. These are not elemental spirits or the old gods, who had a relationship with humanity, but
"immense and terrible personalities" who "deal directly with the soul, and not
indirectly with mere expressions of the soul." This story expresses liminality
as much as *The X-Files* does, exploring the boundary between true and false
views of reality, between belief and skepticism, between the possible and the
impossible, the allowable and the forbidden. It projects the shadow onto a
universe that we regard as "ours," but which may be totally other and alien,
a place where human beings, trapped within their meager space-time environment, are of no consequence whatsoever. For all of its transcendent notions
and extravagant imagery, the text is realistic in its descriptions of landscape
and weather, the actions and interactions of the protagonists, and even in the
supernatural occurrences that intrude into their everyday existence.

In H. P. Lovecraft we find a writer who can also conceive of a universe
freed from the limits imposed by our rudimentary senses and restricted mental capacities. For Lovecraft himself, "time, space, and natural law" held "sug-
gestions of intolerable bondage."[21] The epic world-view of his stories func-
tioned as an attempt to escape this bondage. He is often faulted by literary
critics for his elaborated style, which, in the tradition of Poe, uses language
as much for evocative effect as for objectively depicting scene and action. And

yet, verisimilitude is not lacking in his stories. As Bram Stoker did in *Dracula*, he uses the technique of imaginary journal entries and newspaper articles, as well as artificial scholarly texts and scientific projects, to tie his stories to a recognizable world. His fictions "ranged widely into the unknown," but he was careful to set them "against a meticulously constructed background." "The keynote," he wrote, "should be that of scientific exposition — since that is the normal way of presenting a 'fact' new to existing knowledge — and should not change as the story gradually slides off from the possible into the impossible."[22]

Perhaps Lovecraft's most original achievement was the creation of a mythology called the Cthulhu mythos. Its premise was the existence of a pantheon of unspeakably old and evil beings, otherworldly monsters, known as the Great Old Ones, who were waiting to be called back into the earth's dimension to be lords and masters here again as they had been in eons past. The mythos stories are often set in an area around Arkham and Dunwich, Massachusetts, neither of which are real places. And the Miskatonic River and Miskatonic University, which also enter into these tales, are also imaginary In my credulous early readings of Lovecraft, I fully believed that these places existed, and I half-believed that Lovecraft's dark deities were indeed members of some arcane and ancient mythological system: the Great Cthulhu, "dweller in hidden R'lyeh deep in the sea," Yog-Sothoth, "the all-in-one and one-in-all," Shub-Niggurath, "the black goat of the woods with a thousand young," "Azathoth, a … blight of nethermost confusion which blasphemes and bubbles at the center of all infinity"[23] and Nyarlathotep, "the mad faceless god that howls blindly in the darkness to the piping of two amorphous idiot flute players."[24]

I also believed in the existence of the monstrously terrible secret book *The Necronomicon* and its author, the Mad Arab Abdul Alhazred, in addition to others like the *Pnakotic Manuscripts*, the *R'lyeh Text* and Comte d'Erlette's *Cultes des Goules*. I learned much later that not only did these books and others mentioned in Lovecraft's stories not originally exist, but that some of them were later made up and donated to the mythos by horror writers of the 1920s and '30s who were friends of Lovecraft (Robert Bloch, Clark Ashton Smith). It turns out that I am not the only person who has been captivated and convinced by the Cthuhlu mythos. In Robert Anton Wilson's 1998 guide to popular conspiracies and conspiracy theory, there is an entry for *The Necronomicon*, and a supposedly "real" version of that book has been published.[25] Does it contain the same predictions of and recipes for doom that Lovecraft credits to its pages in "The Dunwich Horror"?

> Nor is it to be thought that man is either the oldest or the last of
> earth's masters, or that the common bulk of life and substance walks
> alone. The Old Ones are, and the Old Ones shall be. Not in the spaces

we know, but *between* them. They walk serene and primal, undimensioned and to us unseen. *Yog-Sothoth* knows the gate. *Yog-Sothoth* is the gate. *Yog-Sothoth* is the key and the guardian of the gate. Past, present, future, all are one in *Yog-Sothoth*. He knows where the Old Ones broke through of old, and where They shall break through again.

In the genre texts that followed Lovecraft's, his concept of a cosmically alien Other was not really recaptured until recent decades, when certain more domestic or more political approximations, like Stephen King's novels *The Shining* and *The Stand*, Clive Barker's film *Hell Raiser* and *The X-Files* television series appeared on the scene. Not surprisingly, attempts to make film adaptations that replicated the numinous dread of Lovecraft's stories have failed miserably. It should be said, however, that the Hell Mouth, a contemporary version of "the gate to the outside," invests TV's *Buffy the Vampire Slayer* with a significant amount of Lovecraftian horror and awe at the close of the '90s. Lovecraft, the dean of American horror writers after Poe, employed genre traditions adapted to the global and existential terrors of the first modern world war. With shadow figures that were more all-encompassing than those of the past, a careful and convincing use of data and realistic detail which echoed his fellows on both sides of the Atlantic, and his own creation of a numinous and compelling mythology, Lovecraft established the ground of the literary climate that has given rise to *The X-Files*.

Horror Fiction After World War II

England suffered the direct effects of both World Wars in a way that North America did not, and the psychic residue of these traumatic events is expressed in Elizabeth Bowen's "The Demon Lover," published in 1945. The almost invisible shadow presence who stalks the woman protagonist is reminiscent of the devilish Peter Quint in "The Turn of the Screw," and it is also in line with the new 20th century development that protagonists not deserve the dreadful fate that (we assume) befalls her. The period is WWII during the London Blitz. Mrs. Drover, whose family has relocated to the country to escape German bombs, has come up to town for the day and decides to drop by and check on her shut-up city home. This comfortably settled British matron and mother of three finds there, to her horror, a note from a former fiancee who had been declared missing and presumed dead in the first World War, twenty-five years earlier.

Since the house had been locked, there was no natural way the message could have appeared, and she remembers with a shudder of terror what her soldier-fiancee had said before leaving for the front lines: "I shall be with you, ... sooner or later. You won't forget that. You need do nothing but wait." She does not remember him fondly, but only as a male presence who pressed her hand "without very much kindness, and painfully, on to one of the breast buttons of his uniform" and who was "faceless," with "spectral glitters instead of eyes." His message reminds her that this is their anniversary and he expects her to keep her promise. She can no longer recall what that promise was, and decides to flee the house immediately, making her way to the nearest taxi stand for safety. Once in the taxi she sees that her driver is, in fact, her demon lover from the past and she continues "to scream freely and to beat with her gloved hands on the glass all round as the taxi, accelerating without mercy, ma[kes] off with her into the hinterland of deserted streets."

The demon lover is an archetype, a figure from folklore and the subject (and title) of an old ballad, but this modern retelling of the legend has something to say about war and its impact on love and the kind of normal life that most of us hope to lead. Like the sins of the fathers, the horrors of war persist down through generations. No matter how prosaic and insulated Kathleen Drover makes herself and her life, she can never escape the forces of disintegration, destruction and chaos. Something within her is kin to those forces, inviting and allowing them, just as we must invite in the vampire before he can enter. The shadow can never be wholly projected onto the evil Other, away from ourselves, as this story shows: The note Kathleen receives from her long lost fiancee is signed with her own initial, "K."

In the 1950s in the United States, another fine supernatural story by a woman — one which is a classic now — evoked the presence of the shadow without actually showing him. Significantly, this was the period just before the feminist 1960s, when the new generation of women began to show a widespread consciousness of their possible status as victims in the social order. The shadowy male presence in Shirley Jackson's *The Haunting of Hill House* is Hugh Crane, the paterfamilias of Hill House, who infuses that edifice with his persona, but never actually makes a ghostly appearance. In a scene from the film adaptation *The Haunting*, however, Eleanor, the central character, dances ritualistically before a statue of Crane, and in another she almost falls to her death as she gazes up at the phallic tower which symbolizes Crane's authority and his ongoing power over Hill House and its occupants. Although he is invisible except for his stone image, Crane as villain is still the individual image of an archetype — in this case the patriarchal father as autocrat, and the house is still a personal icon, as it was in the "house" of Usher. Over the years, as the villain became less the aristocrat or feudal tyrant, his abode evolved into one more like ours. The feudal castle became a haunted house, and that house stands as a metaphor for the haunted psyche.

In Stephen King's *The Shining*, some 20 years later, the shadow becomes larger and assumes a socio-political dimension. His dwelling then turns into a social macrocosm, a resort hotel — but a hotel as isolated in the cold and sterile mountain landscape of Colorado as Dracula's castle is in the primitive

Carpathian back country of Eastern Europe. As the novel begins, Jack Torrance, an out-of-work English teacher and reformed alcoholic, takes a job as the Overlook Hotel's winter caretaker and brings with him his wife Wendy and five-year-old son Danny. The hotel was built in the early years of the twentieth century, and its history since then has been exceptionally lurid and violent. Bought and sold and bought again, its particular evil genius is a Howard Hughes–like self-made "millionaire inventor, pilot, film producer and entrepreneur," Horace Derwent. "Among his patents is a bomb carriage used on the Flying Fortresses that ... rained fire on Hamburg and Dresden and Berlin." His investments have included "a string of munitions factories in New York and New Jersey ... textile mills in New England ... chemical factories in the bankrupt and groaning South," and later have extended to bootlegging, smuggling, prostitution and gambling in other parts of the United States. Further, Derwent's connections in Hollywood and Las Vegas, as well as in the upper echelons of politics, industry and organized crime, represent the most corrupt and contemptible elements of the seamier side of American life. At the time the novel takes place, Horace Derwent, like Dracula and Hugh Crane, is one of the undead. His spirit inhabits the Overlook Hotel, but his death is unconfirmed. And the hotel itself is timeless and universal: "Here in the Overlook things just went on and on. Here in the Overlook all times were one."

Jack Torrance and his family find that a collection of grotesque horrors inhabit the hotel, inside and out. They encounter unnatural perversions of the natural world — the topiary (hedge animals that menace the front lawn and malign) and possessed manufactured objects (an old-fashioned fire hose that flops onto a corridor floor and unrolls itself in malefic pursuit). Not even the childhood world of play is safe, as Danny finds himself hunted and trapped by a child-phantom on the hotel's snowbound playground. Even more to the point, one hotel room is haunted by the bloated corpse of a wealthy aging libertine who committed suicide there; and the blood of a gangland killing spatters the walls of the suite where four U.S. presidents have stayed. The Overlook is, in fact, a compendium of those features of American society which we would prefer to overlook. And Horace Derwent is the apotheosis of opportunism, our ideal of individual autonomy in its shadow form, a decadent and horrific Horatio Alger.

During the climactic scene of the novel, a recurring vision of Danny's is actualized as a monster chases him through the hotel's shadowed halls into a cul-de-sac, slamming the walls with a mallet as it approaches, shouting, "Come out and take your medicine, you little shit!" The voice is his father's, the face his father's, but the dark spirit that animates them belongs to the hotel. The Overlook wants Danny's precognitive, telekinetic and telepathic powers ("the shining" of the book's title). In order to get them, it has corrupted Jack Torrance with alcohol and tempted him with the promise that he will be made the manager as soon as he delivers his son to the hotel by killing him. Thus does the institutionalized selfishness of the socio-economic system work through the personal selfishness of one man. And, just as the hotel stands for the evils of that system, the Torrances suggest the evil possibilities of the nuclear family, that encapsulated pressure chamber, where, all too often, the sins of fathers and mothers are visited upon and passed along to children — for Jack's own father was an alcoholic, a wife-beater, and a child abuser before him.

Although the allegorical content of *The Shining* is quite obvious, Stephen King's abstractions are skillfully clothed in reality and resonate with archetypal force. Also, the symbolic substructure of the novel is rich and supportive. The name Jack Daniel Torrance, for instance, calls to mind both alcohol (Jack Daniels whiskey) and the atavistic madness it can produce (Jack the Ripper — rip/Jack Torrance — tore, torrents). The roque mallet, Jack's eventual weapon, is a metaphor linking him to England's aristocracy: "a British forebear of our croquet ... Croquet is bastardized roque ... ["The Overlook's] may be the finest roque court in America." Jack's final attempted sacrifice of Danny becomes a modern expression of our authoritarian Judeo-Christian heritage, echoing Abraham's unconsummated sacrifice of Isaac, or Jehovah's sacrifice of his son for the sins of humanity. And these are only a scant few strands of the complex web of associations which underscores the central allegory. It is interesting to note that the name Robert Torrence is given to both a scientist and the prisoner who receives his disease-laden package in *The X-Files'* "F. Emasculata" (2X22). The name "Robert" recalls the demonic "Bob" of *Twin Peaks*. At the end of *The Shining*, with the help of some very ordinary folks who have "the shine" to varying degrees, Danny and his mother escape while the hotel and Derwent, its shadow, are consumed in flames. The power to "shine" seems to signify an extension of human consciousness, perhaps an evolutionary one. Those who have it are not wealthy or of noble birth. They are simple people who recognize each other, communicate and care about one another. The shining is a force from within, a force opposed to Jack's selfishness, the worldly power of Horace Derwent and the more universal evil of the hotel itself. The ability to shine springs from unconscious, intuitive sources, and Danny has it in abundance. Thus the reader is left with the hope that Danny, both rational/reflective and attuned to the subconscious, will be able to transcend "the sins of the fathers."

In many ways, the conclusion of *The Shining* echoes that of *Dracula*. The established institutions of society, including the church, play a small part in the eradication of the vampire. That takes place only when a small group of brave men (and one tainted woman) band together and make Dracula's destruction their chivalric quest. Thus the shadow is exorcised by collective action aided by the conscious, reflective thinking that is demonstrated and symbolized by the psychic detective as scientist, Prof. Van Helsing. But the powers of intuition and the subconscious have also contributed, in the form of folkloric magic and Mina Harker's hypnotic trances. In the unconscious, our individual feelings and memories attach themselves to archetypes based in the collective memories of the race, giving us powers that are not available to the conscious mind. The dialectic between rational consciousness and the emotional, intuitive subconscious is one that is continually repeated in the horror genre. The ongoing exchanges between Agents Mulder and Scully in *The X-Files* represent only one of the more recent variations, adapted to the tastes and the expectations of audiences at the end of the 20th century.

Both *Dracula* and *The Shining*, like their predecessor *The Castle of Otranto*, perform a ritual exorcism of our shadow. The two more recent novels, however, do not attempt to control the dark side of our nature by returning to a "safe" authoritarian society, as does *Otranto*. They propose, instead, that our hope for the future lies in brotherhood, collective action and unselfishness. And *The Shining*, further, recognizes that certain of our unexamined beliefs and institutions may be intrinsically dangerous to us in that they nurture our shadow and put it to work in the world. So Stephen King has given our self-consciousness a new, even broader socio-political dimension. He has suggested that in some ways our very society — his metaphorical American hotel — may be "an inhuman place [that] breeds human monsters."

Following an established gothic/horror tradition, then, *The X-Files*, extends the shadow archetype beyond King's hotel into a chronotope that is global and pervasive. The Cabal has no one location. It exists in anonymous business offices and exclusive men's clubs. It has no one nationality, respects no boundaries. It is as mysterious and unimaginable as Lovecraft's dark deities or the MIBs of the Parallax Corporation. Its powers and purposes are matters about which we can only speculate. It reaches into the offices and hearing rooms of agencies and legislative bodies everywhere. It deals in cover-ups (the Majestic 12 documents and countless pieces of X-Files evidence) and assassinations (Deep Throat, Mr. X, Mulder's father, Melissa Scully and others) and it seems to be continually negotiating its sovereignty with equally ill-defined aliens of unknown origins. Although approaching to the threat of Lovecraft's inter-stellar and inter-dimensional monsters, these shadowy dark-suited creatures and their alien allies seem familiar, even prosaic. They live in our space, breathe our air, interpenetrate with our existence. Try as we may to project them out onto an international conspiracy, the earth is round, and they simply roll around it and in again through the back door — taking shape as our military, our corporations, our governmental agencies and our nasty German and Japanese scientists. Our shadow has returned to its origins. And the threat, which may be quite real (or may not), can no longer be projected onto the evil outsider, as it was with *Otranto*'s Italian feudal prince or *Dracula*'s Transylvanian Count, but must be seen for what it is — a part of our own natures, of ourselves.

The X-Files and the Horror Film

Although H. P. Lovecraft and Stephen King continued and expanded gothic horror in important ways, the fulcrum of influence, as far as *The X-Files* is concerned, shifted during the 1920s and '30s from gothic and horror literature in print to similar stories in other media. Theatrical productions that featured traditional figures like the monster and the vampire had been around since the romantic era, and when motion pictures became popular, these scripts and performances were then adapted to, first, silent, and then sound versions of *Dr. Jekyll and Mr. Hyde*, *Dracula*, *Frankenstein* and others. The famous film productions starring Bela Lugosi and Boris Karloff as the latter two monsters were both released early in the sound period and in the same year — 1931.

Throughout the Depression years and into the 1940s, Hollywood's Universal Studios turned out a series of what are now called "classic" horror films featuring the traditional monsters and villains and branching out into stories of mummies returned from hibernation, invisible men, zombies and mad doctors, savage yet pitiable wolf men, and monstrously oversized but also pitiable jungle creatures. Film had a special affinity for the horror tale. Because viewers experience a motion picture in a single sitting, a movie, like a good horror story, can develop strong emotional and aesthetic impact from its cumulative "effect." This "unity of effect" is a quality that Edgar Allan Poe first recognized as an aesthetic advantage of the short story form, and it is particularly desirable in plot-centered genre narratives like suspense fiction. Movies can also arouse visual, sensory, and group-audience responses in an immediate way. Movies show, they don't tell. Group emotions carry individual audience members along, and yet at the same time, the single viewer is isolated, alone in the dark as if in a dream. The movie is happening to the viewer, and it's happening *now*.

The expressionist style of the horror film of the '30s decade translated gothic motifs into a set of recognizable visual conventions: The old dark house, shadows and enclosed spaces, crypts and cemeteries, exotic and depraved "primitive" locations, "wrong" or distorted architecture suggesting madness, monstrous extremes of human ugliness or deformity, terrifying objects (especially those implying forbidden knowledge) and the image of the evil genius — Faustian, vampiric, or scientific — the one who goes too far. Carnival (gypsy camps), masquerade (masks and disguises) and laboratory were also visually configured as sites of license and excess, confinement and unimaginable danger — liminal spaces with their own black shadows and grotesque iconography, outside the law or the normal constructs of morality. Yet these chronotopes of the fantastic still could not approach the extremes of disgust and loathing, on one hand, wonder and numinous dread on the other, that constituted the full spectrum of the horror response as it was conjured up during this period in the images created "on dead paper" by H. P. Lovecraft.

What the classic horror movies of the 1930s did accomplish was to accustom audiences to icons, conventions and formulas that established the look and explored the narrative possibilities of the horror film genre until the next new wave of movie terror arrived in the 1950s, in the form of the science fiction horror film. In the postwar '40s and '50s, the straight horror film in the U.S. dissolved into reflexive parody and pastiche. Like other genre movie types — the Western is a good example — horror films had evolved through an experimental period (in the '20s) when filmmakers were trying out approaches to the genre; a classic period (the '30s) that set the dominant tradition and produced the most artistic and fully realized examples of the type; and then a reflexive stage right after World War II, which made fun of the '30s monsters and traditions because the old imagery and the old stories no longer represented the fears of the new age. During the 1950s and '60s, issue/problem films and science fiction movies began to deal more directly than any other genres with the social and political anxieties of the post-war period in the U.S., which included

> fears of invasion during the Korean War and the Cuban missile crisis, fears of being "taken over" mentally and spiritually during the McCarthy era, a compound of brainwashing, genetic engineering, computerized policing, and bacteriological warfare, as well as growing ecological fears connected with atomic power, aggressive defoliation techniques, various kinds of man-made pollution, the growth of populations, and the penetration of outer space by more and more man-made objects. and at that point, science fiction and horror began to meld, uniting in a single overall terror: fear of the future.[26]

The 1956 version of *Invasion of the Body Snatchers* was the best early film that could lay full claim to being a combined science fiction and true horror film. It is a precedent of *The X-Files* primarily because of its paranoid premise and the way it develops that premise in the ordinary little town of Santa Mira, California (compare to Home, Comity, "Our Town" and the many other *X-Files* small town locations). *Body Snatchers* also introduces full-blown cosmic terror and darkness slowly to the survivors among the town's hapless citizens. Between calm and sun-swept daytime sequences are interspersed night scenes with stark shadows and intense high-key lighting, capturing the highly dramatic look of noir detective/crime dramas of the period and '50s problem or issue films like *Face in the Crowd*. Early on, the doctor-protagonist examines a strangely unfinished-looking body laid out on a friend's pool table. On the wall behind the table is a framed poster with indistinct dark images and, in large, bright letters, MIRROIR NOIR. (My notes say, "Noir goes to the country.") The camera communicates anxiety with obliquely shadowed angle shots, and later heightens dread with claustrophobic points of view — such as long flights of stairs, tunnels and corridors — together with frantic chase scenes, mostly on foot.

The doctor's friend Jack is a writer of detective fiction, who decides that the unformed body will doubtless make a "charming, blood-curdling mystery story." With allusions like this and its *noirish* art direction, the movie declares its affiliation with the pervasive disquietude of the noir text. Still early in the film, someone guesses that the pods that have been discovered are "a weird alien organism" or "an atomic mutation," tying the film to the '50s SF atomic monster genre. In another attempt at explanation, the local psychiatrist suggests that the people who have been complaining that their relatives and friends are *not* their relatives and friends are suffering from a contagious neurosis, probably brought on by what's going on in the world. And another neighbor hopes vainly that whatever is taking place there is *not* happening worldwide. At this point, the movie touches base with the issue film, although "what is going on in the world" is never explored or specified. The emotionless, zombie-like replicants that replace townspeople one by one are related to the zombies of the classic horror films of the '30s and they also recall the evil twin or doppelganger image of the gothic tradition. In this case, the twins are not human flesh and blood nor are they icons of individualism that represent destructive animalistic impulses and instincts. They are plants that grow from spores which have floated down out of the universe, possibly as a colonizing mechanism, and they represent a force opposed to human consciousness and individuation. They were variously interpreted during the '50s as being symbols of the Communist menace or, in a totally opposed reading, of blind bourgeois consumerist conformity. Both of these interpretations relate to the film's emotional and conceptual base: fear of the collective. The "ordinary citizens" who are transformed have, in effect, completely internalized their social controls. They have no questions, no doubts. They are one with each other and one with the invasive power that is using them for an unknown purpose.

As with *The Cabinet of Dr. Caligari*, the *Invasion of the Body Snatchers* as released was not the original version. The distributor mandated a frame around the main action to soften the impact of the original pessimistic conclusion. In the prologue of the revised version, an exhausted and distraught Dr. Bennell makes it to an interstate highway where police pick him up, and he is able to tell his story. The narrative from that point is a flashback — the doctor's story, the film as it was actually made but with a later voiceover by Bennell superimposed. Again as revised, this flashback ends with an epilogue in which a police psychiatrist becomes convinced that Bennell's hysterical story is true and alerts state officials and the FBI. However, in the original version, no one listened or believed, and the film closed with Miles Bennell ricocheting from car to car on the crowded freeway, shouting, "You're next! You're next!" Finish.

Today *The X-Files* has taken the premise of fear of the collective one step further. Among its several significations, the conspiratorial syndicate stands for the network of professional, economic and political discourses that control the minds and lives of citizens. *The X-Files* intimates that these discourses, instead of telling the truth, cover it up and explain it away when it does not serve professional hegemony and survival. Mulder's quest suggests that we are neither individuated nor free if we do not have access to the truth about our situation nor the freedom to act upon it. Those without that truth are the pod-people of consensus reality. It is interesting to consider that one sure sign, in *Invasion of the Body Snatchers*, that someone has become "one of them" is that the person stops trying to tell his or her story, stops attempting to bear personal witness to his or her individual truth.

Although there have been other SF/horror movies that expressed "fear of the future" while constructing a convincing paranoid world, I see Ridley Scott's *Alien* (1979) and John Carpenter's *They Live* (1988) as the intertextual siblings closest, after the 1956 *Body Snatchers*, to the spirit and emotional content of *The X-Files*. Both Scott's and Carpenter's films also reflect the kinds of movies popular in their decades. *Alien* shows SF/horror beginning to demonstrate the high-budget production values, artistic cinematography and thoughtful content for which *2001: A Space Odyssey* (1968) and *Close Encounters of the Third Kind* (1977) had opened the way. *Alien* has also been the referent for several *X-Files* episodes; the volcanic parasite in "Firewalker" (2X09) and the alien monster in "The Beginning" (6X01) both burst from the esophagus of their human hosts much as did the one in *Alien*, and the resulting creature in "The Beginning" assumes a form very like the full-grown alien monster in that film. *They Live* adds another more recent dimension to the SF/horror genre, the muscle-man or tough-guy action formula of the 1980s (think Rambo and the Terminator), making *They Live* a combination of SF, horror and action. *Alien* is much more a genre film than *Space Odyssey* or *Close Encounters*. It also differs in having a purely genre monster, unambiguous and terrifying, much scarier to us than, but related to, the sci-fi movie monsters of the '50s and '60s.

The *Alien* monster and the two major settings of the film, the stranded alien spaceship and the mining-cargo ship from earth, were designed by the Swiss artist Giger, whose conceptions meld the organic and the mechanically industrial. The wrecked alien ship is a gargantuan emptiness that suggests the skeleton and interior of an enormous whale-like animal. In contrast, the Earth vessel as seen from the perspective of space looks random and strictly utilitarian, its bristling metal components linked together above great globular storage tanks in which the ore collected on the Nostromo's mission is transported back to earth.[27] This breast-like design feature underscores the fact that the ship is called "Mother" and is addressed as such through the computer command system. Inside, the vessel is claustrophobic and cluttered, pinkish-orange, fleshy, with intestine-like pipes and ducts built into the walls. Its levels are interleaved with metallic grids, cramped corridors and minimal constructivist floors, ceilings and work spaces — ugly and functional. *Alien* creates its own unique chronotope of space, an enclosed maternal factory of a universe whose verisimilitude is confirmed by characters who work and fight and cry and sweat and bleed in it. Once the alien creature is unleashed, the ship becomes an icon of pure horror — misty, shadowed, confined. Mother protects the crew and employs them, but she also betrays them. She is an extension of the Company, and the Company has informed her that the *Nostromo's* crew is expendable.

In 1983, the editors of *Consumer Guide* published an attractive, glossy, coffee-table book about horror movies. It characterizes *Alien*, made only four years before, as "a stylish, beautiful, brutally effective shocker, already a classic of the genre."[28] Yet the brief article also tells readers that "one of the crewmen — a spy for the 'corporation' — is secretly helping the alien live (presumably so that the corporation can exploit it). This introduction of conspiracy needlessly complicates the story line."[29] Actually, the conspiracy is not needless at all: It is the backbone of the narrative, bringing out essential details of characterization, contributing motivation and suspense. It is also the aspect of this film that brings it closest to *The X-Files*, whose environment is not futuristic but located in the (approximate) here and now. Significantly, the treacherous crewman on the *Nostromo* is Ashe, the science officer. He talks the protagonist Ripley out of recalling the away-team when she learns that the alien message they are responding to may be a warning. He allows the same away-team, after it has contacted the alien ship, to come back into the shuttle without observing the required 24-hour quarantine. Even though the ship's captain, Dallas, did not know Ashe when he came aboard, he allows the science officer to make crucial decisions about the alien presence. The protagonist Ripley, who is second in command, challenges Dallas, asking how this can happen, and he tells her, "It happens, my dear, because that's what the Company wants to happen." She asks about standard procedure and Dallas replies, "Standard procedure is to do whatever they tell you to do."

A crisis arrives when one of the crewmen from the away team "gives birth" to an alien monster-child that has been incubating in his body, reaffirming the traditional scientist/monster horror motif, from *Frankenstein* on, that any child born of a man will be a monster. From this point on, the embattled crew plays a deadly game of hide and seek with the developing creature, which is changing form and becoming bigger, more cunning, and more dangerous as it gets older. After Dallas is killed, Ripley is finally able to break through a "Science Officer Eyes Only" computer lockout and communicate directly with Mother. She finds that the ship was rerouted to new coordinates while the crewmen were in sleep mode during their journey home. The message clearly implies that the Company knows of the alien presence and is aware of its deadly nature. New orders were to investigate any life form found and to gather specimens. Priority One is to ensure the return of the organism for analysis. All other considerations are secondary. The crew is expendable.

After learning the above, Ripley attacks Ashe and finds that he is a robot. He is finally dispatched by Parker, one of the remaining crewmen. Not coincidentally, I think, Parker is played by Veronica Cartwright, who takes the central role of abductee Cassandra Spender in the episodes "The Red and the Black" and "Patient X" (14/15) late in *The X-Files'* fifth season, and in "Two Fathers" and "One Son" (11/12), two episodes shown during the network sweeps period in the middle of the sixth season. After Ashe "dies," Ripley tells Parker that he was protecting the alien creature all along and guesses that the Company must have wanted it for the weapons division. Parker replies, "That's the damn company! What about our lives?" The two manage to repair Ashe's electronic circuitry long enough to ask him how to kill the creature, and he responds, "You can't kill it ... a perfect organism ... a survivor unclouded by conscience, remorse, or the dictates of morality...." Ashe's robot (soulless) scientist echoes the automatons of *Body Snatchers,* but he is much more dangerous because he controls the all-powerful discourse of science, thus is able to achieve the Company's evil purposes on the strength of words alone.

By the time *Alien* came into being, the generalized anxiety of the 1950s had become the full-blown paranoia of the 1970s. The Vietnam war and Watergate convinced many people that high-level institutional deception was not just a possibility but a foregone conclusion. Some of that paranoia, reasonably enough, attached to the bottom-line mentality of large business enterprises. Thus *Alien*'s "Company" could be seen as a perfectly reasonable villain. Note, too, that "The Company" is a nickname of the CIA, whose reputation was suspect in some quarters during the '70s and has generally deteriorated since. In the 1990s, with legal decisions eroding 160 years of antitrust legislation, corporate mergers are escalating. As corporations grow larger, stronger and more global, individuals — especially in the more developed nations — sense that they are less important, more expendable. The resulting fear and suspicion is exacerbated as jobs and even entire factories and operations are moved to foreign locations to take advantage of their low wages and lax regulations. *Alien* did not discover the villainy of the corporation, but the film attaches to that motif the suggestion that the last corporation, the one resulting perhaps from a crescendo of future mergers — the logical outcome of capitalism — would finally come to exercise ultimate economic and political power as the Company, the only company: "A perfect organism — a survivor unclouded by conscience, remorse, or the dictates of morality." Taking the time differential into account, *The X-Files* Syndicate may be seen as this entity in its formative stages.

They Live, unlike *Alien* but similar to *Invasion of the Body Snatchers,* takes place in current reality rather than the future. But this reality is not the placid California small town of the 1950s, but the distressed borderlands of a large, sprawling West Coast metropolis at the end of the 1980s. The protagonist, played by a professional wrestler, is a drifter who lost his job in Colorado and takes the first one he can find in California, working construction by the day. The sights and sounds of a big city create an entirely different sort of chronotope than the industrial space vehicle or the small town of the two other films. The drifter walks down a hill into canyons of steel and glass; the streets and the squatters' camp he enters later are noisy, frantic, conflictive. Early on he passes a blind street preacher whose harangue is the first indication that something is "wrong" in this seemingly normal environment: "They have taken the hearts and minds of our leaders. They have recruited the rich and the powerful. And they have blinded us to the truth. They are our masters. Wake up! They are all around you!" It turns out that this is no religious metaphor.

And the hero is no radical malcontent. A new acquaintance complains about losing his job with a steel company in Detroit, commenting that the golden rule is "he who has the gold makes the rules," but the protagonist rebuffs him: "You ought to have a little more patience with life. I believe in America. You follow the rules...." But he gradually finds out that aliens have taken over most of the major institutions in the U.S. and the world and are working with Earth collaborators to ensure their hegemony and to pacify those who are still unaware of their presence. The aliens disguise their appearance by means of a mind-controlling master signal that goes out to a satellite which blankets the whole world. They also transmit subliminal messages under the cover of this signal, so that every billboard and magazine, beneath their ostensible content, relays commands to OBEY, MARRY AND REPRODUCE, STAY ASLEEP, DO NOT QUESTION AUTHORITY, NO IMAGINATION, WATCH TV, CONSUME, and BUY. All currency is invisibly stamped with the injunction that "THIS IS YOUR GOD." Once his normal view of the world dissolves, once the hero can see the aliens and their messages, he is not safe anywhere. Small surveillance disks patrol the air and all of the alien inhabitants are equipped with communication and transportation devices which can transmit information, or their owners, instantly. Nevertheless, the hero determines to unmask the invaders by destroying their satellite communications link, which would make their true nature and purposes obvious to everyone. In conventional action-adventure fashion, he is able to pull it off—but dies in the attempt.

It should not be supposed that this is an entirely serious movie. But it is a satire rather than the usual parody. Its intent shows in the choice of wrestler Roddy Piper to play the main character and becomes especially apparent in the montage sequence at the end of the film, which shows what happens after the aliens' broadcasting link ceases to function. But the police demolition of Justiceville, the squatters' camp, early in the movie is horrific and convincing, and toward the end of the story, a character who has been transformed from a homeless camp pundit to a tuxedo-clad collaborator offers an explanation of his and others' treachery in joining the aliens: They offer us wealth and power. "Most of us just sign up with them right away. We get promoted.

Our bank accounts get bigger. We start buying new houses, new cars. We'll do anything to be rich." He continues, "Look around you, the environment we live in: carbon dioxide, fluorocarbons, methane…. Earth is being acclimatized." Their environment is replacing ours. "They're free enterprisers. Earth is their third world…. It's business; that's all there is. They own everything, the whole planet. We all sell out every day. It might as well be on the winning side."

The satirical nature of *They Live*, its contemporary chronotope, and its overt political content make it a precursor of *The X-Files* without assuming any direct influence, and that is true of all three of these SF/horror movies from preceding decades. They simply reflect a pattern in the cultural fabric that *The X-Files* shares in an unusually self-conscious, decidedly postmodern fashion. And they share with *The X-Files* a significant shift in the depiction of evil. The personified figure of the shadow, so dominant in the gothic and still existing in some forms of modern horror fiction has, in such texts as the ones described above, become generalized and pervasive rather than romanticized and personified. The villain has changed, and changes in the nature of villainy reflect changes in the cultural climate. The previous and traditional locus of evil is seen clearly in Stuart Kaminsky's schema of the seven branches of the American horror film from the early classics to 1975. The "sources of horror" for each of these branches are very physical manifestations of the shadow. The first four categories feature traditional monster types, number five focuses on the insane or serial killer (who continues from Jack the Ripper to the present day), and numbers six and seven single out two villains resident in the cloned genre of SF/horror. Kaminsky's categories, then, are based on the main evil personage or shadow image in that type. They are: (1) animal drives which threaten man, (2) immortal parasite, (3) witches, corrupt humans who worship evil, (4) resurrected dead, (5) unpredictable madmen, (6) mad scientist and created monster, and (7) creatures from outer space, inside the earth, or from the Id.[30] Motion pictures and *X-Files* episodes falling into each category would be: (1) *Dr. Jekyll and Mr. Hyde* and "Shapes" (1X18); (2) *Dracula* and "Tooms" (1X20); (3) *Rosemary's Baby* and "Terms of Endearment" (6X07); (4) *Night of the Living Dead* and "Kaddish" (4X12); (5) *The Stepfather* and "Paper Hearts" (4X08); (6) *Frankenstein* and "Eve" (1X10); and (7) *Alien* and "Piper Maru"/"Apocrypha" (3X15/16).

Kaminsky's classification works very well for genre movies during the period in which he was writing and before. There is even some "fit" between *X-Files* shows and his schema, showing the relation of the series to the horror film tradition. However, the fit is not close and may be diminishing. Using Kaminsky's "branches" and being generous in my assessment of likenesses, I found about 15 shows in *The X-Files*' Season One that could be classified as belonging to one of his categories. ("Witches" and "resurrected dead" were lacking altogether, but other divisions were well represented.) With Season

Two, I found nine (out of 25) relevant episodes, six in Season Three, nine in Season Four, seven in Season Five, and, well, one or two so far, halfway through Season Six. The instructive aspect of this small analysis is that *The X-Files* has decidedly moved away from the traditional shadow/villain figure toward a different concept, a different representation of evil in the world. This move is both an artistic approach and the expression of the cultural climate of this most interesting pre-millennial decade, a spirit and a worldview which will be examined more closely in the chapter that follows.

Chapter Six

The X-Files and the Zeitgeist of the '90s

If even man himself is a world to other lives, and millions and myriads dwell in the rivers of his blood, and inhabit man's frame as man inhabits earth, common sense ... would suffice to teach that the circumfluent Infinite which you call space — the boundless Impalpable which divides earth from the moon and stars — is filled, also, with its correspondent and appropriate life. Is it not a visible absurdity to suppose that Being is crowded upon every leaf, and yet is absent from the immensities of space?[1]

In 1997, *The New York Post* reported that "President Clinton was intrigued by UFOs and wanted to know if they really existed." According to friends and associate Webb Hubbell, Clinton told him, "If I put you over at Justice I want you to find the answers to two questions for me: One, who killed JFK. And two, are there UFOs." Hubbell reports that "Clinton was dead serious," and that "his [Hubbell's] failure to find out about JFK and UFOs" before leaving the Attorney General's Office "was a big regret."[2] Then, in June of 1998, when Prof. Stephen Hawking addressed a White House Millennium Evening, he conceded the possibility that "UFOs really do contain aliens as many people believe, and the government is hushing it up."[3]

Speculation about the world of alien contact and conspiracies is endemic to much of the global community during the last decade of the century, and UFO sightings worldwide continue to intensify this interest. One symptom of the phenomenon is the likelihood of hearing *"The X-Files"* when someone wishes to infer an alien reality or cover-up. Stephen King once said that his fans often tell him about personal experiences that they say are "just like" one of his story ideas. Many who are not *X-Files* fans or may not even watch the program now compare strange occurrences or conspiratorial suspicions to *X-Files* plots. When Republicans accused Clinton and the Democrats of plotting revenge against them for attempting to impeach the President, Clinton's head attorney commented, "Somebody's been watching too many reruns of *The X-Files.*" The sister of teenager John Greenewald, who has released massive amounts of de-classified UFO documents on the Internet, told a reporter that every day was "like an *X-Files* episode at our house."[4] In the public mind the show has become almost synonymous with paranoid and paranormal premises. Are these premises in line with American beliefs generally?

In some ways, yes, especially where the alien presence is concerned, and in some ways, no. A 1997 Gallup poll for the first time asked whether or not the U.S. government knows more about UFOs than it is telling us.[5] The response was 71 percent in the affirmative. Most people, however, had never seen anything they considered to be a UFO — only 12 percent responded that they had. Asked whether or not they considered UFOs something real, 48 percent said they did, while 31 percent believed they were imaginary and 21 percent had no opinion. There were also 45 percent who believed that UFOs had visited the earth (39 percent No) and 72 percent who believed that there is life on other planets. According to recent polls conducted by other organizations, 50 percent of us believe that people have experienced alien abduction, and .03 percent claim to have been abducted — a seemingly small percentage which nonetheless amounts to over 800,000 people. A summary from the book *UFOs: A Manual for the Millennium* suggests the closeness of UFO belief to a new religion or a modern myth. "For every fundamentalist Christian there are five UFO believers; UFO believers outnumber Roman Catholics by a ratio of better than two-to-one; UFO believers outnumber the voters who placed Reagan, Bush, and Clinton in office, [and] there are three adult Americans who believe that UFOs are real for every two skeptics."[6]

When it comes to the paranormal, the belief levels, according to Gallup, are lower, with 12 percent believing in channeling (64 percent No), 25 percent in Astrology (52 percent No), and 30 percent in Ghosts (50 percent No).[7] These smaller percentages of believers suggest that the millions of people who read Stephen King's fiction, attend movies that feature ghosts and supernatural monsters, and watch *The X-Files* are in some way tuned in to the gothic/horror legacy and appreciate the genre on its own terms, not as a reality, but as a way of symbolically addressing guilts, fears and conflicted mental contents that cannot be accessed or resolved in any direct way. If one is terrified by the prospect of environmental disaster, regretful of personal past mistakes and cruelties, or horrified by news accounts of school massacres or of a black man being dragged to death and dismembered in America in 1999 — what's to be done? The alternative of projecting negative emotions on some other real person or people is socially destructive and simply produces more violence, more guilt and horror. Some things are just too big and too important to be solved directly or by the isolated individual. The horror genre codes all of the standard emotional flashpoints into conventions, formulas and icons that have been accumulating over the past several centuries, as described in Chapter Five. While many do not see the space alien as a creature of the Imaginal, it is among the most recent of these numinous figures, but certainly not the first of its type. Bram Stoker's Dracula was in fact an alien intruder and stood for the same thing: fear of the outsider, of exploding populations, of migration, as well as "anxiety about breeding, miscegenation, and hybridity, about the collapse of distinctions between the alien and ourselves."[8]

What kinds of things do Americans at the turn of the century *know* they fear, or *admit* they fear? According to a 1997 poll, there is a general consensus across race, sex, age, income level and geographic location that the world is a more dangerous place now than it was 20 or more years ago: 90 percent agreed that the world was safer when they were growing up. Four out of ten now feel unsafe taking a walk alone at night within a half-mile of home and seven out of ten have taken some precaution to ensure their safety within the past year. The biggest fears are being in a car crash, having cancer and losing economic security. Also high on the list are Alzheimer's disease and food poisoning from meat, pesticides on food, being a victim of individual violence, being unable to pay current debts and being exposed to foreign viruses.[9] These and a dozen or so others make up the wide range of Americans' immediate and conscious fears, but what of those others that we know about on some level but would rather not think about?

In his White House address, Prof. Hawking mentioned the population explosion as one of the problems that might cause us to legitimately "fear the future."[10] He notes that the current exponential growth (the underlying source of much "alien" terror) cannot continue at its present rate and may result in human beings wiping themselves out by a nuclear or other disaster. In his *The Future in Plain Sight* (1998), Eugene Linden points out that not only is Earth's population increasing by 95 million people a year, but also that this is only one of what he calls "nine clues to the coming instability"; he describes each of these serious problems and then projects each one 50 years into the future. For the past 50 years, he explains, mankind has experienced a period of unprecedented economic, health and climatic stability. With continued stable conditions, we might be able to control the threat of nuclear, biological and chemical weapons and work toward mitigating the further poisoning and destruction of the environment. An extended period of general stability would give us time to deal with desertification and the destruction of eco-systems, mass extinctions of species and climate changes brought about by human activity. He points out that each of these developments is occurring right now and that all are interrelated. The following factors, however, lead him to believe that the stability we need to solve these problems will be lacking in the future:

- Increases in migration and population displacement
- A volatility that is intrinsic to the global market system
- Resurgence of infectious diseases
- Growth and social disintegration of world megacities
- Climate change
- Uncertain food supply and production
- Wage and employment gaps
- Biosphere degradation
- Threat of extremists with rigid, simplistic agendas

Linden discusses the impact of population and migration in terms of the ongoing desperate situations in Haiti, Mexico and China — two of them right next door, and the other, the world's largest nation. Climate change, he points out, is accelerating, melting glaciers and the polar ice cap and creating extremes in weather; 1998 brought a record rise (.3 percent) in the average world temperature and a record series of losses from natural disasters. Food production is reaching its limit. And the world financial system, where large investment funds chase high-yield but low-security profits, is a disaster on its way to happen. Other economic danger signs have to do with the distribution of wealth: In the past 20 years, the real earnings of the poorest 20 percent of U.S. workers dropped by 24 percent, while the upper 20 percent saw an increase in real income of ten percent. Where jobs are concerned, the change has been a bit more democratic. The downsizing which began in the early '80s resulted in 18.7 million white-collar jobs lost up to 1993, and five million jobs have been eliminated in the last 20 years by Fortune Five Hundred companies.[11] And yet, at the end of 1999, the U.S. economy was judged by 89 percent of those polled as being either very good or somewhat good.

As far as the condition of the biosphere is concerned, Linden issues a solemn warning:

> Earth has gone through five major extinction crises during the past few billion years, including the Permian extinctions of 245 million years ago, which wiped out three-quarters of the life forms on earth, and the cataclysm of 65 million years ago, which spelled the doom of the dinosaurs. It is going through one now, and this promises to be a whopper.[12]

As with the economic situation, a serious disjunction between reality and belief shows up in American attitudes toward biosphere degeneration at the end of the century. According to 1998 poll data, Americans believe that emissions from burning fossil fuels, such as that from motor vehicles and power plants, causes global warming. Large majorities (64 percent to 76 percent) also believe that this warming will adversely affect human health, agriculture and the survival of animal and plant species over the next 25 years. However, people do not approve of taking steps to reduce emissions if it would mean increasing energy costs or unemployment, and they don't want the U.S. to take the lead in reducing emissions, even though it leads the world in their production. Most significant is the fact that only 41 percent (down from 60 percent in 1992) believe that global warming is occurring now, and only 25 percent think that global warming will affect them. But 65 percent believe that it will seriously threaten their children and the next generation.

In order to achieve psychic equilibrium on a daily basis, Americans at the end of the '90s are constrained to practice self-deception and accommodate contradictions, as with their view of economic and ecological reality. These are the kinds of conflicted mental contents which art, especially genre fictions, can symbolically, if temporarily, resolve. On a daily basis, contradictions can be handled by resisting and repressing the information that is now pouring into our consciousness from all corners of the globe and a wide variety of sources. As a repairman at my house commented when I told him that I was writing a book about *The X-Files,* "I don't watch that show. I just don't want to think about things like that." He could have meant things that go bump in the night, of course, but I don't think so. I believe that he was referring to the darker, more disturbing symbolic subtext of the series.

In his discussion of the dangers of extremism, Linden foresees an impending struggle between disciplined argument and faith, reason and religion: Mulder and Scully's ongoing argument turned nasty and on a much larger scale. Our trust in science is eroding for several reasons; one is that, according to Linden, scientists have "arrogated to themselves the right to rework the fabric of life, create new organisms, or clone existing ones, with scant heed to the feelings of the community, the potential consequences, or the moral implications of their work"[13] (a concern that is, in fact, directly addressed by *X-Files* episodes). Such news headlines as "Directed evolution 'Mother Nature at Warp Speed': Chemical tricks used to multiply mutations for new drugs, products"[14] do not necessarily elate or comfort us. Scientists are also regarded with deep distrust because of their role in developing weapons of mass destruction, and because they have failed in promises to eliminate disease, achieve free energy and produce worldwide dependable food resources. *The X-Files* affirms this distrust of science by depicting scientists, generally, as the archetypal "one who goes too far" from ancient tragedy and more recent gothic traditions. Although Dr. Scully is a scientist, almost all of the other scientists depicted in the series so far have shown their connection to ancient evil by experimenting on human subjects and being of expatriate German Nazi or Japanese origin — thus "Alien Others." And, of course, extraterrestrial aliens, too, experiment on their abductees, a social factor which "alienates" us further from science and its practitioners.

Science today also seems less and less capable of supplying absolute truth or the ultimate answers to important questions about physical reality. It has withdrawn the comfortable certainty of the old mechanistic or Newtonian picture of physical reality. This paradigm has been superseded by the principles of relativity/quantum physics. Mulder reminds Scully that her dissertation states that the laws of quantum physics do not rule out the possibility of time travel or multidimensionality, which could mean an infinite number of universes and outcomes ("Synchrony," 4X19). Most of us still conceive of the universe in mechanistic terms as an ordered, three-dimensional, empty space occasionally punctuated by discrete atoms and governed by strict causality and predictability. This picture, however, is only an approximation of reality, useful to engineers, but not "true." The new concept of reality is much more complex: four-dimensional, probabalistic, and not governed by fixed and immutable laws. In it, the scientist maps probabilities rather than specifying events. The "indeterminate character of the quantum world ... gives it the openness that was missing in the Newtonian cosmos. The universe at each moment contains the possibility of the unexpected, the new, and even the creative."[15] However, such an expansion of possibilities may not be comforting. In a world of such physical indeterminacy, who can claim to know what is incontrovertibly true, and by what means can it be proven?

Myths and UFOs

> Reports [are] reaching us from all corners of the earth, rumors of round objects that flash through the troposphere and stratosphere and go by the name of Flying Saucers.... Apparently they are changes in the constellation of psychic dominants, of the archetypes, or "gods" as they used to be called, which bring about, or accompany, long-lasting transformations of the collective psyche.[16]

The psychologist Carl Jung considers UFO phenomena to be a visual rumor; that is, he believes that observations and stories of sightings express a changing consciousness in the world. Even though his *Flying Saucers* was published in 1978, it dealt with millennialist concerns, claiming that flying saucers are the projections of a culture that faces a new millennium but considers itself too rational and sophisticated to accept the idea of the direct intervention of God. Jung points out that the circular shape of the craft is that of a mandala, and that this image is a worldwide symbol for the complete and whole individuated self, the psyche with both conscious and subconscious contents integrated. Jung further sees the round and the cigar-shaped UFOs as representations of male and female energies, conjuring up the possible union of polarities. While he does not commit himself to either a physical or metaphysical hypothesis regarding the existence of such objects, he sees them as an explicit demonstration of the individual participating in the spirit of the age:

This particular projection, together with its psychological context, the rumor, is specific of our age and highly characteristic of it. The dominating idea of a mediator and god who became man, after having thrust the old polytheistic beliefs into the background, is now in its turn on the point of evaporating.... A political, social, philosophical, and religious conflict of unprecedented proportions has split the consciousness of our age... . Between the psychic opposites there is generated a "uniting symbol," at first unconscious. This process is running its course in the unconscious of modern man. Between the opposites there arises spontaneously a symbol of unity and wholeness, no matter whether it reaches consciousness or not.[17]

Currently our knowledge base is being challenged by at least two paradigmatic shifts: the religious and the scientific. A shared vision of the mythic and the real functions as the ideational core of any socio–political system, naturalizing and upholding the status quo. Thus in ancient history the patriarchal societies replacing older tribal and matrifocal ones also replaced goddess-centered religions with myths and religious beliefs which supported the new order and its institutions. Since Judeo-Christian thought has been the dominant religious construct in Western civilization for at least 1500 years, it holds a unique position of influence in Anglo-American culture. But now these traditional beliefs are losing their force to bind together the cultural community, just as science is. A changing knowledge base, combined with increasing instability in the world situation, presage not only a crisis of global destruction, but also a crisis of belief. The old religious paradigm is passing, and no one knows what the new one will be. Perhaps, as in Yeats' vision of a "Second Coming," some "rough beast, its hour come round at last,/ Slouches towards Bethlehem to be born."

The UFO phenomenon seems to be related to concepts of both the mythic and the real. Jung sees UFOs as a religio-mythic occurrence, an emblem of change and a symbol of unity projected by the human consciousness in response to the radical divisions and changes that are afflicting the race. And from its inception, UFO discourse has challenged church, state, expert and market control of truth and information. Many UFO researchers are independent; that, of course, means that they are not employed by a foundation, university or corporation, and are not only dealing with an unknown data base, but doing it outside the established discourses (even though they often employ the accepted language forms of the physical, biological or psychological sciences). For the scientific and political establishment to discuss the alien presence openly could (1) undermine their power and call their discourses of control into question, (2) challenge public faith in the essential rightness of the ideals, beliefs and loyalties of the society, and (3) legitimate the discourse of ordinary citizens at the expense of the controlling discourses of major institutions. Nevertheless, the discourse of individual researchers and contactees is gradually gaining a strong presence in this battle of the voices. Jodi Dean puts it this way: "'Scientists' are the ones who have problems with the 'rationality' of those in the UFO community.... Those in positions of power deploy terms like 'reasonable' and 'rational.' Previously, the victims of this deployment, the 'unreasonable' and 'irrational,' remained isolated. They had difficulty getting attention and fighting back. Now, thanks to widespread developments in communication networks, the 'irrational' can get their message out."[18]

Over the years, mainstream science has assessed the validity of UFO evidence several times. The 1968 Colorado Project concluded that no useful purpose would be served by pursuing the topic further. Soon after, in 1970, an American Institute of Aeonautics and Astronautics report recommended further investigation, but using more scientific data collection and analysis. In the summer of 1998, Stanford University hosted a review of UFO data which had been accumulating since the two earlier professional reviews. At Stanford, a panel of physical scientists evaluated reports by eight UFO investigators who had been invited to present their best evidence. The panel focused on incidents that had produced some kind of physical evidence, from photographs to vehicle interference, but did not appear to deal with the most "physical" of UFO-related manifestations: crop circles and animal mutilations. The scientists praised the resourcefulness and commitment of the UFO researchers, but they still judged their studies as lacking objectivity, experimental rigor and a willingness to consider alternative explanations. Among the areas of fruitful research for the future, the panel recommended physical effects on witnesses, like burns or implants; radar sightings, like the one of a huge disc that hovered over Paris in January 1994; repeated or regular sightings of strange lights like those over Marfa, Texas; and gravitational/inertial effects, such as those experienced by an army helicopter in its encounter with a cigar-shaped flying object in 1973.[19]

In February 1999 NBC aired the two-hour television special called *Confirmation,* followed by a subtitle which equivocated by asking, *The Hard Evidence of Aliens Among Us?* The program reviewed proof of sightings from the major periods of UFO occurrence, some of the government reports, interviews with abduction experts and scientific analysis of several implants removed from abductees. While not presenting much in the way of new information, the program did seem positive about the evidence in a restrained way. Not much was said about UFO discourse and the UFO community as a social force, but this is the aspect of the subject that is most relevant to the cultural position of *The X-Files* and has most determined its generally warm reception by television viewers.

UFO Discourse as a Cultural Force[20]

The inescapable profundity of the alien presence has become a source of social pathology in our time. As a culture, we have not yet learned how to tell the truth about something so huge, so strange, and so unexpected. Individuals who make an honest effort to deal with it often discover that their personal stability is at risk. Consequently, the alien presence requires us all to grow, to become stronger and clearer, and to help one another to find our way in a genuinely new world.[21]

The UFO community is a loose grouping of mostly middle-class, middle-income people with overlapping interests, a 50-year history of changes and developments, and a surprising diversity of beliefs. This subculture has produced a wealth of accumulated speculation and information, both in casual sources like the Internet and in more formal publications. *The X-Files* has borrowed liberally from these information sources and rung its own creative touches on some of the, usually more recent, research and reports. According to Jodi Dean, during the Cold War, ufology "established a space from which to resist the expert culture of containment and assert the authority of amateur and civilian opinion and research." Since "military legitimacy rested on a disavowal of the unknown ... that which was unidentified could not be true."[22]

At a 1998 international UFO conference, truth was still a recurring theme for the participants, and one which continued to reflect a strong populist flavor. A speaker from Italy challenged those in attendance, and the larger group of believers worldwide, "to push the world's leaders to tell the truth." A British speaker declared that "truth lies open to everyone. No one has a monopoly on the truth. There is plenty left for future generations." And an American who spoke about the influence of secret societies warned against the persuasiveness of the control phenomena that mark the modern suppression of the truth. The conference speakers told stories and shared theories and information not only on purely UFO subject matter, but also on such topics as alternative archeology, suppressed history, alternate energy forms, prophecy, spirituality, crop circles, out-of-body experiences, fractal phenomena, mind control, secret societies and black budget programs. This diversity also shows up when looking in the books, magazines and other publications that both affect and reflect a substantial amount of public interest here and abroad. These will be reviewed briefly at the end of this section.

Sightings of lights in the sky were around long before the emergence of a so-called UFO community. The first group or wave of such sightings in this country occurred in the 1890s. Some of these included descriptions of what seemed to be airborne vehicles with human-like occupants. Since no flying machines had been developed at that point, such cigar- or disk-shaped craft were often thought to be the inventions of a lone genius, in the style of H. G. Wells or Jules Verne. The next substantial wave of UFO incidents took place during World War II, when U.S. military pilots continually encountered and were tracked by mysterious lights and flying objects they called "Foo

Fighters," which they tended to believe were secret aeronautical devices being produced by the Axis powers, probably those infamous "Nazi Scientists" that still live on *The X-Files* and maybe among us. After the war, sightings began in earnest.

The first major peacetime encounter, again, involved an airplane. On June 24, 1947, a pilot named Kenneth Arnold viewed a grouping of eight flat and round, and one crescent-shaped domed crafts over the Cascade Mountains. He described them later as moving strangely through the air like a "saucer skipped across the water," giving rise to the nickname of flying saucers. Arnold's experience was followed within a month by the well-known incident of a possible UFO crash near the Roswell, New Mexico, base of the 509th Bomber Wing, the only such installation in the country that was nuclear-equipped. The Roswell event and subsequent controversy has assumed such dominance in UFO lore that most people do not realize that on that same date 88 UFOs were reported in other locations, and that during the several-week Roswell period, sightings were reported around the globe — England, Chile, Italy, Japan, Holland. There were 400 from 24 states of the U.S. alone.

After the Air Force denial of the Roswell UFO crash, public interest waned, but unaccountable aerial phenomena continued. Altogether, from 1947 to 1952, 1300 UFO reports were filed in the U.S., and one quarter of those were officially judged to be unknown or unexplained. A number of green fireballs visited and hung over the Los Alamos National Laboratory, arousing the serious concern of scientists and the military. Such intrusions continued to be reported at that and at other nuclear installations, such as Oak Ridge, Tennessee, and the Hanford (Washington) AEC plant. Civilian and military aircraft continued to see UFOs and sometimes official reports indicate that the latter would give chase to the intruders. In 1952 there was a huge rise in the number of reported sightings, culminating in July of that year, when UFOs were seen over Washington, D.C., by hundreds, perhaps thousands of witnesses. One week later, a formation of the craft again hovered and performed maneuvers over the nation's capital.

The original Air Force report of this event is reprinted in Timothy Good's *Beyond Top Secret*. Reading this document, one learns that the Air Force designation for such unidentified objects is "target," as in "a 'very good target' … moved across the [radar] scope from West to East."[23] When the CIA conducted its full inquiry into these targets, its mandate was to debunk UFOs, guided by the question "How do we make this a non-subject?" When their investigation, Project Blue Book, was terminated in 1969, 700 cases were still listed as unexplained. Also during this period, the "targets" or targets like them were making their presence known in other ways. George Adamski's *Flying Saucers Have Landed*, reputedly detailing Adamski's contacts with space aliens, became an international best seller in 1952, and the first Hollywood Hotel UFO Convention was held in 1953/54. After that, the UFO meetings moved to a location in the California desert called Giant Rock, which attracted from three to eight thousand people at a time, a number of whom reported both seeing unidentified flying objects and having contacts with alien beings. These conferences lasted until 1978.

The 1950s alien contacts were with Nordic type extraterrestrials (E.T.s), so-called "Space Brothers" who looked like human beings and warned us about upsetting the balance of nature — a scenario reminiscent of the 1951 science fiction film *The Day the Earth Stood Still*. Perspectives of contactees from the Giant Rock days include the following:

- The aliens' clothing and their craft are organic technology which can "heal" itself.
- Ships are a crystalline life form, made of a dense, incredibly strong material.
- The bell-shaped craft is a transport vessel.
- Some visitors are of a more highly attenuated form of matter (this helps to explain those who claim to be from the inhospitable planet Venus).
- Some beings are multi-dimensional and can step down their vibrational frequencies to visit the Earth plane.
- The Space Brothers first contacted earth governments and told leaders to abandon atomic development and clean up the environment and they would help us.

In the 1960s, the perception of the alien presence began to change. This period saw the first reports of animal mutilations and the beginning of human abductions. Many of the first contactees began to fear that the U.S. government had rejected an alliance with the Space Brothers, and had, instead, struck a deal with less desirable, less altruistic alien visitors in exchange for advanced military and communications technology. Some believed that the government/alien deal involved the permission for aliens to experiment on livestock and a limited number of human subjects. Thus, cattle mutilations and abductions. Abductees usually reported a memory gap or missing time, after which, either on his/her own or through hypnotic regression, the subject would recall being taken by strange beings, examined, manipulated, sometimes implanted with a monitoring device, and then having memories of the incident erased. The abduction marking the beginning of this new contact era was that of Barney and Betty Hill in 1961. Their best-selling book recounting this experience, *The Interrupted Journey,* was published in 1966. Perhaps due to stories like theirs, the attitudes toward E.T.s began to shift through the '60s and '70s. There had always been a disagreement between those who saw the aliens as material beings and their crafts as nuts-and-bolts space ships from other planets and those who saw them as manifestations of less physical, perhaps inter-dimensional, realities. Now, another rift appeared.

Many UFOlogists stopped taking seriously the stories of almost religious or spiritual encounters with tall, blond, Aryan humanoids — the kinds of contacts that had proliferated during the 1950s. Now, moving into the 1970s, a diversity of anomalous creatures appeared, and some of them were hostile. In Europe, the variation of E.T. forms was thought to be due to the psychological needs of the contactee, but in the U.S., following the old nuts-and-bolts concept, the reports tended to homogenize alien sightings into a set of similar, physically real visitors from the stars. The year 1977 brought Steven Spielberg's phenomenally successful film *Close Encounters of the Third Kind*. If the abduction patterns of the '70s were going to persist, adult movie goers seemed to welcome the idea that their abductors would be friendly. Spielberg followed this release with *E.T.* in 1982, reassuring children in the same vein.

By the early '80s, the UFO creature of choice had become the Gray, and abduction had become the typical plotline. In 1981, Bud Hopkins' *Missing Time* marked the beginning of a new kind of abduction: continuous but unrecalled multiple abductions since childhood, as well as the notion of the abductee receiving an implant or being probed. His second book, *Intruders* (1987), reported the forced participation of abductees in breeding experiments that resulted in hybrid children. Hopkins' two books changed the alien scenario: not single, random encounters, but "purposeful, lifelong, genetic manipulation" (Bader 86) to produce mutant offspring. From 1987 on, abductees became active participants in the national discourse. Building on the acceptance of personal stories in psychological analysis, they began writing about their experiences, appearing on talk shows, speaking at conferences and establishing an active Internet presence. During the '90s, the UFO/alien topic became, second to sex, the most frequently accessed subject area on the Net. The rumors that pass back and forth in the UFO community came to include a failed government/alien alliance (echoed in *The X-Files*), a war between aliens and human forces at a secret underground base in the American Southwest (which the humans lost), and resulting government strategies to pursue a hi-tech military build-up in preparation for an alien invasion or colonization attempt sometime during the '90s. At the same time, television series like *V* and *War of the Worlds* showed up, portraying aliens as evil aggressors and, some speculated, sending the TV audience hidden messages suggesting at least part of the truth about the current political situation.

The X-Files has from time to time been included in speculations of government influence. The show has certainly contributed to making the FBI the most popular of U.S. investigative agencies with Americans. During the mid–1990s, applications rose and young middle-class professionals switched careers to join the Bureau, which, coincidentally, just happened to be expanding its ranks. The new volunteers said that they were willing to take a reduction in salary in order to have an interesting job in which they might be able to contribute to the public good, to make a difference. Fox Mulder provides the model. Sorting through the confusing realities of his televisual space, he brings an order to it that is lacking in the cultural sphere of public reality in the '90s. Yet Mulder's control is limited and the order he brings is a fragile construct. In the episode "One Son" (6X12), the narrative suddenly wipes out the major players of the shadowy cabal which collaborated with alien colonizers, along with their family members who had served as hostages to the alien project. The aliens who kill these people are "the rebels," humanoid beings who are opposed to colonization.

Oddly, viewers have not been given a clear picture yet of the alien race that is attempting colonization, aside from the fact that they *may* be Grays. They are more faceless than the "faceless" or "de-faced" rebels who seem to be opposing them. The temporary resolution, or stand-off, between those two is achieved by destroying the past — the agreements, the experiments, the attachments involved and the decisions made — symbolized by the Cabal. Then, in an act of maximum finality, the Smoking Man, a Cabal member who survived the pogrom, shoots FBI Agent Jeffrey Spender, apparently killing his own son. The series odometer is then set back to 00:00, and *The X-Files'* relationship to E.T. realities, if such a relationship exists, must be recalibrated. Similarly, the narrative codes of action, interpretation and symbol are reset to a relatively neutral position. The momentum of the mythic arc is temporarily dampened but not seriously damaged, because the closing-off of one strand of possibilities only opens and broadens the mystery. But to return to the UFO context.

Another wave of sightings took place in the early 1990s, coinciding with the first season of *The X-Files* (in 1993) — another fortunate synchronicity. During this period, large formations of UFOs appeared over many different areas of the world. Residents of Mexico City viewed, and recorded with their video cameras, hundreds of the craft flying together to create patterns or signs in the sky. And, in another development, the '90s saw an alteration in attitudes toward abduction experiences. Whereas the '50s/'60s had contactees, and the '70s/'80s had abductees, in the '90s those who are visited by alien beings more often call themselves experiencers. They may be terrified at first, but then come to know and respect their abductors, and even report positive physical effects from their implants. At the beginning of its 1998-99 season, *The X-Files* introduced an idea that has often been proposed by UFO researchers and is familiar to those with even a nodding acquaintance of the field. In "The Beginning" (6X01), Scully tells Mulder that the same "junk" DNA can be found in Gibson Praise, a telepathic child, in an alien monster, in herself, and ... in all people. This means, she says, that we are all extraterrestrial in origin. This theory of humans having extraterrestrial origins is quite popular in UFO circles, especially in the alternative archeology or hidden history research branches. It posits that the planet Earth was "seeded" by, or primitive life forms here were improved by, the genetic intervention of ET visitors.

Stephen Mehler, an Egyptologist (or Kehmitologist) and Director of Research for the Kinnaman Foundation, is a scholar, writer and investigator who supports the idea of such an intervention, commenting that what human beings really are is "children of apes and of the stars." He also believes that the consciousness of our origins is pre-coded in our DNA, thus is discoverable. In his choice of life work, Mehler typifies the kind of alternative scholar who is working outside the academic and corporate establishment in the '90s. Although Mehler has conventional training and experience in the fields of Natural Science, Prehistory and Ancient History, he is now involved with investigating "all theories of the purposes, construction methods and possible date of construction of the Great Sphinx and major Pyramids of Giza." He differs from mainstream investigators, he feels, because he is pursuing his own personal quest — to find his true identity or blood line, what and who he really is. The search for true knowledge of the past, he regards in large measure to be a search for true knowledge of the self (what Jung would call individuation), and that is what he believes Fox Mulder's quest represents. Mehler discovered his interest in Egypt and UFO phenomena at about the same time and moved through a period in which he became a Rosicrucian and studied metaphysics. As his thinking and study progressed, he came to believe that the gods of the ancient world were, in fact, extraterrestrial beings. He thinks that, at the current time, official preparations are being made for full disclosure of the alien presence on Earth, together with more truthful and complete knowledge about mankind's history. We are on the verge of a dramatic paradigm shift, and new consciousness is being imparted to us now through "myths and story — in the Shaman's way."[24]

Although most people will never attend a UFO conference or access the many "alternative knowledge" sites on the Internet, there has been a massive explosion of information about these matters in the '90s, as well as an increase in positions and points of view that diverge wildly from what we learned in school. The field is vast and various, a sea of interconnected, but disorganized and uncoordinated, data and theories — intriguing and challenging as well as frightening and contradictory. The diversity of publications in UFO/New Age subject areas alone is astounding — a microcosm of that sea of ideas and experiences that surround us today and lap at the eroding shores of consensus reality. Harvard psychologist and UFO researcher John Mack has said that "it is really going to be interesting to see when the official mainstream, the small percentage of elites that determine what we are supposed to think is real, wake up to the fact that the consensus view of reality is gone" (Dean 57).

A survey I made of bookstores in two different cities during the spring and summer of 1998 confirmed to me that the areas of UFO and New Age knowledge overlap and that no set of categories has yet been devised to separate them into discrete areas of knowledge. In a random sample of book shops on Charing Cross Road in London, I found sections called "Beliefs" (books on mysticism, astrology, I-Ching, yoga, Nostradamas, Satan, Feng Shui) and "Odds and Gods" (a small selection of hardback mainstream books like guides to mythology). Other shops had sections variously titled Mysteries, Mind/Body/Spirit, Popular Psychology, Unexplained, New Age, Occult, Astrology and Prediction. The Mysteries or Unexplained sections contained, primarily, works of what might best be called "speculative nonfiction": books using available data to spin a web of theoretical propositions and probabilities regarding the nature of the universe or some portion of it. This kind of work is perhaps even more common in New Age or UFO writings than the personal experience narrative (*Cosmic Warrior*), the fictionalized allegory (*The Celestine Prophecy*), the advice or instructional book (*Urban Shaman*) or the metaphysical explication (*The Tarot*). Several examples will serve to characterize the speculative nonfiction type: John Keel's *Operation Trojan Horse*, which forwards the premise that aliens are actually trickster spirits from another dimension; *Space Aliens from the Pentagon* by William R. Lyne, who charges that Nazis in league with the U.S. government are deceiving us about the alien presence; or *Song of the Greys* by Nigel Kerner, whose thesis of reverse evolution (or devolution — derived from the second law of thermodynamics) leads him to posit aliens as spiritual entities and the Greys as their bio-mechanical operatives on the material plane.

Downtown Denver's Tattered Cover Bookstore offers a much broader selection of alternative titles than the popular London shops surveyed above. This is due not only to the fact that the Denver store is much larger, but also because the Boulder/Denver area is something of a New Age center. Tattered Cover stocks not only a wide selection of books, but also of magazines and popular journals (some glossy, some not), categorized either as Phenomena or Religious/Spiritual/Psychological. In the former are *Nexus* (containing subject areas that include Conspiracies, Behind the News, Health, UFOs and Future Science) and other publications, such as *Body Mind Spirit, Strange, Fortean Times, Atlantis Rising* and *Alternative Therapies*. The Religious/Spiritual/Psychological section contains *Shaman's Drum, Sedona, New Age, Conscious Living, Hope Intuition, Judaism* and *Circle Network News* (Wicca as earth religion), among others.

The Tattered Cover's second floor book area has nine full sections of alternatives, with three bookcases devoted to Alternative Health (nutrition, Deepak Chopra, reflexology, massage, herbals, iridology and much more) and three cases also to Spiritual Growth (L. Ron Hubbard, five editions of *Chicken Soup for the Soul, The Science of Mind, Creating Affluence*, angels and auras, crystal medicine, chakra breathing). New Consciousness and Shamanism takes up only half a bookcase and the topic includes new or strange science, while Channeling, Astrology, Western Esoterica, Phenomena, Wicca/Pagan/Divination and Mythology all occupy one full bookcase.

The mythology section holds the most traditional works — Robert Graves, Edith Hamilton, Joseph Campbell, Irish folk tales, *Beowulf, The New Arthurian Encyclopedia.* The Channeling shelves include William Styron's *The Journey Home,* a metaphysical allegory that seems to be a work of fiction in a non-fiction area, an example of the kind of blending prevalent in these subjects. Phenomena is an unusual section in that it contains seven labeled sub-sections: Phenomena, Afterlife, ESP/Psychic, Hauntings, Lost Continents, Out of Body and UFOs/Conspiracy. This collection seems to be a catchall group. Its subject areas touch on many of the *X-Files'* subject areas, more, in fact, than those in any other section.

It should be noted that in neither the London stores or the well-stocked U.S. bookstore, do non-mainstream offerings such as the above outnumber those in the traditional categories of literature, history, travel, art and so forth. Yet I would venture to say that prior to the 1960s, far fewer books and magazines like these would have been found within the walls of a "respectable" general-interest bookstore in this country or in England. Books like Trevor Ravenscroft's *The Spear of Destiny* (about Adolf Hitler's occult practices, 1968) and Erich von Daniken's *Chariots of the Gods* (the first to propose the idea of ancient astronauts, 1973) are no longer consigned to discount store and supermarket bookracks. Hundreds of similar and newly conceived works of speculative non-fiction have joined them and can be found in numerous upscale locations. Curiosity about and fascination with the unknown has assumed many new forms in the 1990s.

MIBs and Aliens

Reality tends to manifest in channels created by myth and archetype, and, conversely, myth and archetype are ways that individuals organize and make sense of reality. Both fine and popular arts speak to us beyond our immediate understanding and logic by calling up these unconscious elements. Such mythic contents, the symbols and truths of inherited knowledge, are protean or hermetic (in the sense of being shape-shifting yet impervious to outside influences, and magical) and they eventually resist being nailed down to the service of any "official story." They can, however, be manipulated by dominant or insurrectionist ideologies for momentary purposes. The persistence and potency of the shadow or dark man archetype, for one, explains why Americans can be so easily seduced into armed conflict with foreign leaders — Noriega, Qaddafi, Sadaam Hussein, bin Laden, Abdullah Ocalan — who are dark skinned and somehow not "human" like we are.

The Men In Black who contact and threaten abductees and experiencers are also clear, physically obvious expressions of this archetype. In addition to dark clothing, they appear to be non–Caucasian and they are often described as walking and talking in an odd, unnatural manner. These creatures, however, are not the officially designated "devils" of political policy but the shadows of ancient myth personally experienced as reality. The MIB image is not restricted to time or to place. Folklorists link it to past legends of an evil being who was reported to assume the appearance of a tall black man or a man dressed in black. This is a figure that perennially finds its way into art and mysticism. In the "art" film *Orpheus* (1945), by Jean Cocteau (a modernized and loosely interpreted version of the Greek myth), the MIB are imaginatively constructed as messengers to and from the underworld — a couple of motorcycle policemen dressed helmet to boot-tip in black. And in Eastern myth, MIBs have a parallel in the "Brothers of the Shadow," evil beings who try to prevent occult students from learning the great truth.[25] Similarly, the MIB reported worldwide in association with UFO phenomena warn and intimidate individuals to keep them from seeking or telling the truth, that is, from revealing their experiences with UFOs or aliens or pursuing research in extraterrestrial contacts.

UFO researchers Roxanne Carol and Linda Moulton Howe have attempted to classify the types of alien beings reported over the years and both consider MIBs part of the alien presence: Howe, using abductee reports, describes MIBs as wearing clothing from earlier decades. A drawing of one Man in Black by an experiencer shows a pale face with a pointed chin, strange triangular sunglasses, a wide-lapelled dark overcoat, and a very 1940s snap-brimmed hat. This is a figure that closely resembles the (*X-Files*) "Jose Chung" MIBs. Carol describes the traditional vehicle and a perhaps less familiar destination: "'They' are often though not always seen in connection with large, black automobiles, some of which have been seen disappearing into mountains, canyons, or tunnels or … into [or out of] thin air."[26] Carol has examined a wide range of first-hand reports and speculative materials, so she lists more alien types than Howe does and goes into more detail about each one. Her disclaimer, though, is clear: "Groups which have consistently been 'reported' by VARIOUS sources, regardless of any substantial evidence whether such alien groups actually exist or not are related herein."[27] According to Carol's sources, MIBs might be humans under alien control, or synthetic beings, or disguised reptilians. The possibilities for their origins include Sirius "as a major exterran MIB center of activity, with a subterran counterpart existing in ancient antediluvian 'Atlantean' underground complexes which have been re-established beneath the Eastern U.S. seaboard."[28]

Carol reports what she finds "out there"— much of it in Internet sources — and adds some organizational and theoretical concepts to try to clarify a highly diverse corpus of information. Howe, on the other hand, would be considered almost a mainstream researcher in the UFO field, with film documentaries and book-length publications under her belt, and she has done a great deal of on-site investigation for *Facts and Eyewitnesses*, the first volume of her *Glimpses of Other Realities* series. Roxanne Carol could be characterized as a "vernacular" researcher and theorist, paralleling the concept of "a vernacular critic or vernacular criticism," whereas Howe is perhaps more a professional (but not academic) researcher-theorist. Both pursue intellectual roles largely outside of institutionalized expert discourses. The kind of speculative non-fiction they write and the kind of personal experience narratives experiencers tell are the outsider discourses of the 1990s. Howe asks, but doesn't answer, questions suggested by abduction experiences, such as:

- Are a variety of biological species coming and going on our planet?
- Are there other species living underground?
- Are there beings that occupy other dimensional realities?
- Do real species differences exist among aliens? If so, what are they?
- Are there different types or models of aliens for differing work?
- Is this seeming variety of species due to disguises or "screen memories?"
- Or, are holographic projections created by intelligent beings with sophisticated technology being used to make us see what we want to see?

Both Howe and Carol classify alien creatures into similar categories: Howe discusses the species as reported in eyewitness accounts as Humanoid, Gray, or Insectoid/Reptilian. Carol divides the types into two general groups, the Evadamic (Evas) and Draconian (Dracos) neo-saurians or reptilians. She then proceeds to further subdivide the totality into its various species. It's not entirely clear, though, which species are Draconian and which are not, especially where the Grays and Insectoids are concerned. The Evadamics (Adam/Eve) group are humanoid and generally reminiscent of the "Space Brother" figures of early UFO reports. These beings are often referred to by the star system or planet from which they have come (Lyrans, Procyons, Pleiadians, Solarians, etc.). Some are earth natives, often living underground: the giant Telosians, the Sasquan, the Moon-Eyes, the Dwarfin — and these begin to show a connection to the figures of folktale, legend and myth. A small group of the Evadamics may be crossover species connected to the Draconian species — quasi-humans, hybrids, or disguised creatures like the Chameleons or the Iguanas. This latter blending suggests a concept of the universe that is as liminally blurred and borderless as the world of *The X-Files*.

The Grays are by far the largest sub-group in Carol's taxonomy, and she breaks them up into six types, but states that 35 or more different types have been observed so far and that there are reputed to be over 650 Gray species in the universe. The purposes of these creatures vary according to type. Usually they are said to need people — for food or for cloning or for souls — to save their race. Some commentators believe that they are studying us because our diversity and the range of our emotions is unlike that of any other species in the universe. The Insectoids' hive mentality or collective consciousness is seen as a strongly negative feature, maybe due to a lingering terror of "collectivist" Cold War Communism. I mentioned in Chapter Three that a similar connection might lie behind the negative meaning conjured up for the bees of *The X-Files*, which are used as a horror motif. Yet fearing the hive mind may also signal a recognition of the importance of individuation, in the Jungian sense, and the need to escape from invisible discourses of control. As an aside, Howe reports that at least one abductee has seen at least one insectoid creature in a favorable light: a Mantis-like being who seemed to be ancient and a leader, as well as actively intelligent and wise.

Sightings of Dracos or neo-saurians (in Carol's typology) are supposedly the source of vampire stories through the years. There is a link of this vampiric figure, through legend, to horror fiction, in that "Dracule," meaning dragon or devil, was the family name of Vlad Tepeç, (the feudal prince who was the model for Bram Stoker's Count Dracula, see Chapter Five). Looking back even further, the Draconian/Eeptilian races are also related to Biblical lore, especially as they are set off against the humanoid Evadamic races, whose name combines the Adam-and-Eve designations of the Old Testament. These are "soul-matrixed" or "angelic" benevolent beings, and the Draco-reptilians are thought to be "collective," "dark-souled" or "fallen-angelic" beings. Between these two races, a cosmic conflict is in process, one that affects the world for either good or evil and one in which either group may gain control over the other's region of influence.

This traditional battle between the forces of angelic light and the forces of chthonic darkness is a myth pattern that many will recognize as being essentially Judeo-Christian. Joseph Campbell points out that in most cultures the serpent is revered or interpreted in a positive way. The Hopis, for instance, make friends with snakes through ritual and send them back to the hills, for they have come from the hills with messages from nature. In India the Serpent-King of mythology is second in elevation only to Buddha. Campbell maintains that our Biblical tradition, which identifies the serpent with sin, expresses a fear of nature. He points out that a snake flows when it moves, like water, but its flickering tongue suggests fire — unifying opposites, as does the traditional image of the eagle and the serpent. In the Mexican (Aztec) symbol of the eagle holding the serpent in its claws, the bird is not devouring the snake. Together they represent the dynamic union of opposites. "The serpent bound to earth, the eagle in spiritual flight." That conflict is something we all experience. "And then, when the two amalgamate, we get a ... dragon, a serpent with wings."[29] Campbell points out that the images are the same, mean the same thing and are talking about the same nature/spirit conflict worldwide.

The image of a saurian-type alien emerges in *The X-Files* in the sixth season with "The Beginning." It is a large and awesome, a lightning-swift and squealing creature whose genesis and appearance echo the monster in the film *Alien* (discussed in Chapter Five). It seeks out the watery warmth of a nearby power plant, and is discovered there by Mulder as it kills another typical *X-File* MIB (the Dark-haired Man) and turns toward Gibson Praise, the young telepath, as Agent Mulder looks on, powerless to assist the boy. Up to this point, only the black oil organism of the aliens depicted on the show has been unequivocally evil. And this may be intended as a reminder of our own "black oil" and what it is doing to our habitat (to my knowledge, it is not patterned on any corresponding creature in the UFO pantheon). At the very end of "The Beginning" (6X01), Gibson has not been hurt. Bathed in blue light, he watches from a catwalk above the pool that cools the plant's generating rods. Deep within the pool, the creature transforms itself, shedding its skin, snake-like, to become the familiar and almost comforting image of a Gray alien. The dragon has been reborn, as a caterpillar into a butterfly, not in the gentler iconic forms of fairy tales, however, but as a numinous alien figure of contemporary myth.

The serpent has been revered in other cultures because it is able to shed its skin, seeming to be born again, thus to be immortal. So this act is a powerful representation — just as the snake eating its tail is (Scully's tattoo in "Never Again," 4X13) — of the power of life. In the short closing sequence from "The Beginning," *The X-Files* becomes a hermetic field of transformation, reviving the old symbols and combining them with new ones from the current cultural context. The passage of this creature from virus to saurian-reptilian monster to Gray alien exerts much more force in terms of the interpretive and symbolic codes of the narrative than in terms of the action or plot, where it has scarcely any significance at all. The episode summary posted on *The X-Files* website does not even mention this brief closing scene. It also goes beyond the significance that can (yet) be attached to any of the other alien beings seen on the show so far: clones, alien assassins, faceless rebels and certainly the cyclopean Lord Kimbote, some of which seem to have little basis in the UFO literature, whereas the saurian/reptilians and the Grays are key icons.

"All I Want Is the Truth..."

The powerful tell lies believing that they have greater than ordinary understanding of what is at stake; very often, they regard their dupes as having inadequate judgment, or as likely to respond in the wrong way to truthful information....

A certain amount of illusion is needed in order for public servants to be effective. Every government, therefore, has to deceive people to some extent in order to lead them.[30]

As political events progressed through the next to the last year of the decade, the question of truth, its nature and importance, took center stage in a very peculiar way. The attention paid by media and government to President Clinton's affair with Monica Lewinsky lasted for the entire year and far outstripped the amount of time and energy devoted to the character assassination exposed in the McCarthy hearings during the 1950s, the lies of Watergate, the more recent Iran-Contra cover-up, or the many other more official and arguably more harmful lies told by political figures and agencies over the years.

The peculiar aspect of the Clinton-Lewinsky imbroglio was that the American public, though intensely interested, did not really seem to care. Many (73 percent in a February 1999 poll) said that they believed that the President had committed perjury, that he had lied in his grand jury testimony about his relationship with Monica Lewinsky. Yet throughout the impeachment process the percentages remained constant: About a third of U.S. citizens supported Clinton's removal from office and two-thirds opposed it. It appears that, to Americans of the '90s, "Truth is a lot like sunlight: people used to believe it was good for you."[31] Or are our feelings about the relative value of truth — and what constitutes "the truth" and under what conditions — tempered by ideals of individual freedom, how much damage the lying does and to whom, and a hierarchy of public and personal priorities? Most would agree that telling the truth is a philosophical ideal that all should aim for, but one that few of us can adhere to consistently, try as we might.

Of foremost importance to a large majority of citizens, according to pollsters, was the fact that Clinton was a good president. Poll respondents believed that he was doing a good job and supported his policies. Other un-polled factors may reasonably have played a part as well. One of these is empathy, suggested by the Gallup option that removal was unjustified because the charges against him dealt with sexual matters, a statement with which 76 percent of the respondents agreed. Closely associated with this judgment was the opinion that the laws Clinton broke were not serious enough to warrant impeachment (73 percent agreed). These poll results seem to reflect some public resentment, a feeling that, for many, a line had been crossed, violating the right of personal privacy, which is very important to most Americans. Some may have put themselves in the President's shoes. What would I have done in his position? Which is more honorable, to divulge the entire truth or to try, somehow, to protect the other party, one's family and one's own dignity? Thus, identification with the President's dilemma may have played a part as individuals pondered what it might be like to be between that particular "rock and hard place." An Australian, reflecting an empathic view, is said to have commented that Clinton's ordeal made him happy his country had been settled by prisoners and not by Puritans.

According to certain fringe observers, 1998's preoccupation with "the truth" is a symptom of the age — the Aquarian Age. In the 1960s, youthful and other rebels adopted the idea of the recession of the equinoxes, that the earth moves backwards through the astrological signs each epoch (of approximately 2,200 years), and that we are entering the Aquarian Age, the supposed Age of Truth, of revealed hidden matters, and leaving behind the Piscean Age, which marked the birth and spread of Christianity as well as an increasing level of "skepticism and disillusionment." Some Baby Boomers may recall the song about the "dawning of the Age of Aquarius" featured in the '60s Broadway musical *Hair*. These days, the term "New Age" is used more frequently than "Aquarian Age" to refer to the supposed change of consciousness that took place during that tumultuous decade.[32]

The concern with openness and truth-telling that is part of the U.S. legacy from the '60s has taken on even greater importance during the 1990s. More and more of the U.S. government's files and secret documents are being opened up daily under Freedom of Information legislation. By June 1998 the FBI had made 16,000 pages from 37 investigations available on the Internet (the latest is the FBI file on Frank Sinatra). The Bureau intends eventually to put on the Web 1.3 million pages of documents that have already been opened to public scrutiny.[33] This new openness, combined with President Clinton's predicament, and President Nixon's before him, may impel public officials to be more truthful on all fronts in the future. Electronic communications provide instantaneous contact, and official lies and cover-ups have repeatedly been exposed, while other possible deceptions from the past simmer just below the surface, giving rise to a popular film exposé like *JFK* and a television show like *The X-Files*, which repeatedly suggests cover-up and conspiracy, both past and present.

"Subversive" views that challenge official truths are not entirely lacking in TV history. *The Twilight Zone* anticipated *The X-Files'* stance in the early '60s by implying that "behind its mask, our smug normality wasn't all that normal." In those days the show's producer Rod Serling felt constrained to choose "the science fiction genre because it was the only place he could be subversive without scaring off sponsors."[34] Times have changed. Although *The X-Files* has not been free of network interference, it has also enjoyed a great deal of post modern permissiveness. Fortunately, the Fox Network discovered early on that the series' premises of conspiracy, alien visitors and the paranormal were pretty much in line with viewer tastes, if not necessarily their beliefs.

On a practical level, most people realize that they lie and are lied to constantly by everybody from friends and relatives who don't want to hurt their feelings to an uncountable horde of people and institutions who want something from them. Many probably assume the attitude of expecting to be told lies and judging them as "wrong" only when the effect on them personally is undeniably harmful. In this social context, is Mulder's search for the "truth" valid, quixotic, or just a storytelling gimmick? For the first four seasons of the show Mulder believed that the truth, or at least one important truth, was that a Shadow Government, aligned with a military/corporate Cabal, was conspiring to cover up the fact that extraterrestrial beings were not only visiting the earth but engaging in unknown but probably malevolent activities here — such as the abductions of human beings, the cloning of alien/human hybrids or the development of various devices, like diseases, to facilitate colonization of the earth. If Mulder had succeeded in communicating this truth believably to the public at large, would the audience still know the "truth" at the end of the fifth season, when Mulder has changed his mind to believe that extraterrestrial visitations are fabrications of a global military/corporate Syndicate, devised to divert public attention from something that scares us as much or even more than aliens — the development of a secret arsenal of sophisticated and deadly bio-weapons?

Because *The X-Files* is a work of fiction, it is entirely possible that Agent Mulder's quest for the truth is symbolic, something along the line of Diogenes' search for an honest man. It simply signifies our exasperation at living in a society in which lies are ubiquitous and inescapable. Basically, all of the powerful discourses we deal with have their built-in conventions of euphemism, misdirection and doublespeak. Subliminal lies are the special province of advertising and lies are regularly purchased from scientists and other experts by corporations. All government, military, and scientific institutions, in fact, regularly withhold information from us or tells us lies for our own good. This has made the citizen of the '90s a very, very suspicious person, and yet, at the same time, one who relishes hearing and telling stories.

The X-Files and the Case for Personal Truth

> The narrative paradigm ... rejects the notion that only some people are authorized as rational, and assumes instead that all people are innately inclined and qualified not just to "judge the stories that are told for and about them," but also to offer their own accounts and interpretations "of any instance of human choice, including science." Because narrative rationality is concerned with reason, morality, and action — as opposed to traditional rationality's concern with logical structures and subject-matter expertise — and because it invites all members of a community to participate as co-authors of public narratives, ... it is more consistent with democratic ideals and hence more desirable.[35]

At the conclusion of "Quagmire" (3X22), Scully tells Mulder, "There's still hope. That's why these myths and stories have endured. People want to believe." The position of *The X-Files* is that individuals want to believe in the existence of numinous mysteries and in each other. They want to achieve a community of knowledge and conjecture of their own, one that allows for emotion and imagination, that does not set rigid dividing lines between polarities — true or false, wrong or right, fact or fantasy. They want to be heard. Expert and professional discourses have restricted individuals both pragmatically and creatively, and many people, struggling with multiplicity and contradiction and confusion as the millennium approaches, are attempting to escape the limits imposed by these structures and to find some kind of personally satisfying order for themselves and for their own lives.

One widespread manifestation of this attempt to gain control is the current tendency to go outside the boundaries of traditional medicine and to try alternative therapies, such as acupuncture, massage, and aromatherapy. When the FDA threatened to restrict the sale and purchase of herbal supplements and medications, it brought on the largest amount of opposing mail that the agency had ever received. There appears to be an ongoing drive (whether or not it will succeed is yet to be seen) to unseat the professional discourses of power and control as the source of truth and replace or at least balance them with the common language, authentic discourse of ordinary people following their own path as much as possible and telling their own stories. "Witnessing" is the religious term for it. The importance of one's own truth has come to the fore over the past 30 years for a variety of reasons. One source of this development rests, I believe, in specific changes in methods of teaching writing in public schools and colleges during that period.

I began teaching written composition to middle school and high school students at the end of the 1960s. The book that I used in my classes was *Writing to be Read*. It was written by a journalist, Ken Macrorie, and has now been in print without interruption since its original publication in 1968 — an astoundingly long time for a composition textbook. Teaching English in the public schools during the '60s and early '70s was an invigorating experience. A majority of my students were intellectually curious, idealistic and socially aware. And Macrorie's approach to writing suited them. His methods included asking students to write freely 10 to15 minutes at a time and telling them not to worry about mechanics or getting just the right word, but to allow the words to flow in a stream of consciousness that, it turned out, both filled pages and improved fluency. Macrorie's method was a departure from the restricted and formalistic five-paragraph essay, grammar and usage exercises, and obsession with correctness that had been the chief approach to teaching writing in the 1950s and early '60s. He pioneered the writing workshop, in which student writers read their pieces aloud to their peers, in order to share their ideas and to give and receive feedback for revision. Macrorie insisted that writers have one basic aim, to tell the truth:

> All good writers speak in honest voices and tell the truth.... This is the
> first requirement for good writing: truth; not *the* truth (whoever knows

surely what that is?), but some kind of truth — a connection between the things written about, the words used in the writing, and the author's real experience in the world he knows well — whether in fact or dream or imagination.... Part of growing up is learning to tell lies, big and little, sophisticated and crude, conscious and unconscious. The good writer differs from the bad one in that he constantly tries to shake the habit. He holds himself to the highest standard of truth telling.[36]

Macrorie's way of authentic self-expression became the new way, the progressive way, to teach writing. It lent itself well to the kind of eight-week units that English teachers were being forced to design to attract students into English classes. This was a period in which economy-minded legislatures began cutting the years of required high school English, from four to two in many states. Macrorie's techniques began to receive a lot of professional and theoretical attention, and once teachers were receiving student journals and papers that they *wanted* to read (a clear bonus of the program), many adopted Macrorie's methods and goals. Although never a universal doctrine, it gradually infiltrated a broad cross-section of American schools and has since become the fundamental approach upon which more analytic and formal teaching strategies are based. Given the fact that English language arts classes are the most common offerings of the K-12 curriculum, even stretching into the college years, and given the 30-year spread of this methodology, millions of Americans have been exposed to Macrorie's ideas on some level. Colleges have for years had classes in autobiography writing or, for extended learning students, such courses as Writing Your Own Life. Students in middle and high schools and in college keep learning journals, in which their personal responses are supposed to interpenetrate with course materials being studied. This technique leads to a more full integration of subject matter, and at the same time provokes questions, affective reactions, and dissent — a particularly American classroom ideal.

My point in recounting this little history is that many American children and adults over the past 30 years have been encouraged to tell their own truth in their own way — and not just in written discourse. The National Council of Teachers of English, the largest professional education organization in the U.S., also produced during this period a statement supporting "students' right to their own language," the purpose of which was to level the playing field for language- or dialect-different students in language arts classes. More and more, various voices were being encouraged to speak and to write their ideas and their experiences in educational settings, and this has contributed to the explosion of voices currently being heard in many areas of American life: on television talk shows, on the Internet, and in the proliferation of abduction narratives, all of which are developments of just the past ten years. Jodi Dean's recent *Aliens in America*, sets the watershed year as 1987, the year that content controls on television programming were loosened and Whitney Streiber's *Communion* and Bud Hopkins' *Intruders*, both non-fiction accounts of alien abductions, made best-seller lists. She points out that the Internet soon took off, too, providing yet another setting for free-wheeling public discourse.

Several episodes of *The X-Files* focus on personal experience narratives or comment on them in some way. One motif that runs through the series as a whole is that people who have had inexplicable experiences are willing to tell their stories to Mulder because they have heard (or come to realize) that he will not dismiss or scoff at what they have been through. "Jose Chung's *From Outer Space* (3X20), a satirical episode, deals directly with the question of truth where the personal experience story is concerned. Many of the individuals that the author Chung interviews tell contradictory stories and Chrissy, who is hypnotically regressed twice to recall her abduction, contradicts her first story (aliens abducted her and stole her memory) with her second (the U.S. military did it). Mulder and Scully are seen by quintessential loser Blaine Faulkner as MIBs, and the owner of a diner, where Mulder remembers conferring with an Air Force pilot, recalls that Mulder was alone and ate an entire pie. (I suspect an oblique reference to FBI Agent Cooper's fondness for pie in *Twin Peaks*.)

Jose Chung believes that "truth is as subjective as reality," and the reality in this episode shifts all over the place, depending upon whose point of view is being represented. The clear implication is that people may have differing versions of the same reality due to some very non-conspiratorial reasons — differing sensory capabilities, previous experiences, their motives and beliefs, their level of attention, where they were during the incident, what their expectations were, their emotional state and suggestibility and so forth. Although these differences can never be completely reconciled, they can be recorded in a straightforward manner, producing the genuine artifact of an event or experience with all of the bumps and crevices intact. The "authentic" document, then would be a compilation or compendium, retaining even those data that appear subjective, contradictory or just plain weird. Otherwise, "the truth" gets packed into a pre-formed box of consensus reality and "the official story."

"El Mundo Gira" (4X11) is an episode which features stories and storytelling in subtle but significant ways. The first way is to manipulate the point of view, not skew it in many varied directions the way "Jose Chung" does, but to make the teller of tales a middle-aged Mexican woman in a migrant worker's shanty town. There are candles, red light and chatter in Spanish; when she begins speaking, a guitar starts to play and the chatter subsides. She begins her story: It was awful, and she saw it with her own eyes. The scene recreates the setting and atmosphere of traditional oral storytelling, the earliest beginning of horror tales. It also has the aura of another type of tale-telling. The assembled listeners are all women and, except for the spooky atmosphere of darkness and candles, we could simply be listening in on a village gossip session. So Flakita tells the story, and there seem to be no notable distortions until almost the end of Act Five, when she reports seeing aliens/chupacabras descending on the shanty town through the mist. Someone objects: That's not the way it happened according to Gabrielle. At that point another woman takes over the tale briefly and revises the ending somewhat, with both brothers turning into the legendary chupacabra figure and the aliens in the mist transformed into a hazardous materials corps in protective gear. They have moved in to disinfect the area, cleansing it of deadly fungal infestations. Mulder and Scully reporting their unaccountable story to Skinner close the show, so Flakita and Gabrielle's tale seems to be theirs as well.

"El Mundo Gira" is one of those busy episodes that pull in lots of premises: aliens (both extraterrestrial and illegal), a fortean event (yellow rain), a folk superstition (the chupacabra), pesticides attacking the immune system of migrant workers and making them more susceptible to fungus attacks, the disease-related fears that have been with us through the 1990s and will be into the future. Mulder also connects the bright flash before the yellow rain with the exsanguination and mutilation of animals associated with UFO phenomena. The sly juxtaposition of illegal alien workers and space aliens is pointed up several times when both the local INS officer and then Scully (to Skinner) remark that the illegal workers are invisible to most people. The government officer himself plays a role that is also used in the episode "Hell Money" (3X19). When the member of an ethnic minority goes to work for The Man, it would seem to be only a matter of time until he is disposed of: Sgt. Andy Taylor (black) in "Home," Detective Chao in "Hell Money" and Conrad Lazano, "El Mundo Gira's" Mexican-American border officer.

Not only is "El Mundo Gira" a story told by two Mexican women, and in Spanish, but Lazano also comments on the existence of such stories and their importance to his people. They tell stories, he explains, because their lives are limited and they are out of place, and, later, he says that his people use stories to keep them sane while they wait to get work. And finally, when Mulder spins out an explanation for the fungus disease that includes an extraterrestrial origin, the detective observes that you (we assume Anglos) have your stories, too. Although Scully and Mulder are characters in someone else's story in this episode, as far as viewers can tell neither their characters nor the events have been distorted by the tale tellers' superstition or lack of education. Their tale is the one the audience sees and hears, and we are led to believe that this is the same story that Scully and Mulder tell Skinner in the end. The migrants', the agents', and our stories — like *The X-Files* itself — serve a personal and social need, as stories with that numinous factor of supernatural horror always do.

The stories told in the migrants' camp bind the community and create a shared mythic truth, a truth to the imagination as much as a truth based on observation and accurate recall. Imaginative truth operates in both folk and literary tales. Sometimes a literary text will validate the imagination directly, showing what the powers of the imagination are good for, as Jack London does in his story "To Build a Fire." The unnamed main character is out on the trail in the Yukon wilderness in temperatures that he realizes are at least 50 degrees below zero, maybe even lower. He is in trouble, but not because he lacks adequate information or equipment. London tells us that "he was a newcomer in the land ... and this was his first winter. The trouble with him was that he was without imagination. He was quick and alert in the things of life, but only in the things, and not in the significances."

The novels of Carlos Casteneda, on the other hand, see values in the imagination that are more spiritual, less immediately practical. Casteneda, who was very much a writer of the 1960s, not only expresses that decade's imaginative revival, but marks a return, along with the Herman Hesse of *Sidhartha* and *Beneath the Wheel*, to the philosophical and mystical in popular literature. His novels have remained in print and continued to be read to the present day, and when he died in 1998, a news report called him the "godfather of America's New Age movement" and described his works as "a strange alchemy of anthropology, parapsychology, ethnography, Buddhism, and perhaps great fiction." And (literary) author Joyce Carol Oates commented that though they seem to be anthropological studies, his writings were really "remarkable works of art, on the Hesse-like theme of a young man's initiation into 'another way' of reality." A critic observed of his work that "it isn't necessary to believe to get swept up in Casteneda's other-worldly narrative. Like myth, it works a strange and beautiful magic beyond the realm of belief."[37] Casteneda, with his blurred boundaries between information and imagination, is as much a post modern writer as Pynchon and Vonnegut, as much a magical realist as Borges or Marquez. In ways that are perhaps more folk than formal, the storytellers and explicators of the UFO sub-culture participate in the same tradition.

The Stories Are Out There

> Finding truth depends on finding someone to trust.... During his live broadcast from Area 51, Nevada, Larry King asked: "How much stock do you put in the word of your fellow man? This is the central question of the UFO debate." Incredible, the alien implicates everyone in conspiracies to produce and suppress, reveal and deny an always fugitive truth.[38]

Mia's Story[39]

Mia Adams was a speaker at the UFO Summer Seminar in Laughlin, Nevada, in August 1998. Ten years before, she was living in a condominium complex in Florida where she began to experience strange occurrences, including what she believed was surveillance from high frequency microwave bursts which interfered with her sleeping. Thinking her problems might originate with an annoying FBI agent who lived in her building (think Morris Fletcher from "Dreamland I and II", 6X5/6), she wrote a complaint to the Agency and was then contacted by an Agent Jordan Perez, who told her, "In the Bureau they call me The X-Files Man. I'm in a special division called Unit Five, specializing in MIBs." Perez also furnished the information that he had attended Duke University on a naval scholarship, served in naval intelligence, and then served in the CIA before joining the FBI.

Over a period of time, Mia developed a very close relationship with Agent Perez. As she saw it, he seemed almost like her in many uncanny ways, and she felt bonded to him. He told her that he knew he was under surveillance and she became aware that she was being watched as well — even more than she had been previously. Gradually she began to recall a forgotten incident of her college days, when she had also lived in Florida. As more and more of that incident returned to memory, she began to realize that she had been abducted by a joint government-alien effort in 1962, and that during the abduction, her own ova had been harvested. She then came to believe that Jordan Perez was her child, part of an alien effort to see if emotional energy connected mother and child outside of direct physical contact. That was the reason he had been assigned to her case.[40]

JONATHAN'S STORY

On November 18, 1998, the Art Bell radio show featured an interview with Dr. Jonathan Reed, a psychologist who recounted an 1996 experience he had had with what seemed to be an alien creature. Reed was living in the Pacific Northwest at the time and was taking a day hike in the Cascade Mountains with his golden retriever Suzy. The dog ran off and then began barking frantically. Jonathan picked up a large branch beside the trail and rushed up and over a rise as the dog's bark changed into a yelping or howling. When he saw her, she was obscured by a presence that seemed to be vibrating intensely all around her. She grabbed the arm of the vibrating creature and it took hold of her head and tore it back, exposing the dog's jawbone. Jonathan lunged forward, swung the branch he was carrying, and hit the creature, whose rate of vibration had slowed so that he could see it more clearly. It was a small Gray alien with red tinted eyes, wearing a dark one-piece garment. When hit, it shrieked and collapsed. Suzy had died and was beginning to implode.

Jonathan found a strange dark obelisk floating three or four feet off the ground nearby. It was surrounded by an intense electromagnetic charge. He wrapped the alien body in a survival blanket and carried it back to his car. At home, he put the body in a locked freezer and called a friend. They spent the next few days examining it, taking videos and photos and trying to contact someone from MUFON or the local university who would tell them how to proceed or would come look at it. Incredibly, the creature appeared to be reviving in the freezer. Meanwhile, both Jonathan and his friend were being followed. They were almost run off the road by a large blue-black van, and their houses were searched. Finally, nine days after Jonathan's encounter, there was a major destructive ransacking of his home, and his locked freezer was taken. His friend Gary disappeared. Jonathan has not seen him for two years and doesn't know where he is.[41]

Thomas' Story

Thomas Castellano worked in security for a time at the secret underground base near Dulce, New Mexico. One day he was assigned to take a foreign dignitary on a tour of the Dulce complex and that included a trip down "the long tunnel to Taos, which headed off through a portal marked with the symbol for marshlands (a Z superimposed by a =). When he began driving through the tunnel, he understood why that symbol was used. The walls were decorated with colorful depictions of a wild tropical landscape, painted in relief, with unfamiliar mountains rising in the distance. Driving through miles and miles of trees, vines, meadows and blossoms, he thought that every plant on earth must have been represented. There were no animals or people. He decided to slow down and try to see if the artwork was signed, but saw no signature or writing of any kind. Was this a museum? A shrine? He felt that it couldn't have been created by modern man, although it was carved in minute detail and appeared new.

No source could be seen for the soft illumination. It came from everywhere. He stopped the electric car and got out for a closer look. The walls were covered with some kind of transparent coating, maybe as much as a foot thick. The slightest touch would set the surface quivering in a wave of light that was somehow inside the glass. At that point he began to hear sounds "starting as a soft gentle harmonic sound that resonated with the shimmering lights and grew to a bone deep vibration that was subtle and surprisingly invasive.... The tunnel echoed with musical tones. I struggled to isolate the difference between what I was hearing and what I was feeling. I could not separate them." He felt that the tones were transmitting information in a very old language. At first the progression of notes was fast, all running together, but as they continued, he started to recognize what seemed to be separate sounds, separate words. He was certain that what he was hearing was a "lost language." When he got back in the car, he began driving again but felt dizzy and disoriented. Although the flow of sounds was like a kind of music, it was very intense, and the vibrations penetrated his mind and body deeply, unceasingly, until he reached the end of the tunnel and exited. Concluding his story, he comments: "It was one of the most profound experiences of my life, but I wouldn't want to do it again."[42]

Story and the Construction of Reality

So how are we to take the preceding stories? I contend that they can be "read"— that is, interpreted, appreciated, and enjoyed — like any popular genre or literary text. A storyteller's deep consciousness of basic mythic forms (the descent to and return from the underworld) and archetypes (the trickster or the shadow) can be shaped by the near-conscious and socially-influenced components of formula and convention to produce a text based on and further enriched by the author's knowledge and personal real-life and imaginary experiences. These details ring changes upon genre elements and fulfill the requirements of a popular culture document — that it be a unique and living statement of its life and times. Listeners, readers and viewers find comfort in the familiar old patterns and images but are intrigued by what is new, individual and unique. I should note that some would regard the imaginal as a function of deep consciousness, but I disagree. Although the realm of the human imagination can access all levels of consciousness, it is the primary source of originality, inalterably connected to the persona of the creator and to the here-and-now. In other words, the individual's experiences, because they arise from a direct connection with both the material and the imaginal, have meaning and *count for something* in the world of public reality.

Basic generic structures, like the contents of the archetypal unconscious, change slowly and gradually, but the data of material and imaginal personal experience are constantly shifting. These latter take on myriad forms and are capable of an infinite variety of combinations. In the fictional "composed" stories of popular and elite art, and in "vernacular" human personal experience stories, three levels of consciousness come into play. The relationships among these levels could be modeled as follows, from the most to the least accessible:

Experiential level: Individual
MATERIAL AND IMAGINAL MANIFESTATIONS
(interwoven and interrelated)

Representational level: Social and Temporal
ARTISTIC CODES
FORMULAS, CONVENTIONS, AND ICONS
IDEOLOGICAL CONSTRUCTS

Intuitive level: Universal, Cosmic
IDEA FORMS, BASIC GENRE STRUCTURES
ARCHETYPES
THE COLLECTIVE UNCONSCIOUS

In the genre text, the second, intermediate or "representational" level interacts with imaginative and material reality from the first level in such a way as to make the individualistic elements supplied by the creators available for general understanding. The second level helps shape idiosyncratic elements so that they can be understood and accepted, at least partially, into consensus reality (by having such features as having a beginning, middle and end, for instance). The influences among these three levels of mental creation go in all of the directions; they are only arranged hierarchically in the model to show that the lowest level is the one least accessible to conscious thought and the uppermost is the level where that consciousness operates, the level upon which we experience, see, think, feel, reason, create. This is the environment in which we ourselves, as individuals, engage in the drama of the perceptible and the imaginable. The other levels help to determine how material from the experiential plane will be interpreted and even what form it will take. What seem to be boundaries between levels are not lines but areas, not borders that are clear and discrete, but indistinct areas that allow for overlaps and inter-penetrations. It should be understood that this is not a complete model of human mental processing, but one that concentrates primarily on the function of stories in the construction of reality.

Those who have studied philosophy will recognize the approximation of the above to Plato's theory of forms. The base "universal or cosmic" level is the site of Plato's ideal forms, which are general notions, ideas, concepts. He claimed that such forms, and not ephemeral manifestations of the real, were the essence of reality. In the above model, too, surface reality is apprehended on the level of exterior consciousness. Plato, though, was not interested in the relationships between form/idea and human experience as such, and he had very little respect for story as it was developing in his time into a form of entertainment. Poetry, including drama, would not be allowed in his ideal state, for it was third-hand knowledge, two steps removed from the ideal form, or the idea, and one step away from the physical object (persons in action) which it imitated. Plato held that artistic creation was a sort of insanity. That opinion accords with the current suspicion in some circles that the imagination is a source of delusion rather than a useful and legitimate mental capability. Although tapping into certain artistic codes, like the gothic, and accessing archetypal figures and concepts like the shadow, can seem a kind of "madness" to some; it is also true that all three levels of consciousness play a part in what we commonly call "creative inspiration."

The above model is also relevant to questions of truth and reality in UFO and related debates. Extreme possibilities are produced by individual consciousness by means of whatever imaginal and material reality the experiencer believes and understands. This combination of the two kinds of experience then trues itself up as best it can with the structures of consensus reality. It accepts the explanatory structures it can and discards what it cannot accept. Many experiencers are now telling their stories. These stories then influence external reality; that is, they become new experiential evidence that is drawn into the unconscious, gradually accumulating in the subconscious of the race. The tangled question of whether any non-consensus experiences or ideas are "true" or not means less than the fact that the telling and hearing of these stories gives people leverage against the discourses of power. Such alternative discourses as the abduction narrative take individual human consciousness into account, in fact, put it at the center, or maybe on top. Who is believable? Why or why not? What kind of evidence, if any, do we need in order to believe? It's easy to see, I think, that alternative narratives ask us to use human reason, to judge and often to reserve judgment until more is known. Thus they offer a locus for intellectual activity that is almost always lacking in the impositions of "expert" discourse or the propositions of lowest common denominator reality. Extreme possibilities stimulate us to entertain serious questions about human understanding and existence. As part of this process, *The X-Files* is involved in mainstreaming information and language that is liminal and esoteric — the discourse of UFO, paranormal, and conspiracy lore, alternative constructs that stimulate *both* creative thinking and logical analysis.

Carl Gustav Jung Revisited

Obviously, C. G. Jung, who died in 1961, does not qualify as a member of today's UFO or New Age community, but his explorations in philosophy and psychology make him a figure of some influence where both of these groups or movements are concerned. Playing on the obituary description of Carlos Casteneda as the "godfather of the new age," I would perhaps call Jung the Grandfather of the New Age. Jung's ideas have made it more possible to talk about experiences that are strange and unusual or to have an interest in possibilities that are extreme. From a Swiss family with a long history of preternatural experiences, he had his own first encounter with such things at the age of seven. Yet he was trained as a medical doctor, was a respected colleague of Sigmund Freud, and is considered a pioneer in the field of modern psychology. He was also an artist, a writer and an original thinker who investigated spiritualists and mediums and the Chinese divinatory system — the I Ching — as well as Western astrology, which he believed represented "the sum of all the psychological knowledge of antiquity."[43]

Jung studied history, folklore, art and dreams to come to his own particular understanding of both humanity and metaphysics, and he wrote a book in which he examined the UFO phenomena in relationship to art, to dreams and to the collective unconscious. As I have mentioned often, my interpretation of *The X-Files* leans heavily on Jung's ideas about human individuation and his theories of the archetypal unconscious, especially in discussing its codes of symbolism and characterization. This is as it should be, for Jung is a large part of the world-view — sometimes as interpreted by Joseph Campbell — that has made television viewers so receptive to *The X-Files* as a popular narrative.

Jung has written much about his own experiences with paranormal phenomena, and comments that "exceptions are just as real as probabilities. The premise of probability simultaneously postulates the existence of the improbable."[44] While many people on both sides of the Atlantic pursued an intense interest in mediums, ghosts, and supernatural manifestations during the 19th century, Jung personally studied the work of at least eight mediums and declared that what he found was totally explainable by scientific laws, a view that would shift as he later explored an a-causal principle that he called "synchronicity." To describe nature, he believed, "we need a principle of discontinuity. In psychology this is the drive to individuation. In biology it is differentiation, but in nature it is the 'meaningful coincidence,' that is to say, synchronicity" (Main 119). Jung came to believe that this principle was harmonious with the new probabalistic science of Einstein and others, and that it accounted for many kinds of unexplainable events and experiences that people regarded as paranormal. "The collective unconscious is simply Nature — and since Nature contains everything it also contains the unknown" (108). To describe nature, he believed, we should not rely on mechanistic science or pure (experimental) cause and effect: "Pure causality is only meaningful when used for the creation and functioning of an efficient instrument or machine by an intelligence standing outside this process and independent of it" (116). Mechanistic science, he thought, could have little useful to say about the unique and the extraordinary because "science gives us only an average picture of the world, but not a true one" (117).

After Jung began an association with Freud in 1907, his preoccupation with the paranormal continued. At first Freud was quite skeptical, exhorting Jung to make his (Freud's) sexual theory "'a dogma, an unshakable bulwark' against 'the black tide of mud ... of occultism'" (4). One evening in March 1909, Freud told Jung that he regarded him as his successor, like an eldest son. But later that evening, the men began to quarrel about the nature and possibility of the paranormal, and, suddenly, a loud explosive noise erupted from Jung's bookcase. Freud dismissed Jung's paranormal interpretation of the event, and Jung responded that if they continued to argue, the noise would occur again, which, to Freud's amazement, it did. Later, in a letter to Jung, Freud confessed that the incident had impressed him greatly. He explained that it immediately cast him out of the kingly, paternalistic role he had assumed in making Jung his professional heir. A commentator remarks that this event is emblematic of the divergence of thinking between the two psychologists, that, in fact, they moved apart due largely to their disagreement about paranormal phenomena.

In 1958, Jung stated his position definitively, as follows: "There is in nature a background of acausality, freedom, and meaningfulness which behaves complementarily to determinism, mechanism and meaninglessness; and it is to be assumed that such phenomena are observable. *Owing to their peculiar nature, however, they will hardly be prevailed upon to lay aside the chance character that makes them so questionable* [emphasis mine]. If they did this they would no longer be what they are — acausal, undetermined, meaningful" (116). This explanation sounds very much like the Italian UFO investigator who described extraterrestrial aliens as "visitors, beings of many races, who never manifest publicly but always in an occult or hidden way."[45] This "peculiar nature" applies to all paranormal and UFO events. These occurrences cannot be isolated in a laboratory and subjected to quantifiable measurements in order to determine their validity and reliability, as in a proper experimental study. It is possible, though, to capture their numinous strangeness in the familiar conventional forms of genre literature — as *The X-Files* does. And the best reason for doing so is that these experiences on the far ends of the bell-shaped curve tell us more about who we are and allow us to live more richly and fully, in our emotions, our imaginations, and our senses, than do the ways we all resemble each other — the usual, the expected, the "average."

An Ideological Postscript

Baby boomers of the '60s and '70s came of age during a time when they were bound to encounter progressive ideas about economic and social injustice that spanned the preceding century, from Karl Marx to the Black Panthers. In this way, so-called boomers became sensitive to the notion that the material world and the individual's position in it matters, means something, that nobody is born to be or deserves to be abused, exploited or oppressed by the economic and political institutions of any system.

On the other hand, the '60s and '70s also marked a rediscovery of a spiritual dimension in human beings and fostered a wide-ranging exploration of concepts and traditions quite outside the Judeo/Christian/Catholic belief systems that were then considered normal. Influenced by Eastern religions and New Age thought, ideas that would never have reached the mainstream in the preceding decade began to creep into established academic disciplines. As suggested in the previous section, in psychology, Carl Jung's theories about archetypes, individuation, and consciousness were displacing Sigmund Freud's family romance as a nexus of popular interest and belief. And even in the very conservative field of education, the new approaches and philosophical positions of the period roughly 1965 to 1975 ran the gamut from Macrorie's naturalistic writing program to Neil Postman and Charles Weingartner's *Teaching as a Subversive Activity* to George Leonard's *Education and Ecstasy*, delineating the possibilities for education to teach self expression, foster a kind of critical thinking which might bring about change in the material world, and also expand the potentials of the human psyche. Whereas the first aim is personal and the second, social and political, the third is spiritual in a way that focuses attention away from social realities. Socio-political or personal/spiritual: These are polarities of identification and belief that many *X-Files* viewers still carry around, articles of faith, as it were, about who they *ought to be* that are unconscious and seemingly incompatible.

The figure of Mulder, then, attempts to harmonize these competing visions of the self in relation to the world. He is an idealist who nurtures a transcendent vision of a truth that must be learned and shared with the community. He continually poses the question "Who is in control?" and is alert to the doubtful legitimacy of any locus of control which presents itself. As a trickster, an ironist, and a questioner, Mulder is taking the role of Postman and Weingartner's "crap detector." Earlier in this study, Mulder is referred to as the repository of our collective post–World War II memory, and just over his shoulder, I think, we can glimpse the shadow of the killings at Kent State — and those of students in Rome and Paris and Mexico City who died during the same period. This succession of incidents, although they took place before many young *X-Files* viewers were born, still resonate in the cultural consciousness, as suggested by a fan who is commenting on the red and black color symbolism in *The X-Files* series:

> Red and Black is also the title of an important song in the musical *Les Misérables*. In case you aren't familiar, it's about a group of young people trying to fight against the mighty French army. And they don't have a chance except each other and their own belief that they are doing the right thing. Also there are many who want them dead and who will betray them to their powerful enemies. Sound familiar?[46]

In *The X-Files*, Agent Mulder represents the metaphysical importance of faith and principles, of a spiritual and cosmological matrix which interweaves with yet extends far beyond the time-based confines of the physical world and the limited senses with which we apprehend it. While an opposition between the spiritual and the problems and demands of material reality may seem to be a dichotomy that is built into the nature of the universe, it is also possible that this seeming opposition is merely an interpretation of reality based on ideology rather than on any objective truth. Mulder reminds us that spiritual and physical existence may not be naturally separate, but only look to be so because of certain Western habits of seeing and thinking. Through him we achieve realization of both our spiritual *and* political/physical nature, *and* we don't even have to lose our sense of humor to do it.

We are now entering the last season of *The X-Files* (Season Seven). Numerologically, seven is a good number for seeing the quest to its close.

While the numbers one through six reference the range of possibilities offered by the material world, the numbers seven through nine are associated with the spiritual plane. The number seven is the number of "the teacher, the Christ number." Seven signifies alchemy, challenge, a change of direction. These meanings could apply to the legacy and the closure of the series. The text could, of course, experience a miraculous recovery and go on to number eight, but I don't anticipate it. As is typical for a genre text, the series has run through its exploratory stage (Season One), its brilliant classic period (Seasons Two through Five), and at least one reflexive or self-conscious period (Season Six). And thus far *The X-Files* is a singularity — an entity formed from many genres that constitutes a genre all to itself. Its cultural moment — the decade at the end of the 20th century — is passing. Yet for those who have accepted its weekly invitation, it has explored a universe that combines the real and the imaginal unlike any televisual event has done before. Not only has this text responded to the postmodern impulse of the era artistically and imaginatively, but it has also drawn from and found inspiration in a long, rich tradition of gothic/horror literature in many media. *The X-Files*, as a recorded cultural artifact, will always reflect a 1990s world populated with our past fears as well as our fears of the future. It will always suggest creative and hopeful dimensions of human possibilities, some extreme and some not. And, with its motto "The truth is out there," it will always examine seriously (but not too seriously) the importance, as well as the difficulty, of telling and knowing the truth.

Appendix 1.
Episode Titles
in Order of Broadcast
(with Brief Annotations)

1. 1X00 "Pilot." 09/10/93. UFO, small town, teenagers.
2. 1X01 "Deep Throat." 09/17/93. UFO, narration by Scully begins.
3. 1X02 "Squeeze." 09/24/93. Mutant human. Cannibalism, liver eater. Body distortion.
4. 1X03 "Conduit." 10/01/93. UFO, abduction, family (Samantha).
5. 1X04 "The Jersey Devil." 10/08/93. Beast-monster in nature, Scully personal.
6. 1X05 "Shadows." 10/22/93. Ghost, poltergeist, revenge/protection motive.
7. 1X06 "Ghost in the Machine." 10/29/93. Horrible object (C.O.S.) and inventor.
8. 1X07 "Ice." 11/05/93. Monstrous worm (*The Thing* echo), remote place.
9. 1X08 "Space." 11/12/93. Ghost from space — face on Mars. NASA.
10. 1X09 "Fallen Angel." 11/19/93. UFO abductee, NICAP (Max Fenig).
11. 1X10 "Eve." 12/10/93. Cloning, nasty children (girls product of genetic research).
12. 1X11 "Fire." 12/17/93. Fire-starter, paranormal, class resentment, Mulder personal.
13. 1X12 "Beyond the Sea." 01/07/94. Family, Scully father, psychic abilities.

14. 1X13 "Genderbender." 01/21/94. Alien community, shape-shifter, Scully personal.
15. 1X14 "Lazarus." 02/04/94. Soul switch at death, Scully first kills, Scully personal.
16. 1X15 "Young at Heart." 02/11/94. Revenge, proto-cloning, Mulder first kills.
17. 1X16 "E.B.E." 02/18/94. UFO, Lone Gunmen introduced.
18. 1X17 "Miracle Man." 03/18/94. Family/religion, visions (Mulder).
19. 1X18 "Shapes." 04/01/94. Monster. werewolf/manitou, traditional and Native American.
20. 1X19 "Darkness Falls." 04/15/94. Issue — environment, new life form.
21. 1X20 "Tooms." 04/22/94. Genetic mutant. Cannibalism. See "Squeeze" on previous page.
22. 1X21 "Born Again." 04/29/94. Revenge plot. Reincarnation/psychokinesis.
23. 1X22 "Roland." 05/07/94. Family (Mulder). Twins (clonelike). Dreams. Scientists.
24. 1X23 "The Erlenmeyer Flask." 05/13/94. Alien DNA, assassin. Government testing,
25. 2X01 "Little Green Men." 09/16/94. Family. Alien.
26. 2X02 "The Host." 09/23/94. Ecology issue. Radioactive waste/mutant. Fluke creature.
27. 2X03 "Blood." 09/30/94. Small town. Scary inanimate objects.
28. 2X04 "Sleepless." 10/07/94. Government experiment. Psychic powers.
29. 2X05 "Duane Barry." 10/14/94. (1) Alien abductee. Hostage situation.
30. 2X06 "Ascension." 10/21/94. (2) UFO, Scully abduction.
31. 2X07 "3." 11/04/94. Mulder personal. Vampires (ambiguous).
32. 2X08 "One Breath." 11/11/94. UFO. Family.
33. 2X09 "Firewalker." 11/18/94. FBI called to remote place. New life form. Obsession.
34. 2X10 "Red Museum." 12/09/94. Small town. Teens. Alien DNA experiment.
35. 2X11 "Excelsius Dei." 12/16/94. Issue: Nursing homes. Aging. Experiment.
36. 2X12 "Aubrey." 01/06/95. Serial killer. Genetic transference.
37. 2X13 "Irresistible." 01/13/95. Psychotic. Erotic fixation on dead. Taboo.
38. 2X14 "Die Hand Die Verletzt." 01/27/95. Small town. Teens. Demon summoned.
39. 2X15 "Fresh Bones." 02/03/95. Contemporary issue: internment camp. Voodoo.
40. 2X16 "Colony." 02/10/95. (1) UFO. Clones. Shape-shifting alien.
41. 2X17 "End Game." 02/17/95. (2). Genetic interference. UFO.

42. 2X18 "Fearful Symmetry." 02/24/95. Ecology, contemporary institution/issue: zoo.
43. 2X19 "Dod Kalm." 03/10/95. Nebulous UFO. Issues: fresh water, aging. Remote area.
44. 2X20 "Humbug." 03/31/95. Freaks, doppelganger (brother). Humor.
45. 2X21 "The Calusari." 04/14/95. Demon possession (*The Exorcist, The Omen* echo).
46. 2X22 "F. Emasculata." 04/28/95. Prison. Plague. Corporate experiment.
47. 2X23 "Soft Light." 05/05/95. Perils of science. Government experiment.
48. 2X24 "Our Town." 05/12/95. Small town. Factory. Cannibalism.
49. 2X25 "Anasazi." 05/19/95. (1) UFO Family. Genetics experiment. Conspiracy.
50. 3X01 "The Blessing Way." 09/22/95. (2) UFO. Family. American Indian.
51. 3X02 "Paper Clip." 09/29/95. (3) UFO. Alien/human hybrid.
52. 3X03 "D.P.O." 10/06/95. Paranormal powers. Teen controls lightning. Small town.
53. 3X04 "Clyde Bruckman's Final Repose" 10/13/95. Psychic. Serial killer. Humor.
54. 3X05 "The List." 10/20/95. Prison. Revenge plot. Ghost. Black characters, culture.
55. 3X06 "2Shy." 11/03/95. Contemporary monster: "fat-sucking vampire."
56. 3X07 "The Walk." 11/10/95. Military hospital, paraplegic veteran, astral projection.
57. 3X08 "Oubliette." 11/17/95. Serial abductor, teenage girl, empathic transference.
58. 3X09 "Nisei." 11/24/95. (1) UFO. Alien abduction. Experiments on humans or clones.
59. 3X10 "731." 12/01/95. (2) Leper colony. Files underground. Aliens.
60. 3X11 "Revelations." 12/15/95. Stigmatic. Scully psychic. Corporate killer.
61. 3X12 "War of the Coprophages." 01/05/96. Mulder voiceover. Cockroaches.
62. 3X13 "Syzygy." 01/26/96. Small town. Astrology. Teens, same birthday.
63. 3X14 "Grotesque." 02/02/96. Demonic force. Serial killer.
64. 3X15 "Piper Maru." 02/09/96. (1) Atomic/alien/disease (black oil). Family.
65. 3X16 "Apocrypha." 02/16/96. (2) Family, myth, alien/UFO.
66. 3X17 "Pusher." 02/23/96. Killer with paranormal psychokinetic powers.
67. 3X18 "Teso Dos Bichos." 03/08/96. South American artifact. Killer animals.

68. 3X19 "Hell Money." 03/29/96. Issue: organ harvesting. Asian cast.
69. 3X20 "Jose Chung's *From Outer Space*." 04/12/96. UFO/aliens. Perspective shifts.
70. 3X21 "Avatar." 04/26/96. Succubus. Red raincoat (*Don't Look Now* echo). Skinner.
71. 3X22 "Quagmire." 05/03/96. Traditional monster: sea serpent. Mulder/Scully personal.
72. 3X23 "Wetwired." 05/10/96. Small town, TV mind control experiment.
{ 73. 3X24 "Talitha Cumi." 05/17/96. (1) Alien bounty hunter, Mulder family.
74. 4X01 "Herrenvolk." 10/04/96. (2) Bees, clones, cataloguing citizens.
75. 4X02 "Unruhe." 10/27/96. Incestuous child abuse, serial killer — distorted photo images.
76. 4X03 "Home." 10/11/96. Ultimate dysfunctional family. Incest taboo. Satire.
77. 4X04 "Teliko." 10/18/96. African myth, air spirit — parasite must kill to live.
78. 4X05 "The Field Where I Died." 11/03/96. Reincarnation, Cult. Mulder personal.
79. 4X06 "Sanguinarium." 11/10/96. Hospital, plastic surgery, ritual magic, shape shifting.
80. 4X07 "Musings of a Cigarette Smoking Man." 11/17/96. Family. Conspiracy.
{ 81. 4X09 "Tunguska." 11/24/96 (1) Conspiracy. Space worms, black oil. Senate hearing.
82. 4X10 "Terma." 12/02/96. (2) Krycek loses arm. UFO in missile silo. Remote area.
83. 4X08 "Paper Hearts." 12/15/96. Serial child killer with link to Mulder.
84. 4X11 "El Mundo Gira." 01/12/97. Chupacabra — Latin American folk monster. L.A. cast.
85. 4X12 "Kaddish." 02/16/97. Golem. City violence, racism, teenage fascists.
86. 4X13 "Never Again." 02/02/97. Possession, poison, pop cult (tattooing). Scully personal.
87. 4X14 "Leonard Betts." 01/26/97. Human monster. Genetic mutation, cancer eater.
88. 4X15 "Memento Mori." 02/07/97. Experiment, clones. Scully cancer.
89. 4X16 "Unrequited." 02/21/97. Military. Revenge plot. Invisibility. Issue: MIAs.
{ 90. 4X17 "Tempus Fugit." 03/16/97. (1) UFO, military coverup, plane crash (Max Fenig).
91. 4X18 "Max." 03/23/97. (2) UFO intercept, military coverup (Max Fenig).

92. 4X19 "Synchrony." 04/06/97. Time travel. Issue: science.

93. 4X20 "Small Potatoes." 04/20/97. Shape shifter, baby with tail, Mulder/Scully personal. Satire.

94. 4X21 "Zero-Sum." 04/27/97. Disease (smallpox), insects (bees), Syndicate/Skinner.

95. 4X22 "Elegy." 05/04/97. Death omen/spirit, obsession, mental institution.

96. 4X23 "Demons." 05/11/97. Mulder personal, obsessive-compulsive, past regression.

97. 4X24 "Gethsemane." 05/18/97. (1) UFO/alien, Scully cancer, family, Mulder suicide.

98. 5X01 "Unusual Suspects." 11/16/97. Government conspiracy, Lone Gunmen. Past.

99. 5X02 "Redux." 11/02/97. (2) Military/corporate biowarfare, alien coverup story.

100. 5X03 "Redux II." 11/09/97. (3) Corporate conspiracy, syndicate, Scully cancer.

101. 5X04 "Detour." 11/23/97. Hostile nature elementals. Reverse evolution.

102. 5X05 "Christmas Carol." (1) 12/07/97. Ghost, dreams, Scully personal and family, clone.

103. 5X06 "Post-Modern Prometheus." 11/30/97. Frankenstein, B & W, reflexive.

104. 5X07 "Emily." 12/14/97. (2) Family, Scully daughter ill, cloning, corporate experimentation.

105. 5X08 "Kitsunegari." 01/04/98. Pusher (mind control), twins.

106. 5X09 "Schizogeny." 01/11/98. Teens/child abuse, insane counselor.

107. 5X10 "Chinga." 02/08/98. Small town. Evil doll. Scully alone on case. Stephen King.

108. 5X11 "Kill Switch." 02/15/98. Object (computer) menace, cyberpunk. William Gibson.

109. 5X12 "Bad Blood." 02/22/98. Vampire RV community. Humor, Mulder/Scully personal.

110. 5X13 "Patient X." 03/01/98. (1) Black oil/vaccine, new faceless aliens, burnings.

111. 5X14 "The Red and the Black." 03/08/98. (2) Alien rebels, hypno-regression.

112. 5X15 "Travelers." 03/29/98. McCarthy era, Mulder father, experiment/monster. Flashback.

113. 5X16 "Minds Eye." 04/19/98. Blind girl "sees" murder by man who killed mother.

114. 5X17 "All Souls." 04/26/98. Religious. Misbegotten girls killed. Scully personal.

115. 5X18 "The Pine Bluff Variant." 05/03/98. Virus, two terrorist groups, Mulder infiltrates.
116. 5X19 "Folie a Deux." 05/10/98. Employees see bosses as monsters.
117. 5X20 "The End." 05/17/98. (1) Gifted child. *Alien* link. Mulder personal, CSM family.

Appendix 2.
Episode Titles in
Alphabetical Order

The first number following each title is its season number. The second number indicates where it fell in the series (1, 2, 3, etc.).

Agua Mala, 6X13, 130

All Souls, 5X17, 114

Alpha, 6X16, 133

Anasazi (1) 2X25, 49

Apocrypha (2), 3X16, 65

Arcadia, 6X15, 132

Ascension (3), 2X06, 30

Aubrey, 2X12, 36

Avatar, 3X21, 70

Bad Blood, 5X12, 109

The Beginning, 6X01, 118

Beyond the Sea, 1X12, 13

The Blessing Way (2), 3X01, 50

Blood, 2X03, 27

Born Again, 1X21, 22

The Calusari, 2X21, 45

Chinga, 5X10, 107

Christmas Carol (1), 5X05, 102

Clyde Bruckman's Final Repose, 3X04, 53

Colony (1), 2X16, 40

Conduit, 1X03, 4

D.P.O., 3X03, 52

Darkness Falls, 1X19, 20

Deep Throat, 1X01, 2

Demons, 4X23, 96

Detour, 5X04, 101

Die Hand Die Verletzt, 2X14, 38

Dod Kalm, 2X19, 43

Dreamland I, 6X04, 121

Dreamland II, 6X05, 122

Drive, 6X02, 119

Duane Barry (1), 2X05, 29

EBE, 1X16, 17

El Mundo Gira, 4X11, 84

Elegy, 4X22, 95

Emily, 5X07 (2), 104

Notes

CHAPTER ONE. *THE X-FILES*:
MYTHOS, VISION AND PERSONA

    1. Dave Barry, "No Loopholes Here: Flat Tax Has Fat Chance," *Denver Post Empire Magazine*, 25 February 1996, 7.
    2. "Resurgent Sci-Fi Shows Find Fresh Ideas, Complex Themes," *Denver Post*, 8 March 1996, 19F.
    3. Brian Lowry, *Trust No One: The Official Third Season Guide to "The X-Files"* (New York: Harper, 1996), 171.
    4. *Denver Post*, 7 June–11 July 1997.
    5. Ibid.
    6. "Watchdog Group Finds Wholesome TV at Every Turn," *Denver Post*, 7 January 1996, 2F.
    7. *Denver Post*, 26, 28 January 1996.
    8. Brian Lowry, *The Truth Is Out There: The Official Guide to "The X-Files"* (New York: Harper, 1995), 27.
    9. Al Franken, *Rush Limbaugh Is a Big Fat Idiot* (New York: Delacort Press, 1996), 104.
    10. Ruth Rosen, "The Sinister Images of *The X-Files*," *The Chronicle of Higher Education*, 11 July 1997, B7.
    11. "'Are You Now or Have You Ever Been?' Conspiracy Theory and *The X-Files*," in *Deny All Knowledge: Reading "The X-Files*," ed. David Lavery *et al.* (Syracuse, NY: Syracuse University Press, 1996), 58.
    12. Awareness of these structures of control may be a symptom of the dawning of reflective thought, what psychologist C.G. Jung calls individuation, on the part of more and more individuals. Personal experience stories and other manifestations of individuation as cultural change will be explored in more detail in chapters of the Context section. Michel Foucault, however, would warn

against describing the effects of power in such negative terms as *excluding, repressing, abstracting* or *concealing.* Instead, power *creates.* It structures reality and our view of the world, and it thereby determines what we conceive of as "the truth."

13. Trans. Alan Sheridan (New York: Vintage Books, 1979), 194.

14. Good will, good character and good sense are the three markers of ethical proof, according to Aristotle. A speaker's credibility with an audience is influenced by whether or not he or she seems to possess these ethical qualities.

15. Jimmie L. Reeves, Mark C. Rodgers and Michael Epstein, "The Cult Files" in *Deny All Knowledge: Reading "The X-Files,"* ed. David Lavery *et al.* (Syracuse, NY: Syracuse University Press, 1996), 35.

16. "Contemporary Horror Fiction, 1950–88," *Horror Literature: A Reader's Guide,* ed. Neil Barron (New York: Garland, 1990), 165.

17. Lowry, *The Truth Is Out There,* 167.

18. Lowry, *Trust No One,* 217.

19. Lowry, *The Truth Is Out There,* 118.

20. Robert Stam, Robert Burgoyne and Sandy Flitterman-Lewis, *New Vocabularies in Film Semiotics* (New York: Routledge, 1993), 217.

21. In mid–1997, *Mad TV,* a Fox Network competitor of *Saturday Night Live,* aired a three-minute send-up that adroitly replicated the style that has become a hallmark of the series.

22. *From Caligari to Hitler: A Psychological History of the German Film* (Princeton, NJ: Princeton University Press, 1947), 10.

23. *The Haunted Screen* (Berkeley: University of California Press, 1952), 21.

24. J. P. Telotte, *Voices in the Dark: The Narrative Patterns of Film Noir* (Urbana, IL: University of Illinois Press, 1989), 4–17.

25. Ibid.

26. "X-Philes Speak," *USA Weekend,* 14–16 July 1995, 7.

27. Graham, "Are You Now or Have You Ever Been?", 57.

28. Ibid., 58.

29. See Graham for a brief but enlightening discussion of the inter-textual connections of such conspiracy films as *The Conversation, The Parallax View* and *Klute,* as well as a couple of 1950s science fiction movies.

30. Having to do with interpretation. A. A. Berger states that a hermeneutic interpreter regards a text as a self-contained universe and "wishes to experience this universe imaginatively rather than analyze it intellectually." *Cultural Criticism* (Thousand Oaks, CA: Sage Publications, 1995), 18.

31. *TV Guide,* 20–26 June 1998, 20.

32. Berger, citing Russian literary theorist Viktor Saklovsky, *Cultural Criticism,* 34.

33. Michael Kammen, "The Study of Popular Culture Has Acquired Legitimacy, but Still Lacks Cohesion," *The Chronicle of Higher Education,* 3 July 1998, B5.

34. "Canons and Close Readings," in *Falling Into Theory,* ed. David H. Richter (Boston: Bedford Books of St. Martin's Press, 1994), 219.

35. "Scully's Song: Sunday's Episode," *Fox Fan Forum*, 5 September 1998, http://xfox.proxicom.com/xfox

36. "Communication, M&S Style," Ibid.

37. "Teaching the Intellectual Merits of Stephen King's Fiction," *The Chronicle of Higher Education*, 19 June 1998, B7.

38. *The Mixtake Files* (London, UK: Summersdale, No Date) reports on "mistakes of every shape and form: continuity errors, logical inconsistencies, subject matter, plot discrepancies..." from the first three seasons; *The Nitpicker's Guide for X-Philes* (New York: Bantam Doubleday Dell, 1997) ferrets out "equipment flubs, changed premises, plot oversights" and other content problems up to Season Five.

CHAPTER TWO. THE *X-FILES* PLOT:
THE ARTISTRY OF ESCAPE

1. "The Big Chiller," 28 February 1987, 258. Author and professor George Stade, writing about horror fiction in *The Nation* over a decade ago, thus described the harmony of popular literature with democratic principles.

2. (Chicago: University of Chicago Press, 1976), 16.

3. Ibid., 46.

4. Ibid., 35.

5. This compendium of critical activities was adapted from *The Harper Handbook to Literature*, 2d ed. (New York: Longman, 1997), 134.

6. "Bending the Truth," 58–9.

7. Andy Meisler, *I Want to Believe: The Official Fourth Season Guide to "The X-Files"* (New York: Harper, 1998), 9.

8. Ibid.

9. Brian Lowry, *Trust No One: The Official Third Season Guide to "The X-Files"* (New York: Harper, 1996), 126.

10. Rhythmic repetitions are items or patterns of dialogue that are used to punctuate and sometimes conclude episodes. One example is the humorous "whatever" from "Syzygy," the phrase, "He is one" from "Red Museum," carried over to "Nisei," and "I just knew" from "Eve" and other shows.

11. "Biography of William Scully," http://www.thex-files.com/biowil.html

12. Michael Shayerson, "David Duchovny's X-Factor," *Vanity Fair*, June 1998, 212.

13. Roland Barthes demonstrates his theory of narrative codes particularly in *S/Z*, trans. R. Miller (New York: Hill and Wang, 1975), and Vladimir Propp, in *Morphology of the Folktale*, 2d ed. (Austin: University of Texas Press, 1968), forwards a similar idea of action/character units he calls "functions."

14. Radiation hazards are foregrounded in the "black oil" episodes "Piper Maru" (3X15), "Apocrypha" (3X16), "Tunguska" (4X09) and "Terma" (4X10).

15. The Majestic 12 documents, supposedly compiled for President Truman after the Roswell UFO incident, are reputed to prove that a secret organization exists which is devoted to concealing any contacts with extraterrestrials. Lowry in *The Truth Is Out There* (227) points out that in "Anasazi" the conspiracy to

keep these documents secret is obviously an international one, rather than just a US government plot.

16. "You Only Expose Your Father," in *Deny All Knowledge: Reading "The X-Files,"* ed. David Lavery *et al.* (Syracuse, NY: Syracuse University Press, 1996), 194.

17. The possible content of what such an exposé might reveal is still one of the series' perennial secrets. Even if Mulder, in his commitment to the truth, were willing to acknowledge his father's crimes, he can never separate himself from the World of the Father in which he lives and works.

18. John G. Cawelti, *Adventure, Mystery, and Romance* (Chicago: The University of Chicago Press, 1976), 34.

19. Ibid., 17.

CHAPTER THREE. GENRE AND CONTENT

1. Shadow on *X-Files Fan Forum*, 15 July 1998, http://xfox.proxicom.com/xfox

2. Chris Baldick, *The Concise Oxford Dictionary of Literary Terms* (Oxford: Oxford University Press, 1991), 200.

3. Northrup Frye *et al.*, *The Harper Handbook to Literature* (New York: Longman, 1997), 420.

4. (New York: Greenwood Press, 1986), 108.

5. Ibid., 110.

6. Michael White's *The Science of "The X-Files"* (London: Random House, 1996), promises to look "at the weird world of the paranormal and show ... how unbelievable things can remain within the limits of science," yet the book seemed to me to be more of a debunking of *X-Files'* science than not.

7. "Dark Fantasy" in *The Encyclopedia of Fantasy,* eds. John Clute and John Grant (New York: St. Martin's Press, 1997), 909.

8. Ibid.

9. Chris Baldick, *The Concise Oxford Dictionary of Literary Terms*, 128.

10. *Fantasy: The Literature of Subversion* (London: Methuen, 1981), 4.

11. From *The Poetics.*

12. Greek tragic heroes could be males, as Agamemnon or Oedipus, and rarely but sometimes females, such as Oedipus' daughter Antigone.

13. Brian Lowry, *Trust No One: The Official Third Season Guide to "The X-Files"* (New York: Harper, 1996), 90.

14. Roger Ebert, "*Psycho* Connects with Viewer's Deepest Fears," *Denver Post,* 6 December 1998, 4-I.

15. "The Masque of the Red Death." Similarly, during the Cold War, an underground facility was built on the grounds of a luxury hotel resort in Virginia that was big enough to house and protect Washington politicians and government officials in the event of a national (military) emergency.

16. Horror-suspense writer Dean Koontz in *Intensity:* "Sensation in all its glories is the reason that we're here."

17. In keeping with *The X-Files'* consciousness of other horror texts, this sequence echoes another that takes place in a bathtub in David Cronenberg's film *They Came from Within* (alternately titled *The Parasite Murders* or *Shivers*), which also featured a disgusting and phallicly suggestive parasite.

18. *Consuming Pleasures: Active Audiences and Serial Fictions from Dickens to Soap Opera* (Lexington KY: University Press of Kentucky, 1997), 4.

19. Susan Clerc, "DDEB, GATB, MPPB, and Ratboy: *The X-Files'* Media Fandom, Online and Off," in *Deny All Knowledge,* eds. David Lavery *et al.* (New York: Syracuse University Press, 1996), 48–9.

20. Rhonda Wilcox and J.P. Williams, "What Do You Think?" in *Deny All Knowledge,* Lavery *et al.,* 107.

21. Ibid., 104.

22. Elizabeth Kubek, "You Only Expose Your Father," in *Deny All Knowledge,* Laverly *et al.,* 195.

23. International Forum Address, University of Colorado, Boulder, CO, 25 September 1992.

24. Rob Tannenbaum, "Scully and Mulder's Excellent Adventure," *Details Magazine* (UK), June 1998, 130.

25. *Fantasy: The Literature of Subversion* (New York: Methuen, 1981), 177.

26. Ibid., 3.

27. Brian Lowry, *The Truth Is Out There: The Official Guide to "The X-Files"* (New York: Harper, 1995), 168.

28. Leslie Jones, "Last Week We Had an Omen," in *Deny All Knowledge,* Laverly *et al.,* 79.

29. This is the story upon which Alfred Hitchcock constructed his baroque 1963 foray into the wonderful world of special effects.

30. *Living in Fear* (New York: Charles Scribner's Sons), 210.

31. Andy Meisler, *I Want to Believe: The Official Fourth Season Guide to "The X-Files"* (New York: Harper, 1998), 26.

32. *Denver Post,* 22 October 1998, 13A.

CHAPTER FOUR. CHARACTER, STYLE AND THEME

1. Quote taken from "Inside *The X-Files,*" a series of brief promotional documentaries and interviews shown before *X-Files* reruns on the Fox Television Network in 1998.

2. Casting is one of those production areas in which *The X-Files* excels. Actors are obviously chosen with care and skill and do indeed invariably look like what they are supposed to be. Chris Carter has said that the show is only as scary as it is believable, and that "name actors" are usually avoided because their recognizable image makes it harder for viewers to lose themselves in the show. In *Trust No One: The Official Third Season Guide to "The X-Files"* (New York: Harper, 1996), 97.

3. Sam Smiley, *Playwriting: The Structure of Action* (Englewood Cliffs, NJ: Prentice-Hall, Inc., 1971), 84–88. My discussion of character traits, based on an Aristotelian model, is derived from this source.

4. Barbara Walker, *The Woman's Encyclopedia of Myths and Secrets* (New York: HarperCollins Publishers, 1983), 208.

5. Andy Meisler, *I Want to Believe: The Official Fourth Season Guide to "The X-Files"* (New York: Harper, 1998), 73.

6. Thank you to numerologist Timothy Masterson for drawing my attention to this aspect of *The X-Files'* name magic.

7. Rosemary Ellen Guiley, *Harper's Encyclopedia of Mystical and Paranormal Experience* (New York: Castle Books, 1991), 409–10.

8. Television show *Sabrina the Teenage Witch*, 23 May 1997.

9. An oblique reference from *The New York Times* to that other cult TV sex symbol Captain Jean Luc Picard of the *Starship Enterprise*.

10. BBC Internet source, original quote from *The New Republic*. CultTV:XFs, feature.bbc.co.uk/cult/archive/33xfiles

11. Stuart M. Kaminsky and Jeffrey H. Mahan, *American Television Genres* (Chicago: Nelson Hall, 1985), 58.

12. Gary Totten, "Bakhtin and Genre Theory," paper presented at the annual meeting of the RMMLA, Denver, CO, 1997; and Frederic Jameson, International Forum Address delivered at the University of Colorado, Boulder, CO, 25 September 1992.

13. *Adventure, Mystery, and Romance: Formula Stories as Art and Popular Culture* (Chicago: The University of Chicago Press, 1976), 11.

14. *A Literary Symbiosis: Science Fiction/Fantasy Mystery* (Westport, CT: Greenwood Press, 1983), 226.

15. Ibid., 228, 223.

16. http://cgi.pathfinder.com/ew/features/981225/bestandworst/besttv.html

17. A description applied to Jung's concept of synchronicity in Allan Combs and Mark Holland, *Synchronicity: Science, Myth, and the Trickster* (New York: Marlowe and Company, 1996), 94.

18. Carl Gustav Jung, *Four Archetypes: Mother, Rebirth, Spirit, Trickster*, trans. R.F.C. Hull (Princeton, NJ: Princeton University Press, 1969), 146.

19. Ibid., 136.

20. Kaminsky and Mahan, *American Television Genres*, 66.

21. Ross McDonald, "On Crime Writing," (1973), quoted in Pierce, *A Literary Symbiosis*, 10.

22. Jung, *Four Archetypes*, 151.

23. Inside *"The X-Files."*

24. "Special Agent or Monstrosity? Finding the Feminine in *The X-Files*," in *Deny All Knowledge: Reading "The X-Files,"* ed. David Lavery *et al.* (Syracuse, NY: Syracuse University Press, 1996), 129, 122.

25. Ibid., 138.

26. *Scotland Press and Journal*, 24 February 1998, 10.

27. Jung, *Four Archetypes*, 136.

28. In an article with the subheading "Religious seek miracles in an age of materialism," Gustav Niebuhr writes, "For all the secular materialism that distinguishes late 20th century culture, belief in the miraculous, in divine signs and wonders, remains very much alive." And R. Scott Appleby, who directs the Cusha

Center for the Study of American Catholicism at Notre Dame, says that "over the past 150 years, along with the rise of industrialization, capitalism and democracy, there have been more claims of appearances by the Virgin Mary to individuals than at any time since the Middle Ages." "Faithful flocking to girl in coma," *Denver Post*, 30 August 1998, 7A.

29. Walker, *The Woman's Encyclopedia*, 612–13. The quotation is from *The Fear of Women* (New York: Harcourt Brace Jovanovich Inc., 1968), 179.

30. "Saint Scully ... YES!" *X-Files Forum*, http://xfox.proxicom.com/sfox ?sid, 22 July 1998.

31. Walker, *The Woman's Encyclopedia*, 179

32. Skit on National Public Radio's *Prairie Home Companion*, 14 June 1998.

33. Chris Carter himself appears briefly as an FBI "Suit" in the episode "Anasazi" (2X25); and in "Young at Heart" (1X15), Mulder observes that the men in "bad suits" hovering over a hospital patient must be CIA agents.

34. Hayward, Jennifer Poole. *Consuming Pleasures: Active Audiences and Serial Fictions from Dickens to Soap Opera* (Lexington, KY: The University Press of Kentucky, 1997), 131.

35. Ibid., 192.

36. Umbro Apollonio, "Expressionism," in Vol. 5 of *The Encyclopedia of World Art*, (New York: McGraw-Hill, 1961), 31.

37. J. A. Place and L. S. Peterson, "Some Visual Motifs of Film Noir," *Film Comment*, January 1974, 30.

38. "Graphic Designers Jump Aboard Out-of-Focus Bandwagon," *Denver Post*, 4 January 1996, 3E.

39. Ibid.

40. Alain Silver and Elizabeth Ward, *Film Noir: An Encyclopedic Reference to the American Style* (Woodstock, NY: The Overlook Press, 1979), 58.

41. Andy Meisler, *I Want to Believe*, 37.

42. Brian Lowry, *The Truth Is Out There: The Official Guide to "The X-Files"* (New York: Harper, 1995), 148.

43. Bakhtin, M. M., *The Dialogic Imagination*, ed. Michael Holquist, trans. Caryl Emerson and Michael Holquist (Austin: University of Texas Press, 1981), 254.

44. Ibid., 245.

45. Ibid., 248.

46. E. F. Bleiler, *The Guide to Supernatural Fiction.* (Kent, Ohio: Kent State University Press, 1983), 553.

47. Ibid., 553–4.

CHAPTER FIVE. *THE X-FILES*
AND THE GOTHIC HORROR TRADITION

1. G. Richard Thompson, ed., *The Gothic Imagination* (Pullman: Washington State University Press, 1974), 3.

2. Totten, Gary L. "Bakhtin and Genre Theory" (paper presented at the

annual meeting of the Rocky Mountain Modern Language Association, Denver, CO, October 1997), 5.

3. Ibid., 7, 5.

4. Quoted in the introduction to H. P. Lovecraft, *The Dunwich Horror and Others* (Sauk City, WI: Arkham House Publishers, 1963), xx.

5. *Three Gothic Novels*, E. F. Bleiler, ed. (New York: Dover Publications, 1966), 18.

6. *The Fantastic: A Structural Approach to a Literary Genre*, trans. Richard Howard (Ithaca, NY: Cornell University Press, 1975).

7. Frederick S. Frank, "The Early Gothic," in *Horror Literature: A Reader's Guide*, ed. Neil Barron (New York: Garland Publishers Inc., 1990), 8–9.

8. Ibid., 9.

9. *Two Essays on Analytic Psychology* (New York: Pantheon, 1963), 94.

10. D. P. Varma, *The Gothic Flame* (New York, Russell and Russell, 1966), 46.

11. For a full explication of these ideas see C. G. Jung, *Man and His Symbols* (New York: Dell, 1978).

12. The British historian Edward Hallett Carr discusses the rise to consciousness of western man in *What is History?* (Knopff, 1963). History, he writes, is "the break with nature caused by the awakening of consciousness," 178, and "modern man is to an unprecedented degree self-conscious," 179.

13. The character's name was also used by Byron's ex-mistress, Lady Caroline Lamb, when she portrayed the poet as Ruthwen Glenarvon in her novel *Glenarvon*.

14. *The Vampire* (New York: Award Books, 1962), 130.

15. Brian Stapleford, "The Later Gothic Tradition," in *Horror Literature: A Reader's Guide*, ed. Neil Barron (New York: Garland Publishers Inc., 1990), 62.

16. Ibid., 60.

17. Historical background, quotations and references to the life of Charlotte Perkins Gilman are taken from Barbara Ehrenreich and Deirdre English, *For Her Own Good: 150 Years of the Experts' Advice to Women* (Garden City, NY: Anchor Press/Doubleday, 1978), 14–93.

18. Everett Franklin Bleiler, *The Guide to Supernatural Fiction* (Kent, Ohio: Kent State University Press, 1983), 553.

19. Stapleford, in Barron, *Horror Literature*, 97.

20. Ibid. 96.

21. H. P. Lovecraft, *The Dunwich Horror and Others*, xx.

22. Ibid., xvi.

23. Ibid., xiv.

24. Ibid., "Rats in the Walls," 51. Either intentional or synchronistic echoes on the part of *The X-Files* may explain why this story, one of Lovecraft's most famous, states in its first line that the location is Exham Priory, the "X" equaling the unknown, the Priory being a reincarnation of the traditional gothic building.

25. *Everything is Under Control: Conspiracies, Cults, and Cover-Ups* (New York: HarperPerennial, 1998).

26. S. S. Prawer, *Caligari's Children* (Oxford: Oxford University Press, 1980), 13.

27. The name of the cargo ship is also the title of a novel by Joseph Conrad.

28. Darrell Moore, *The Best, Worst, and Most Unusual: Horror Films* (Skokie, IL: Publications International, Ltd., 1983), 73.

29. Ibid., 72.

30. Stuart M.Kaminsky, *American Film Genres* (New York: Dell Publishing Co., 1977), 152.

CHAPTER SIX. *THE X-FILES* AND THE ZEITGEIST OF THE '90S

1. Bulwer-Lytton, *Zanoni*, 1842. Quoted in D. J. Enright, *The Oxford Book of the Supernatural* (Oxford: Oxford University Press, 1995), 514.

2. Deborah Orin, http://members.aol.com/nsp97/news/nypost.htm. Conspiracy buffs, looking at the size of Clinton's proposed 1999 military budget, would undoubtedly speculate that the President obviously knows about UFOs now, because this funding request, enormous for peacetime, must be hiding a number of "black budget" expenditures having to do with alien contact.

3. C Span Television, http://members.aol.com/nsp97/news/hawking2.htm

4. *Confirmation: The Hard Evidence of Aliens Among Us?* NBC Television Network, Wednesday, 17 February 1999. Greenewald's web site is The Black Vault.

5. All Gallup data cited in this chapter may be accessed on the Internet at http://205.219.140.75/POLL-ARCHIVES, unless another source is indicated.

6. Jodi Dean, *Aliens in America: Conspiracy Cultures from Outerspace to Cyberspace* (Ithaca, New York: Cornell University Press, 1997), 10.

7. "Some Want to Believe, Some Don't," http://www.parascope.com/articles/0597/gallup.htm

8. Dean, *Aliens in America*, 17.

9. Gavin de Becker, "Conquering What Scares Us," *USA Weekend*, 22–24 August 1997, 5.

10. The prescient title of *The X-Files* movie.

11. National Public Radio *Evening Edition*, 17 February 1999.

12. Eugene Linden, *The Future in Plain Sight: Nine Clues to the Coming Instability* (New York: Simon and Schuster, 1998), 94.

13. Ibid., 129.

14. *Denver Post*, 24 April 1999, 35A.

15. Allan Combs and Mark Holland, *Synchronicity: Science, Myth, and the Trickster* (New York: Marlowe and Company, 1996), xxxii.

16. C. G. Jung, *Flying Saucers: A Modern Myth of Things Seen in the Skies*, trans. R.F.C. Hull (Princeton, NJ: Princeton University Press, 1978), 5.

17. Ibid., 108.

18. Dean, *Aliens in America*, 9.

19. "'Evidence' of UFOs Reviewed," *Denver Post*, 29 June 1998, 2A, 9A. Also on the Internet at http://exosci.comnews/79.html

20. This section was drawn from several sources, most notably Dean's *Aliens in America*; Chris Bader's "The UFO Contact Movement from the 1950s to the

Present" in *Studies in Popular Culture* 17 (1995): 73–90; material from the Second Annual UFO Summer Seminar, *Learning About Man's Place in the Cosmos*, held 1–8 August 1998, in Laughlin, Nevada (relevant sources, speakers and page numbers are cited in the text); and from *Confirmation: The Hard Evidence of Aliens Among Us?* NBC-TV, 17 February 1999, 7–9 P.M.

21. Michael Lindemann, quoted in Linda Moulton Howe, *Glimpses of Other Realities, Vol. 1, Facts and Eyewitnesses* (Cheyenne, WY: LMH Productions, 1993), 301.

22. Jodi Dean, *Aliens in America*, 41.

23. Timothy Good, *Beyond Top Secret* (London: Pan Books, 1996), 334.

24. Stephen Mehler, "The Coming Paradigm Shift," interview by author in Denver, CO, 21 February 1999.

25. Rosemary Ellen Guiley, *Harper's Encyclopedia of Mystical and Paranormal Experience* (New York: Castle Books, 1991), 362.

26. Roxanne Carol, "ETs, Aliens or Angels: Who's Who in the Zoo," Denver, CO (1998, Photocopy), 12.

27. Ibid. Continuing in the same vein, Carol cautions readers that "the following synopsis of the various 'alien' groups is based upon hundreds of corroborating accounts of encounters with Terran, Subterran or Exterran groups over a period of years yet which should nevertheless be weighed by the reader in light of their corroborative elements, documentation, *the sincerity and reputation of the numerous witnesses* [emphasis added], and other evidences both physical and circumstantial."

28. Ibid.

29. Joseph Campbell, *The Power of Myth* (New York: Doubleday, 1988), 45.

30. Editorial by Sue O'Brien, quoting Sissela Bok's *Lying: Moral Choice in Public and Private Life* (1978), in the *Denver Post*, 12 June 1998, 4H.

31. *King of the Hill*, Fox Network television program, Autumn 1998.

32. Guiley, *Harper's Encyclopedia of Mystical and Paranormal Experience*, 3.

33. "FBI Puts Files on 'Net So People May Know," *Denver Post*, 17 June 1998, 2A.

34. Alison Gwin, *The 100 Greatest TV Shows of All Time* (New York: Entertainment Weekly Books, 1998), 37.

35. Elizabeth Ervin, "Academics and the Negotiation of Local Knowledge," *College English* 61, no. 4, (1999): 457. The quoted material is from Walter Fisher, *Human Communication as Narration: Toward a Philosophy of Reason, Value, and Action* (Columbia: University of South Carolina Press, 1987), 66.

36. (Rochelle Park, NJ: Hayden Book Company, Inc., 1968.), 5.

37. *Denver Post*, 19 June 1998, 2A.

38. Dean, *Aliens in America*, 55.

39. To be faithful to the spirit and effect of the personal experience stories told here, I should probably use the first person point of view (I) rather than the third person (she or he). However, these versions are shortened rather drastically from the original and paraphrased, so that the exact words used are not the storyteller's, but mine, so I decided that to use the first person would be presumptuous as well as inauthentic.

40. Incident related at the Second Annual Summer Seminar, *Learning About Man's Place in the Cosmos*, Laughlin, Nevada, 1–8 August 1998. This incident also comprises a section of Mia Adams' book *The Excycles*.

41. *Art Bell Web Page*, http://6bs.rowlandnet.com/cgi-bin/WebX?14@^382526 @.ee75a4e/0

42. BRANTON, *The DULCE Book*, http://www.eagle-net.org/dulce

43. Roderick Main, ed., *Jung on Synchronicity and the Paranormal* (London: Routledge, 1997), 84.

44. Ibid. Further quotes in this section are from the same source, and page numbers are given in parentheses.

45. Giorgio Bongiovanni at the *Second Annual UFO Summer Seminar*, Laughlin, Nevada, 6 August 1998.

46. Chelsey, *X-Files* Fan Forum, 7/14/98. Http://xfox.proxicom.com/xfox? sid=OJ27Riqi&msg=19%3a3374&t=forum%2fshow. Currently, *Les Misérables* is being advertised for its 1999 US tour as the "World's Most Popular Musical, the Musical of the Century."

Bibliography

Apollonio, Umbro. "Expressionism." Vol. 5 of *The Encyclopedia of World Art.* New York: McGraw-Hill, 1961.

Bader, Chris. "The UFO Contact Movement from the 1950s to the Present." *Studies in Popular Culture* 17 (1995): 73–90.

Bakhtin, M. M. *The Dialogic Imagination.* Edited by Michael Holquist. Translated by Caryl Emerson and Michael Holquist. Austin: University of Texas Press, 1981.

Baldick, Chris. *The Concise Oxford Dictionary of Literary Terms.* Oxford: Oxford University Press, 1991.

Barry, Dave. "No loopholes Here: Flat Tax Has Fat Chance." *Denver Post Empire Magazine,* 25 February 1996.

"Bending the Truth." *Focus Magazine* (UK), October 1997.

Berger, Arthur Asa. *Narratives in Popular Culture, Media, and Everyday Life.* Thousand Oaks, California: Sage Publications, 1997.

_____. *Cultural Criticism.* Thousand Oaks, California: Sage Publications, 1995.

Bleiler, Everett Franklin. *The Guide to Supernatural Fiction.* Kent, Ohio: Kent State University Press, 1983.

_____. *Three Gothic Novels.* New York: Dover Publications, 1966,

Campbell, Joseph. *The Power of Myth.* New York: Doubleday, 1988.

Carol, Roxanne. "ETs, Aliens or Angels: Who's Who in the Zoo?" Denver, Colorado: 1998. Photocopy.

Carr, Edward Hallett. *What Is History?* New York: Knopff, 1963.

Cawelti, John G. *Adventure, Mystery, and Romance: Formula Stories as Art and Popular Culture.* Chicago: The University of Chicago Press, 1976.

Clute, John and John Grant, eds. *The Encyclopedia of Fantasy.* New York: St. Martin's Press, 1997.

Clerk, Susan. "DDEB, GATB, MPPB, and Ratboy: *The X-Files*' Media Fandom, Online and Off." In *Deny All Knowledge: Reading* The X-Files. Edited by David Laverly, Angela Hague and Marla Cartwright, 36–51. Syracuse, New York: Syracuse University Press, 1996.

Combs, Allan, and Mark Holland. *Synchronicity: Science, Myth, and the Trickster.* New York: Marlowe, 1996.

Confirmation: The Hard Evidence of Aliens Among Us? NBC-TV: 17 February 1999, 7–9 P.M.

Daniels, Les. *Living in Fear: A History of Horror in the Mass Media.* New York: Charles Scribner's Sons, 1975.

Dean, Jodi. *Aliens in America: Conspiracy Cultures from Outerspace to Cyberspace.* Ithaca, New York: Cornell University Press, 1997.

de Becker, Gavin. "Conquering What Scares Us." *USA Weekend*, 22–24 August 1997.

Denver Post. January 1995–April 1999.

Ehrenreich, Barbara, and Deirdre English. *For Her Own Good: 150 Years of the Experts' Advice to Women.* Garden City, New York: Anchor Press/Doubleday, 1978.

Eisner, Lotte H. *The Haunted Screen.* Berkeley: University of California Press, 1952.

Enright, D. J. *The Oxford Book of the Supernatural.* Oxford: Oxford University Press, 1994.

Ervin, Elizabeth. "Academics and the Negotiation of Local Knowledge." *College English* 61, no. 4 (1999): 448–470.

Foucault, Michel. *Discipline and Punish: The Birth of the Prison.* Translated by Alan Sheridan. New York: Vintage Books, 1979.

Frank, Frederick S. "The Early Gothic." In *Horror Literature: A Reader's Guide.* Edited by Neil Barron, 3–57. New York: Garland, 1990.

Franken, Al. *Rush Limbaugh Is a Big Fat Idiot.* New York: Delacort Press, 1996.

Good, Timothy. *Beyond Top Secret: The Worldwide UFO Security Threat.* London: Pan Books, 1996.

Graham, Allison. "'Are You Now or Have You Ever Been?' Conspiracy Theory and *The X-Files*." In *Deny All Knowledge: Reading* The X-Files. Edited by David Laverly, Angela Hague and Marla Cartwright, 52–62. Syracuse, New York: Syracuse University Press, 1996.

Guiley, Rosemary Ellen. *Harper's Encyclopedia of Mystical and Paranormal Experience.* New York: Castle Books, 1991.

Hayward, Jennifer Poole. *Consuming Pleasures: Active Audiences and Serial Fictions from Dickens to Soap Opera.* Lexington, Kentucky: The University Press of Kentucky, 1997.

Howe, Linda Moulton. *Glimpses of Other Realities.* Vol. 1, *Facts and Eyewitnesses.* Cheyenne, WY: LMH Productions, 1993.

Jackson, Rosemary. *Fantasy: The Literature of Subversion.* New York: Methuen, 1981.

Jones, Leslie. "Last Week We Had an Omen." In *Deny All Knowledge: Reading* The X-Files. Edited by David Laverly, Angela Hague and Marla Cartwright, 77–98. Syracuse, New York: Syracuse University Press, 1996.

Jung, C. G. *Flying Saucers: A Modern Myth of Things Seen in the Skies.* Translated by R.F.C. Hull. Princeton, New Jersey: Princeton University Press, 1978.

_____. *Four Archetypes: Mother, Rebirth, Spirit, Trickster.* Translated by R.F.C. Hull. Princeton, New Jersey: Princeton University Press, 1969.

_____. *Man and His Symbols.* New York: Dell, 1978.

Kaminsky, Stuart M. *American Film Genres.* New York: Dell, 1977.

_____, and Jeffrey H. Mahan. *American Television Genres.* Chicago: Nelson Hall, 1985.

Kammen, Michael. "The Study of Popular Culture Has Acquired Legitimacy, but Still Lacks Cohesion." *The Chronicle of Higher Education* (July 1998): B5.

King, Stephen. *Danse Macabre.* New York: Berkley Books, 1982.

Kracauer, Siegfried. *From Caligari to Hitler: A Psychological History of the German Film.* Princeton, New Jersey: Princeton University Press, 1947.

Kubek, Elizabeth. "You Only Expose Your Father." In *Deny All Knowledge: Reading* The X-Files. Edited by David Laverly, Angela Hague and Marla Cartwright, 168–204. Syracuse, New York: Syracuse University Press, 1996.

Learning About Man's Place in the Cosmos. Second Annual UFO Summer Seminar. Laughlin, Nevada: International UFO Congress, 1–8 August 1998.

Linden, Eugene. *The Future in Plain Sight: Nine Clues to the Coming Instability.* New York: Simon and Schuster, 1998.

Lovecraft, H. P. *The Dunwich Horror and Others.* Sauk City, Wisconsin: Arkham House, 1963.

Lowry, Brian. *Trust No One: The Official Third Season Guide to* The X-Files. New York: Harper, 1996.

_____. *The Truth Is Out There: The Official Guide to* The X-Files. New York: Harper, 1995.

Magistrale, Tony. "Teaching the Intellectual Merits of Stephen King's Fiction." *The Chronicle of Higher Education* (19 June 1998): B7.

Main, Roderick, ed. *Jung on Synchronicity and the Paranormal.* London: Routledge, 1997.

Mehler, Stephen. Interview conducted in Denver, Colorado, 21 February 1999.

Meisler, Andy. *I Want to Believe: The Official Fourth Season Guide to* The X-Files. New York: Harper, 1998.

Moore, Darrell. *The Best, Worst, and Most Unusual: Horror Films.* Skokie, Illinois: Publications International, 1983.

Neilson, Keith. "Contemporary Horror Fiction, 1950–88." In *Horror Literature: A Reader's Guide.* Edited by Neil Barron, 160–214. New York: Garland, 1990.

O'Brien, Sue. Quoting from Sissela Bok's *Lying: Moral Choice in Public and Private Life* (1978). Editorial in the *Denver Post* (12 June 1998): 4H.

Parks, Lisa. "Special Agent or Monstrosity? Finding the Feminine in The X-Files." In *Deny All Knowledge: Reading* The X-Files. Edited by David Lavery, Angela Hague and Marla Cartwright, 121–134. Syracuse, New York: Syracuse University Press, 1996.

Pierce, Hazel Beasley. *A Literary Symbiosis: Science Fiction/Fantasy Mystery.* Westport, Connecticut: Greenwood Press, 1983.

Place, J. A., and L. S. Peterson. "Some Visual Motifs of Film Noir." *Film Comment*, January 1974.

Prawer, S. S. *Caligari's Children: The Film as a Tale of Terror.* Oxford: Oxford University Press, 1989.

Propp, Vladimir. *Morphology of the Folktale.* 2d ed. Translated by L. Scott. Austin: University of Texas Press, 1968.

Rabinowitz, Peter. "Canons and Close Readings." In *Falling into Theory: Conflicting Views on Reading Literature.* Edited by David H Richter, 218–221. Boston: Bedford Books of St. Martin's Press, 1994.

Reeves, Jimmie L., Mark C. Rodgers, and Michael Epstein. "The Cult Files." In *Deny All Knowledge: Reading* The X-Files. Edited by David Laverly, Angela Hague and Marla Cartwright, 22–35. Syracuse, New York: Syracuse University Press, 1996.

Rosen, Ruth. "The Sinister Images of *The X-Files.*" *The Chronicle of Higher Education* (11 July 1997): B7.

Shayerson, Michael. "David Duchovny's X-Factor." *Vanity Fair,* June 1998.

Silver, Alain, and Elizabeth Ward, eds. *Film Noir: An Encyclopedic Reference to the American Style.* Woodstock, New York: The Overlook Press, 1979.

Smiley, Sam. *Playwriting: The Structure of Action.* Englewood Cliffs, New Jersey: Prentice-Hall, 1971.

Stade, George. "The Big Chiller." *The Nation* (28 February 1987): 258.

Stam, Robert, Robert Burgoyne, and Sandy Flitterman-Lewis. *New Vocabularies in Film Semiotics.* New York: Routledge, 1993.

Stapleford, Brian. "The Later Gothic Tradition, 1825–96" and "Early Modern Horror Fiction, 1897–1949." In *Horror Literature: A Reader's Guide.* Edited by Neil Barron, 58–67, 93–104. New York: Garland, 1990.

Tannenbaum, Rob. "Scully and Mulder's Excellent Adventure." *Details Magazine* (UK), June 1998.

Telotte, J. P. *Voices in the Dark: The Narrative Patterns of Film Noir.* Urbana, Illinois: University of Illinois Press, 1989.

Thompson, G. Richard, ed. *The Gothic Imagination.* Pullman: Washington State University Press, 1974.

Totten, Gary L. "Bakhtin and Genre Theory." Paper presented at the annual meeting of the Rocky Mountain Modern Language Association, Denver, Colorado, 1997.

Varma, D. P. *The Gothic Flame*. New York: Russell and Russell, 1966.

Volta, Ornella. *The Vampire*. Translated by Raymond Rudorff. New York: Award Books, 1962.

Walker, Barbara. *The Woman's Encyclopedia of Myths and Secrets*. New York: HarperCollins, 1983.

Willen, Gerald, ed. *A Casebook on Henry James's* The Turn of the Screw. 2d ed. Binghamton, NY: Thomas Y. Crowell, 1969.

Wilson, Colin. *Alien Dawn: An Investigation into the Contact Experience*. New York: Fromm International, 1998.

Wilson, Robert Anton. *Everything Is Under Control: Conspiracies, Cults, and Cover-ups*. New York: HarperPerennial, 1998.

Wolfe, Gary K. *Critical Terms for Science Fiction and Fantasy: A Glossary and Guide to Scholarship*. New York: Greenwood Press, 1986.

"X-Philes Speak." *U.S.A. Weekend*. 14–16 July 1995.

Index

conspiracy 16, 22, 24, 52, 89–90, 172;
  conspiracy literature 40
critical study 36–37
criticism 37

"The Demon Lover" 163, 164
detective fiction: physical beatings in
  43; plot in 83; private investigator
  (Mulder's similarity to) 102–3; psychic detective 104, 156–67, 166; role of
  the detective 49
dialectic 41, 114
Dickens, Charles 156, 157
Discourse of the Father see fathers,
  world of the father
Dr. Jekyll and Mr. Hyde 146, 168
Dracula 98, 147–49, 151–52, 157, 162,
  166, 167, 168, 195
Duchovny, David (actor) 48, 127
du Maurier, Daphne 86

Eliot, T. S. 159
episodes: aspects of tragedy in 67–68;
  bound 8–9, 15, 44, 49, 106; free 44,
  49, 73, 106, 145; list of 8–13; mythological 8–13; reflexive 81, 106, 158;
  titles of 84
escapist fiction 35; formula fiction, plot
  36; see also popular literature
ET 188
Expressionism 25, 121–22; Edvard
  Munch, "The Scream" 121; German
  21–22

"The Fall of the House of Usher" 138
family history 10
family values 118–19, 120; nuclear family 166
fans' views and comments 30, 61, 212
fantastic literature 83; dark fantasy 65
fathers 10–11; of Mulder 53–54, 117, 118,
  141; of Scully 46–47, 54, 117, 118, "sins
  of the father" 166; structure of control 156; the symbolic order 83–84,
  119; world of the father 81, 100, 104
  117–18, 119–20, 142, 154, 155
FBI 188, 198; informants 17
fears: contemporary 179–80; development of 72–73
files 15, 23
film noir 18, 21, 22, 23, 25, 38, 122, 123,

124, 169–70; detectives 89; heroes 23;
  use of voice-over narration 114, 115,
  116; women 26
film techniques: blurred graphics 124;
  TV shows in background 125–26
folktales: chupacabra 203; Hansel and
  Gretel 25
formulas 39, 40–42; see also plot conventions
Foucault, Michel 17, 20, 151; disciplinary society 17
Frankenstein 168, 172

gender 25–26, 80, 111, 114; idealization
  of women 155
genre, definition of 37
Ghostbusters 58
Gilman, Charlotte Perkins 140, 153–54,
  155–56
Gothic forms 137–41
Gothic genre 64, 93; see also horror,
  supernatural horror, dark fantasy
Gothic motifs 135; Byronic hero 147;
  the dark man 142, 145, 192–93; dread
  135; entrapment 138, 139, 150, 151; the
  forbidden book 139–40; genealogy
  141; ghosts 150, 151, 156–58; madness
  151–52, 153–54, 175; the other 135;
  premature burial 151; the supernatural 139; "the unexplained" 159
Gothic tradition 132–76
The Government: control 17–18; distrust 16–17, 73; Freedom of Information Act 198; and UFOs 186–88, 191

Hammer Studios horror movies 78
The Haunting 164
The Haunting of Hill House 140, 164
Hawking, Professor Stephen J. 177, 179
hegemony 31, 36; corporate and professional 142, 171, 173, 175; and exploitation, with magical realism 65–66;
  hegemonic discourse 31–32, 209; of
  language 53
Hellraiser 58, 78, 163
heroes: Byronic 147; mythic 47–48;
  noir 23; Prometheus 56, 105–6;
  sacrificial 105; scribe of 26; seeker
  106; victim 106; western 102–3
Hesse, Herman 204
Hoover, J. Edgar 17